SINGING
FOR NOTHING

SINGING FOR NOTHING

*selected nonfiction
as literary memoir*

WALLY SWIST

the operating system
brooklyn new york
c.2018

the operating system print//document
SINGING FOR NOTHING

ISBN: 978-1-946031-31-0
Library of Congress Control Number: 2018948542
copyright © 2018 by Wally Swist
edited by Lynne DeSilva-Johnson
text design by Michael Flatt with Lynne DeSilva-Johnson

is released under a Creative Commons CC-BY-NC-ND (Attribution, Non Commercial, No Derivatives) License: its reproduction is encouraged for those who otherwise could not afford its purchase in the case of academic, personal, and other creative usage from which no profit will accrue.

Complete rules and restrictions are available at:
http://creativecommons.org/licenses/by-nc-nd/3.0/

For additional questions regarding reproduction, quotation, or to request a pdf for review contact operator@theoperatingsystem.org

This text was set in Europa, Gill Sans, Minion, Franchise, and OCR-A Standard.

Books from The Operating System are distributed to the trade by SPD/Small Press Distribution, with ePub and POD via Ingram, with production by Spencer Printing, in Honesdale, PA, in the USA.

Cover Art by Lynne DeSilva-Johnson;
Cover and author photos by Betty Wilda

The operating system is a member of the Radical Open Access Collective, a community of scholar-led, not-for-profit presses, journals and other open access projects. Now consisting of 40 members, we promote a progressive vision for open publishing in the humanities and social sciences. Learn more at: http://radicaloa.disruptivemedia.org.uk/about/

Your donation makes our publications, platform and programs possible!
We <3 You.
bit.ly/growtheoperatingsystem

the operating system
141 Spencer Street #203
Brooklyn, NY 11205
www.theoperatingsystem.org
operator@theoperatingsystem.org

For the Readers of This Book

*and in the memory of
Robert M. Palter, Professor Emeritus,
Charles A. Dana Professor of History of Science,
Trinity College, Hartford, Connecticut,
Bibliophile, Scholar, and Veritable Renaissance Man*

"Be like the rain
that wears a ragged coat
and finds the lamp
in the smallest stone
and sings for nothing
from street to street"

—BERT MEYERS, "These Days"

Contents

Author's Preface — xv

1. Essays and Reviews: Regarding Poetry and Poets — 1

    Poetic Alchemy: Wislawa Szymborska's Map: Collected and Last Poems — 10

    Tuning Fork on the Sidewalk of Dreams: Bert Meyers's The Wild Olive Tree *and* the Blue Café — 18

    The Art and Necessity of Festschrift: Fair Warning: Leo Connellan and His Poetry *and a Review of Leo Connellan's* Death in Lobsterland — 27

    Lyrical Mathematics: The Kingfisher's Reign *by Jonas Zdanys* — 34

2. Journey to the East: The Way of Haiku — 39

    The Windbreak Pine: *An Introduction* — 45

    Imagistic Perpetuity: The Haiku of Adele Kenny — 52

    The Watershed of "Just as It Is:" Mountain *by John Wills* — 55

    The Poetics of Walking — 59

    The Conclusion of the Grail Legend, Trout Fishing, and the Art of Writing Haiku Poetry — 63

    The International Saijiki: *The Legacy of William J. Higginson* — 67

    Western Haiku as American Poetry: Nicholas A. Virigilio — 73

CONTENTS

3. Selected Reviews: Espousing a Few Books
   I Have Loved 77

   An Elucidation of the Science of Geology:
   John McPhee's Basin and Range 89

   Political Memoir as Eastern European History:
   Native Realm *by Czeslaw Milosz* 95

   Aging, Identity, and Time: Being Here
   by Robert Penn Warren 100

   An Iconic Literary History of the Great Depression:
   The Dream of the Golden Mountains
   by Malcolm Cowley 105

   Elegy, Epiphany, and Song: Field Work
   by Seamus Heaney 110

   Spellbound by the Supernatural: Mirabell: Books
   of Number *by James Merrill* 116

4. Towards an Active Perseverance: A Feature Article
   that May Not Have Been Otherwise Written 123

   A Salute to the Varied Career of Rudolph F. Zallinger 131

5. Reveling in What is Salvageable: Writing What
   an Editor Wants 139

   Big Data: Uncorking the Genie from the Bottle 145

   *How We Progress Over Time in Conjunction
   with How We Are Affected by the Evolution of
   Technology—or What Constitutes the Foundation
   for a Measure of Success Relevant to Pop Culture* 167

   The Science and Art of Measurement 175

   *The History of Retirement in America: Epilogue
   to the American Dream, A Socio-Economic and
   Political Retrospective* 186

6. Biographical Literary Monograph: The Friendship
   of Robert Francis and Robert Frost 223

   *High Pressure Weather and Country Air:
   The Friendship of Robert Francis and Robert Frost* 235

CONTENTS

7. What Is Psychospirituality? Infusing the Blog
   with Literary Panache — 275

   Anxiety, Time, and Being Present in the Moment — 287

   Anxiety: Not Being Needed and What to Do about It — 290

   Anxiety and Synchronicity: Living in the Real World — 293

   Attachment: How It Affects You and How Your Parents Are Culpable — 296

   Origins of the Inner Voice: Difference between Divinity, Consciousness, and Madness — 300

   Post-Election Collective Trauma: How to Manage the Stress of Having an Autocratic President — 303

8. A Pair of Forewords and a Meditation:
   Towards an Active Spirituality — 307

   Co-Translator's Preface: The Daodejing: A New Interpretation — 314

   Foreword to A Staff to a Pilgrim: Meditations on the Way with Nine Celtic Saints — 319

   Guided Chakra Meditation — 322

Wally Swist in Conversation
with Lynne DeSilva-Johnson — 329

Acknowledgments — 335

About the Author — 339

Author's Preface

I have led a rather bookish life. I have willingly, and quite gladly, lived a life reading books and writing them. I have needed to live frugally but my life through books has largely been a source of nearly constant satisfaction. That intrinsically has been a boon and a burden. Leading a literary life may be fulfilling, with respect to nourishing one's soul, but getting used to little, or no, remuneration for persevering to adhere to the writer's craft is quite another. After reading Irving Stone's fictional biography of Jack London, *Sailor on Horseback,* in my late teens, I saw that there was a possibility of my becoming a writer—only if I read luminously—as London did. Of course he had the guidance of Ina Coolbrith, a librarian at Oakland Public Library. Joseph Campbell also invested himself in becoming a luminous reader. Campbell would glean an encyclopedic knowledge regarding mythology and comparative religion with the generosity of a bookseller in New York City, who didn't ask for the balance on Campbell's account for the years he holed up in Woodstock, New York during the Great Depression before he began his distinguished teaching career of some 37 years at Sarah Lawrence College, in Bronxville, NY.

My first real job, in 1973, at the age of twenty, was as in a small, but rarefied, and somewhat legendary, bookstore in New Haven, called Book World, on Chapel Street, next to the Yale Art & Architecture building. I suppose it was characteristic of my first autumn working at Book World that I was reading Ayn Rand's *The Fountainhead* during my lunch breaks on the steps of the Yale A & A, which connected with an adjacent wall of Book World. I read *The Fountainhead* not as a political, or economical, tract, but as a biography of what it was to be an artist, as I believed Howard Roark

AUTHOR'S PREFACE

essentially was, overcoming one challenge after another, only to forge on to practice and to further his craft.

The staff at Book World became mentors to me. Ed Bednar, who would go on to found the New Haven Zen Center, was studying with the imminent literary critic Harold Bloom, in finishing his Ph.D. thesis on D. H. Lawrence. The manager and lead buyer, George Wagner, a storied bookperson I would go on to work with over the next seven years, was respected and admired in the Yale community for his knowledge of books, and had been a mainstay around the Yale campus for at least a decade and a half before he hired me to take the place of a valued staff person who left to move to San Francisco, and who, within weeks, was hired for a job working at City Lights Bookstore along with owner and iconic beat poet Lawrence Ferlinghetti.

Entering this milieu for me was indeed breathing in some rather heady air. As a goal, I read at least two books a week, and for several years I realized my aim of reading more than a hundred books a year. In some circles, this would not amount to not much at all to report about, but I was making a valid attempt to read—and to write, as well.

In 1975, after my own literary homage to San Francisco and the Bay Area, in which I worked at one of the other initial paperback bookstores, The Cottage Bookshop, on Fourth Street, in San Rafael, I began writing for the arts section of *The New Haven Advocate*, upon my return to New Haven. My stint there, contributing copy along with some of the best writers who made up the staff of the newspaper, often graduates of Yale, lasted through 1980. It was there I had the opportunity to practice writing a sentence, with Joan Didion's *Slouching toward Bethlehem* on my writing table. It was during this time, I indentured myself in acquiring the craft of writing a lead paragraph, with William Zinsser's *On Writing Well* by my side. During the 1970s, Zinsser, a former veteran journalist with

AUTHOR'S PREFACE

The New York Herald Tribune, taught writing at Yale and was a Master of Branford College.

When I left New Haven, in January 1981, I moved to semirural western Massachusetts where I have largely made my home ever since, with the exception of four years I spent working at Trinity College, in Hartford, Connecticut where I managed a small college general bookstore, Gallows Hill Bookstore, from the autumn of 1998 through early spring 2002. Urban living is not something I found myself suited to again even after spending most of my twenties in New Haven. The rolling hills, meadows, and brooks of the Pioneer Valley in western Massachusetts and the Berkshires, farther west, were to be my main source of inspiration not only as a writer but also since nature provided me an essential touchstone to an active spiritual life.

Managing bookstores was primarily how I made my living for most of my working years. I had the occasion of usually being lead buyer in the stores I managed in Connecticut and in Northampton, Massachusetts, across the Connecticut River where I have lived in Amherst. Although I did continue to write, I did so after coming home after my shift at whatever bookstore I was employed in—only to remove my coat, hang it on the back of the chair of my writing table, and then begin, often before having dinner, if not sometimes through my normal dinner time, and then after.

Ostensibly, that was my life through 2008, when I left the book business, after some thirty years, with the occasion of having a few other jobs in between. Since that time, I have considered myself a full-time writer. Although I am primarily known as a poet, I have written a considerable amount of nonfiction, including articles, essays, reviews, and a slew of press releases, which are actually quite literary. I used the latter to double in promoting my author event and reading series, which I conducted at the bookstores I managed, but also as introductions

AUTHOR'S PREFACE

to the readings themselves. Some of these press releases were thought of well enough that they were requested by a former curator of Special Collections at the Jones Library, in Amherst, so that they would be included in the file boxes of my materials archived there.

One of the authors I hosted, when I was at Trinity College, shortly thereafter began a nationwide tour for his book. Some months later, I needed to ask the author a question and phoned him. Upon answering the phone, and before he even addressed my question, he commented that he had been on radio, TV, and in many bookstores on his tour but didn't experience the kind of felicity that I had provided him with in the launch of his book. I knew myself what a writer, or an artist, required to keep them focused and to be made to feel comfortable, since I was a working writer myself.

So, why write this book? If you have read this preface thus far, you might be thinking if my main focus in my writing life has been poetry, then why assemble a collection of *Selected Nonfiction?* Why is that necessary, in an age of such a plethora of books, some of which I myself don't find necessary at all?

When I was at Trinity College one spring afternoon, with the weeping cherry tree blooming in front of Gallows Hill Bookstore, a longstanding friend walked into my office and literally whisked me away for a reading a mutual friend of ours was giving on campus that I wasn't aware of. I shouldn't have been surprised when our mutual friend acknowledged us in the audience before she gave the presentation of her lecture on the poetry of Emily Dickinson. The paper from which the woman read from appeared to be some three pages in length, but as a poet herself, she was not only impassioned as to the influence Dickinson had on her life as an adolescent, when she first came upon her work, but also as a mature and much celebrated poet.

AUTHOR'S PREFACE

Writers who are poets are not necessarily known for writing James Michener-like epics. We use words differently and often sprinkle metaphors and similes throughout our prose. Roger Hahn, a staff writer for *The New Haven Advocate* in the late 1970s, who went on to write for *The New York Post,* once commented on one of my stories in *The Advocate* by saying, "Lots of nice similes in that article."

Writing nonfiction, for me, especially since 2008, has been indicative of my either making a living or augmenting my finances in what are now my years of benefitting from collecting Social Security. Writing nonfiction is similar to breathing. Writing poetry honors the soul and what sings there, as well as the cognitive mind. Writing nonfiction pays tribute to the spirit and our daily bread, so to speak. Nonfiction can be ordinary, but it sometimes it can be extraordinary, and it assists us in catching the train we want to take. Poetry often is the train itself, and when it isn't, it is then certainly the speed of the train, the G-force of it. However, it was nonfiction that took us there.

Regarding the *why* of this book and my considering what is included in it, which took several drafts and a year or two critical discernment, its writing and compilation required my assessing what nonfiction I wrote and selecting not just the best of it but the best of what still matters. Writing nonfiction sometimes took me away from experiencing the speed of the train—of poetry itself. Managing bookstores kept me away from writing itself but it was what I did as my livelihood. When I stopped doing that, I depended on my writing nonfiction to get me to the station on time. So, I could take the train, when life, and soul, demanded it.

What nonfiction I include in this book is as essential as to the many pieces I didn't collect in this book that were accomplished enough also to be offered here. I decided to only include the reviews of books, for instance, that were specific to my own

AUTHOR'S PREFACE

particular literary memoir, and which could be directly associated with a significant anecdote that just may be enough interest to you, dear reader.

The direction that Editor Lynne DeSilva-Johnson, founder and publisher of The Operating System, provided was actually more challenge than guidance. However, I took on the challenge. She was discerning enough to see that an earlier draft of this book had some literary value to it, and suggested, as is the ethos of her press, to push the boundaries of both nonfiction and memoir. Lynne has as much credit in creating this book, as it is, as I do. It was her voice, *as muse*, that precipitated what became my own *revisioning* of the *why* and the *what* of the book as it is now. Lynne's redirection is tantamount to the best of what might be achieved here.

The question then begs itself as to what might be achieved here, if anything at all. To some what may be offered here may resemble a ragtag assortment of nonfiction held together by a montage of literary anecdotes. If so, then I have failed, miserably. What I do intend for this book is for it to be a treasure trove of my own life in books, of which I hope is a humble enough offering but also one in which you might revel and find some delight.

In a life of having worked with books on perhaps every conceivable level—from sewing copies of signatures of fine letterpress books by hand to boxing up children's books for a book fair to writing lead paragraphs with an old friend for our separate book reviews on the floor of her living room on a Sunday afternoon in New Haven amid pages of the Sunday *New York Times*—books have not been just a meager part of my life but they also have, indeed, made up the entirety of my life.

By making the selections I have for this book, I am sharing with you the best of my life with books. I had occasion to work with an absolutely fascinating woman, named Mrs. R. Mrs. R's

AUTHOR'S PREFACE

name was actually Mrs. Alberta Robinson. No one dared call her Alberta. So, she was known as Mrs. R. She had a twenty year career at Springfield Library in Springfield, Massachusetts. In the late 1960s, she began her second career as the manager and lead book buyer at Johnson's Secondhand Bookshop, once an anchor store on Main Street in Springfield for more than a century. After Mrs. R. retired, I was hired as manager, in the mid-1980s. In my time working at Johnson's I made some changes, which Mrs. R. didn't agree with, such as shelving the books with the titles spined vertically, whereas, she used to shelve them horizontally, so you could read them more easily.

However there were also some things I made sure to honor just as they were. One of the things I left the same was the Books on Books table, where a reader would find just that: informative *and* delightful books regarding books themselves, in multitudinous ways. I would often display fine press material, bibliographies, and literary criticism there after I returned from a book auction. Although not quite fitting any of the rubrics above, I believe the book I have written here might be best displayed on the Books on Books table of Mrs. R's. Or at least I hope so; and if a bookseller should shelve this book in a literary subsection in the sociology aisle *that* in itself would make my writing this book quite worthwhile, especially considering the study I enclose herein regarding "The History of Retirement of America." My intent in this essay, by making use of historical references, although based on non-partisan research, is to inflect a stance that is progressive in the best of socio-political contexts. Actually, I dream of the day a new and relevant WPA Program might be instituted. America could benefit immensely by the utility of such a program—one that is intelligently administered, as was FDR's during the Great Depression.

Mrs. R. always often enough repeated the phrase, "The road to hell is paved with the best intentions." This *Selected Nonfiction as Literary Memoir* is one of my best intentions. It is, as I have

AUTHOR'S PREFACE

offered, nonfiction written by a writer who is primarily at least thought of as first being a poet. If you should read this book and find yourself infused with the resonance that I am a nonfiction writer worth reading, and a writer whose nonfiction will get you to the train on time to sometimes experience the essence of poetry, which is the rush of the train itself, then I would be not only delighted but also be grateful that you decided to take a ride that was possibly worth going on.

WALLY SWIST
South Amherst, Massachusetts
July 2017

SINGING
FOR NOTHING

1. Essays and Reviews
REGARDING POETRY AND POETS

In June 2015, Steven Schroeder, Editor of Virtual Artists Collective and of *all roads will lead you home* suggested, as by way of invitation, that I might contribute a review to this online journal, which exhibits a multidisciplinary vision. I had just finished reading the late Nobel Laureate Wislawa Szymborska's Map: Collected and Last Poems. I could hardly refuse the invitation, most especially since I had been reading Szymborska for some years and my having an opportunity to honor her work with some of my insights was inexplicably delicious to me. Steve published the piece in his second number of all roads will lead you home, an annual publication. However, he indicated that a consensus among him and the other editors was that the Szymborska piece was more of an essay than a review. He furthered that I might think of writing more of the same—which planted the initial seed in me for such a presentation of work in that vein that might be assembled into a collection for a book.

Many years earlier, I contributed a true essay on the work of the late Southern California poet Bert Meyers for a special issue of *Poetry East*, called "Praises," published in 1992. Bert Meyers was the poet who completely threw open the doors for me as to what poetry could be. Reading Bert Meyers not only enabled me to see clearly, in a poetic sense, but he also provided me with the key—which was his unmistakable genius in constructing images that were perfect in every sense and vibrant within themselves in a remarkable resonance, and often written with crystal clear simplicity. I had the occasion to speak with Bert on the phone once when I worked as a cataloger for Hugh Miller, Bookseller in New Haven in 1977, and it was a privilege to do so. High and I were working on publishing a book of his, entitled Windowsills, and I thank Hugh to this day for the opportunity to make my small contribution in his consulting me on some aspects of the publication of the book, but also in the tacit and palpable activity of folding Fabriano wrappers for the book's cover. The Fabriano was canary-yellow, and it seemed quite an apt choice of color for the book since there were so many imagistic references to light in Bert's poetry. Despite the joy found in the work, what saddens me still was that while we were on the final leg of finishing production, Odette Meyers, Bert's wife, phoned us and informed us that Bert had lost his battle with lung cancer—that he had died. He didn't live to see Windowsills and certainly not the long-awaited volume of his Selected Poems, entitled In a Dybbuk's Raincoat; however, the images he created in his poetry and the poetry itself do certainly live on. The word perpetuity is emblematic of the work of Bert Meyers, and I am eternally grateful that I had the experience of reading his work when I was young enough—in my early to mid-twenties—that it would make a significant difference in my own writing. The essay enclosed herein was revised and updated in 2016.

Leo Connellan was a poet I met when I directed my first reading series at The Theatre and the Space, on the corner of Orange Street and Chapel Streets in New Haven, where it was housed in a large loft with its expansive windows facing east. Leo had just published his First Selected Poems with University of Pittsburg Press, which still publishes some of the finest American poets. Leo and I shared an emotional history in that both his mother and mine died in our respective childhoods, and made our lives all the more intensely sadder than they needed to be—making our psychological scars similar. However, when I met Leo I was 23, in 1975, and he was 47. Although he was old enough to be my father, I resisted that chronological reference point. However, I did respect his work and the man who was the writer who created a poetry that was deeply rooted in the resin of the American grain, such as his poetry was.

Leo intimated to me on more than one occasion that someday when I was older than he was I might have a chance to either include his work in an anthology or to write an essay regarding his contribution to American poetry. I never really ever forgot that inkling that he inculcated within me all those years ago that has veritably rung softly like a glass bell for me to take notice of ever since. Leo and I also shared the fact that we both left college before we gained our degrees and practiced our literary craft largely among academics that, as Leo might intone, had a number of letters after their names. However, Leo earned has earned his place on the heights of America's version of Mount Olympus. His poems are worthy of the ethos of what it is to be American in our culture. If you have lost your way in assessing who you are in your being American, you will find your own specific identity in the poetry of Leo Connellan—or at least through your reading of it.

Jonas Zdanys and I had a mutual friend when we lived in New Haven in the late 1970s. I would hear about him from this friend, and he would also hear from her about me. Actually, I now remember his face, as I passed him in the streets that delineated the blocks that constitute Yale campus. We have come to know each other, initially, through our reading of each other's poetry over the years; and, finally, met, in April 2013, when he invited me to read and be a Visiting Writer at Sacred Heart University where he teaches writing in the English Department. I am grateful for our easy colleagueship and friendship. Also, I am appreciative for his own fine poetry, which is deserving of a much wider readership than it currently has. Although not unlike myself, who enjoys working in multiple genres, Jonas is a renowned translator, a lyric poet, and as evidence of the writing in Kingfisher's Reign, which I review here, he is, in my opinion, a magisterial talent in writing prose poems, in conjunction with his other poetic talents.

As suggested by Lynne DeSilva-Johnson, I am including some of my own poems, scrupulously selected among the prose offered in this book. Initially, I thought it unbecoming to include poems of my own, since it first seemed to me to be something that would indicate a lack of humility. However, after much consideration, I don't believe readers will mind if I segue a couple of my own poems here—one being a poem I wrote for Bert Meyers and one in which I had labored over for at least ten years before I finally felt I might have the images in it just right enough. The other poem I include is a political poem, not necessary influenced by my reading Wislawa Szymborska, but one written that same summer I had written the essay regarding her work that appears in this book.

As the poems vary, the first one was finally published in the mid-1990s, but initially composed many years before, when I was working my way through a period in which I wrote many drafts of a single poem. The second poem is from the summer of 2015, and the mature period I now write in, which is marked by fewer drafts, after my having learned something, I believe, with respect to craft, over the decades—a time in which I write more freely, finishing a poem, for the better intent and purpose, in a handful of revisions. May these poems not spoil the reading of the prose, but may they offer an indication of what long and large shadows I have chosen to pursue my own work in, since both Meyers and Szymborska are modern masters, and I am in the very least indebted to them to have had the opportunity to choose so well in my being open to actively loving their work as much as I do.

Before Dawn
for Bert Meyers

Wind turns and turns again like a man
in his sleep. A mouse rummages

in the bureau, jarring the familiar
and the forgotten from drawer to drawer.

Birds canvass about existence;
the alarm clock buzzes like a dentist's drill.

The wind's a semi
that's driven all night past the poplars.

* * * *

Future History Books

How curious we may all appear
to those in the future
and how our era might be judged
by those who will own
the vantage point of looking backward,
giving perspective to where
we had the opportunities to guide
our own eternal present
in seeking what was truly in harmony
with the benefit of all of the people
and in honor of the nature of the planet
and her ways, or to misapprehend
what was necessary and beneficent
in lieu of profit, money, and greed.

Will the future history books
call this the Age of Entitlement, even
mention the insanity

of the drivers in their cars, before cars
could drive themselves,
correlating a particular automotive
body language of the individuals who
operated them, in
nearly driving other cars off the road,
just to get ahead, only
to need to stop at the same traffic light,
where the car they just passed
pulls up beside them.

What will those books relay
about the obfuscation by the Tea Party
and the open racism
against President Obama? What will
be written about the press
who just seemed to step aside instead
of reporting it?

Will the books make reference to how
the Koch Brothers bought the press,
how they manipulated the strings
of the marionettes of the Republican
party? Will those books point to
McConnell and Boehner whose energy
policies crippled nature conservation
and further paved the way for
the conservative movement, without
any one of them ever needing to wear
black armbands?

How will the history of our country
be interpreted
in relation to those who discounted
global warming? Will those who
write those books be able to drink

potable water? Will they be able
to look up into the same sky
and stand beneath the towering
beauty of forested trees?

What about breathing the freshness
of the air?
What will the future history books
reveal about what we did
to ourselves and to the planet, or
will what is already happening now
happen then,
and will the truth about today be
redacted on the pages of tomorrow?

POETIC ALCHEMY: WISLAWA SZYMBORSKA'S
MAP: COLLECTED AND LAST POEMS

It may seem to be unwise, if not imprudent, to categorize not only an author's photograph but especially one that appears on the front cover of a poet's collected poems. However, on the dust jacket of *Map: Collected and Last Poems,* Wislawa Szymborska appears to be watching someone, perhaps studying a person from above, from the perch of the concrete porch, with a steel rail, of her apartment complex.

It is quite a telling, quite a revealing portrait, because her literary reputation rests upon observing history, and ourselves, not to mention how we have behaved throughout it, as she does in one of her last poems, "Someone I've Been Watching for a While." The poem is from the collection she was working on when she passed from this life, entitled *Enough,* which was her final compilation of scrupulously crafted poems, bursting with ironies and insight.

Only this posthumous collection was even shorter than the others, since it was unfinished, as it was left, containing just thirteen poems. However, each of these poems is a precious and a qualitatively substantial addition to this eminent Polish poet's *oeuvre*.

The focus of her observation in this poem is someone "Unremarked./ Unspectacular./ He's employed by City Sanitation." So, the reader thinks, that this is who she has been watching from above from her poetic aerie, "At first light/ from the site of the event/ he sweeps up, carries off, tosses in the truck,/ what's been hammered onto half-dead trees,/ trampled into the exhausted grass." Of the detritus are: "Tattered banners,/ broken bottles,/ burned effigies,/ gnawed bones,/ rosaries, whistles, and condoms."

All of this tragic-comedic litany, which is not unlike some of the imagery of the magical surrealism of Gabriel Garcia Marquez, which has pirated the reader's attention, is driven home by the inimitable poetic alchemy of Szymborska, who could be also referred to as sister to the Brothers Grimm, in her portrayal of what Jean-Paul Sartre dubbed as the paralyzing psycho-social ailment humankind suffered from in his mid-20th-century philosophical classic, *Nausea*.

Although Szymborska's vision and imagery offers her own particular gold stamp: an inscrutable resonance which haunts the reader forever with her offering of the transmutable and what is perennially transfixed, as in the conclusion of this poem: "Once he found a dove cage in the bushes./ He took it home/ so he could/ keep it empty." So be it: we are charmed and we have also been augmented. We understand intuitively but are unsure why. Szymborska leaves us with what Rilke intimated were the questions, and which he suggested that we come to know initially before ascertaining the answers themselves. If literature such as this changes, or alters us, as does Szymborska in her poems, with such consistency and high art, then we are affected by one of its true masters.

Map collects some three hundred fifty poems of Szymborska. When asked why she published so relatively few poems, she answered, typifying her impishness, "I have a trash bin at home." Many poets write many poems; however, Szymborska's poems are not necessarily just poems at all, they are poetical *events*. Szymborska's poems are high-wire acts, the coloratura of a lyrical aria sung by a gifted soprano, children's games (she did write comic works, such as *rymowanki*, or limericks and nursery rhymes; and *polsuchance*, or what she referred to as *eavesdroppings*, which are uncollected here, since she did not want them included). Szymborska's poems are themselves cultural events and they inspired other artists to not only incorporate them in their own work but her poems also informed those works, such as the concluding film in the trilogy, directed by Krzystof Kieslowski, *Three Colors: Red*, which was inspired by Szymborska's poem, "Love At First Sight." The poem's portrayal of romantic relationship, or marriage, is intra-generational. It is profound, balancing humor and tragedy as does a circus bear that steadies himself in the air, as he rolls a large medicine ball beneath his feet. It is Pasternak's Zhivago and Laura, post-romance, who in Szymborska's poem "don't remember—a moment face to face/ in some revolving door," and who find at the poem's end, "Every beginning/ is only a sequel, after all,/ and the book of events/ is always open halfway through."

Born in 1923, Szymborska, who died in her sleep in 2012, was initiated into her adulthood, as were so many other Poles, by the invasion by Nazi Germany in September 1939. Although she was one of the more fortunate of her countrymen, since she was given a job working as a railroad employee, whereas many others were enlisted into forced labor. However, she began studying in underground classes, and eventually, in 1943 enrolled at Jagiellonian University in Krakow, where she switched from her studies of Polish literature to sociology. Although she did not finish a degree, she did become involved in writing groups, and, most felicitously met Czeslaw Milosz, and came under his influence, at least initially—two future Nobel Prize recipients briefly passing each other in the shadow of WWII.

As with Miloz's work, whose memoir *Native Realm* can be read as a layperson's history of eastern Europe or the biography of a member of the resistance written in lyrical prose, Szymborska's life and literary legacy was incontrovertibly shaped by surviving these bleak war years. In her survival, whether innate characteristics or not, her heightened senses of piquant irony and keen observation became fashioned into sophisticated poetic tools. She developed an elfin and puckish characteristic in her poetry the way Edmond Rostand may have introduced the word *panache* into the English language, since his character *Cyrano de Bergerac* is known for his display of it.

Szymborska also needed to weather the apprenticeship and journeyman stages of most writer's literary careers in that her first book, that was to be published in 1949, "did not meet socialist requirement," whose parameters were established by the new Soviet state. So, her obstacles were not only of a similar norm as for other writers of her generation, they were made more extraordinary, since she was groomed to support socialist themes. Although her debut poetry collection, *Why We Live,* included a poem entitled "Lenin" (not included in *Map*), published in 1952, she diverted herself from such staunch authoritarianism and established her own world view, whose vision remains penetrating. Eventually, in 1966, she officially left the party and actively began to affiliate herself with dissidents, such as Jerzy Giedroyc, Editor of the Paris-based émigré journal, *Kultura,* as early as 1957. Szymborska's struggles were imposing ones and she rose above them. It is no wonder she possessed such a knowing and disarming smile, worthy as much of candor as it was of sly mischief.

However, beginning in the late 1950s, Szymborska's voice took shape with the inconoclastic collection *Calling Out to Yeti,* and as she writes in the poem, "Rehabilitation," regarding the power of words, in her atypical and uncommon assessment, "I can't even restore them to half-breath,/ a Sisyphus assigned to the hell of poetry.// They come to us. Sharp as diamonds,/ they pass along shop windows lit in front,/ along the windowpanes of cozy houses,/ along rose-colored glasses, along the glass/ of hearts and brains, quietly cutting."

ESSAYS AND REVIEWS

The poem is as much criticism as much as it is affirmation: Szymborska's own "quietly cutting" vision, so balanced with the way of the world that she can't "even restore them to half-breath." That "half-breath" is so full of itself: a modifier of the living of life itself under one government of oppression or another.

In another poem, appearing in the 1967 collection, *No End of Fun,* entitled "Railroad Station," we don't need to wonder too much if her experience in working for the railroad during the war for the Nazis left any affect on her. The action in the poem nearly takes place vicariously, as if the narrator is estranged from herself: "My absence joined the throng/ as it made its way toward the exit." The poem concludes in a similar existentialist fashion. However, Szymborska transcends what may be mere absurdist *de rigueur* by actually becoming more real than real: "Even a rendezvous/ took place as planned.// Beyond the reach/ of our presence.// In the paradise lost/ of probability.// Somewhere else./ Somewhere else./ How these little words ring."

Szymborska's talent for crystallization is as abundant as her narrative poems are layered with crystallized images. In the 1986 collection, *The People on the Bridge,* the poem "View with a Grain of Sand" is emblematic of her prowess for discovering what is a spiritual maxim of what is small in what is large and what is large in what is small. The poem also served as a title poem for an earlier *Selected Poems* that were translated into English by the provident and accomplished team of Clare Cavanagh and Stanislaw Baranczak, of whom only Cavanagh is responsible for creating the present volume, since Baranczak has been ill, and whose translations into English apparently are the ones that Szymborska favored. In the poem, not unlike Whitman and his *Leaves of Grass,* Szymborska views grains of sand, "The lake's floor exists floorlessly,/ and its shore exists shorelessly," in her amplitude of incisive playfulness. She goes on to propose that all this occurs "beneath a sky by nature skyless/ in which the sun sets without setting at all," which precipitates the thought that Szymborska and her countryman Nikolaus Copernicus would have been quite delighted with each other. The poem concludes with its imprimatur of aplomb, lightly but raising some cosmological dust just the same: "Time has passed like a courier with urgent news./ But that's just our simile./ The character is invented, his haste is make-believe,/ his news inhuman."

Szymborska's perception regarding "that's just our simile" is her broad vision of historical perspective. The *Mise-en-scene* here could be a tableau for a *denouement* in an Agatha Christie mystery in which Hercule Poirot is treading the boards of the stage itself as he explicates each character's role in the crime. However, if it were possible, Szymborska's craft and her poetic gifts only increased with age. In the poem, "Sky," form the 1993 collection, *The End and the Beginning*, we easily see how her magician's tricks acquire such literary technique that they are clearly deserving of her lengthy list of literary awards. "Sky" is similar in its ontological inspection as "View in a Grain of Sand;" however, this poem is even more refined, more distilled, more of a metaphor of itself. She writes an ode to the sky without ostensibly giving it even faint praise: "I don't have to wait for a starry night,/ I don't have to crane my neck/ to get a look of it."

Although the realist in her portrays the ever present dome above our heads as "Grainy, gritty, liquid,/ inflamed, or volatile," it is also "everywhere,/ even in the dark beneath your skin." If any reader, by now, can't see that reading a poem by Szymborska is *like* a roller coaster ride, then just wait until the car plunges down the track at such an unexpected angle and rate of speed, as in her conclusion of "Sky:" "Division into sky and earth—/ it's not the proper way/ to contemplate this wholeness./ It simply lets me go on living/ at a more exact address/ where I can be reached promptly/ if I'm sought./ My identifying features/ are rapture and despair." Here we have arrived again at the beginning of the ride itself, exhausted by both our humanity and the human condition.

Although Szymborska's vision only continues to deepen with age, and she also further develops her predilection for metaphor as space, as in the 2002 collection, *Moment,* and in the poem "Clouds." Her playfulness alerts us only to her underlying seriousness, as she opens the poem, "I'd have to be really quick/ to describe clouds—/ a split second's enough/ for them to start being something else." She continues, tongue-in-cheek, one hand tugging at our shirt sleeve: "Their trademark:/ they don't repeat a single/ shape, shade, pose, arrangement."

With her hold on us now, she can extrapolate almost extemporaneously, and we believe her: "Next to clouds,/ even a stone seems like a brother." She insists, "Let people exist if they want,/ and then die, one after another:/ clouds simply don't care." Upon which we are nearly ready, but not quite, for the lighthearted lamentation at the poem's conclusion, regarding "Clouds," "They aren't obliged to vanish when we're gone./ They don't have to be seen while sailing on."

Perhaps the poem "Monologue of a Dog Ensnared in History" from the 2005 collection, *Colon,* may be offered as a lasting, and final, example, here, of the breadth of the work of this European master. We can only truly marvel at both the simplicity and depth of the poem's initial line: "There are dogs and dogs. I was among the chosen." We also are aware that "there are dog poems and poems that are dogs," which is my own inventiveness and a gloss on Szymborska's, which she just might have smiled at. It is interesting, in light of that comment, that she writes in this poem that we should "Take care, though—beware comparisons." Although I suspect Szymborska was an atheist, or an agnostic, her sense of spirituality was as imminent as those who might make ostentation of their own religious views, and most spiritual teachers will relay that comparisons are not part of the path. However, the dog in Szymborska's poem is at first well-groomed by its master, then eschewed by the invading army. In this first person portrayal, the dog in the poem betrays its own sense of lost equilibrium, in barking out that "Someone tore my silver-trimmed collar off,/ someone kicked my bowl, empty for days." Then another "someone" leans out of the car window, one who "shot me twice." The poem concludes, "He couldn't even shoot straight,/ since I died for a long time, in pain,/ to the buzz of impertinent flies./ I, the dog of my master." Szymborska is not beyond having mastered a Brechtian instinct for the poem as cabaret.

Translator Clare Cavanaugh mentions in her afterword that Marina Tsvetaeva spoke of "poets with a history and poets without a history," and that Szymborska, she writes, was "a poet with a history"—how true. However, Szymborska's sense of history, not unlike that of Milosz, possessed a sense of humility; and, perhaps, quite unlike Milosz, she also specialized in a rigorously disciplined sense of humor, as well.

Returning to the trope of the author's photograph, which began this essay, if we look at the photograph of Szymborska's that is on the inside of the book's back flap, we can see a woman who is possibly self-absorbed, however quite fully aware—someone who may be representative of sheer ebullience; and certainly that smile is that of an alchemist, someone who has discovered how to turn the lead of history and the dross of personal experience, thereof, into the gold of a poetic literature—that, if it is anything, will remain as significant to us as it is, in turns, that are both impish and irrevocably brilliant.

TUNING FORK ON THE SIDEWALK OF DREAMS: BERT MEYERS'S *THE WILD OLIVE TREE* AND *THE BLUE CAFÉ*

For many years the poetry of Bert Meyers was out of print. That seemed impossible in an age where the small press was as visible and vocal as it was. Considered by many to be a prominent American poet, if not one of the foremost American imagist poets, Bert Meyers still deserves a wider readership, even though *In a Dybbuk's Raincoat: Collected Poems* was published by University of Mexico Press in 2007.

Meyers's book *Windowsills* helped form many of my notions about what poetry is and what it could be. I was involved in its publication back in the spring of 1979, as assistant and cataloguer for publisher Hugh Miller of Common Table Press, in New Haven. One April afternoon, our publication date imminent, we received a phone call informing us that Bert Meyers had lost his fight with cancer. Hugh and I finished work that day with a strange steadiness, two young men bonded by significant circumstance and a common goal. This was one the origins of my deep love for the poetry of Bert Meyers.

The year Myers died, we published *Windowsills* and the West Coast Poetry Review Press issued *The Wild Olive Tree*. Three years later in 1982, these two books formed the core of poems collected in *The Wild Olive Tree and The Blue Café*, co-published by Jazz Press and PapaBach Editions. Though the volume was assembled after Meyers's death, it is a tight collection. It is very close to being a selected poems; the poems flow together quite naturally. Robert Frost once commented that if there were twenty-four poems in a book the twenty-fifth should be the book itself. Because Meyers's life work is so seamless, his editors had little trouble producing, from several sources, a book of amazing coherence and power. "Signature," the book's prefatory poem, plants the seeds of transcendence in his lovely posthumous volume:

> *I watch the world decay*
> *on every page on every face*
> *it's a sick man's clouded eye*
> *that rolls around in space*
>
> *And my obsession's*
> *a line I can't revise*
> *to be a gardener*
> *in paradise*

The integrity of Meyers's imagery is the cornerstone of his work. His deepest images are often rooted in the ordinary, day to day existence. What is special about a Meyers's image is that it is *exact*. His images often straddle the sometimes indistinguishable line between the startling and the cliché. Simply, put, Meyers's images are palpable, as in these lines from "These Days."

> Be like the rain
> that wears a ragged coat
> and finds the lamp
> in the smallest stone
> and sings for nothing
> from street to street

I think Meyers's poetry remains vital because—to borrow a phrase from Joseph Campbell—"these things just sing to you." Although Campbell was speaking of the symbols in myth, the images that "just sing" to us in Meyers's work are similarly valuable. Campbell stressed the importance of poetic vision to a culture's edification and survival.

Meyers often deals thematically with political and social issues. His poems frequently point to the individual's struggle to remain afloat among the wreckage of contemporary society and are marked by a poignant realism, but almost never without a nurturing possibility, a kind of buoyant resonance.

> Somehow, we created hope,
> reliable drum
> in the shadow's wrist;
> a tuning fork
> on the sidewalk of dreams.
> —"Gently, Gently"

As genuine as is his focus on society at large, when it switches to the individual, and especially to themes of old age and death, what emerges is a tenderness and compassion that compare with the lyrics of Theodore Roethke. An exquisite example is Meyers's portrayal of the loneliness of the elderly:

> Their children are gone:
> almost everyone
> they loved and half
> of what they understood,
> has disappeared.
> But the door's still open,
> the porch light's on;
> a little wind at night
> and they hear footsteps
> when a few leaves fall.
> —"Old"

In Rilke's poem "Archaic Torso of Apollo" is the command, "you must change your life." Meyers, too, knows the value of the edict for one's personal salvation, but Meyers states it in first person. He knows that functioning in society can arouse a dramatic, visceral response. In "A Citizen," he is "a coat hanger/ twisted by rage" and "a swastika, the headless man/ whose iron limbs grind the world." And it he can't save himself, then how can he save anybody else? "I want to change./ Even a wall gets painted again."

The last poem of this opening section, "All Around Me," is a paean to the survivor in all of us. Meyers is someone who has gone full circle, like the Zen Buddhist after the moment of satori, when the things of the world are the things of the world but emerge from the depths of their own radiance:

> All around me, butterflies
> ecstatic hinges,
> hunt for the ideal door.
> A cicada's ratchet
> tightens a place in the yard.
> Everything's warmed
> by a wave from a tree.

Even though he is witness to a kind of heaven on earth, Meyers puts the condition of the human species into perspective. The Buddhist says, "Life is suffering." Meyers echoes this universal truth, quite humanly, at the end of this plaintive lament.

> We do marvelous things
> without knowing how,
> like the chicken whose bronze shit
> builds a shrine under his coop.
> But, even so,
> one gets depressed.
> This morning, a field,
> a flock of stones
> asleep in its mist . . .
> The world's painted
> on a glass that has
> to break.

ESSAYS AND REVIEWS

As with Francis Ponge, the topics of many of Meyers's prose poems are *things*. We are re-introduced to some of the commonplace household items most of us own, and we are made to see them with a new awareness. A pair of pliers is the "contour of fish, or a donkey's intractable head." Notice the intriguing cubist element of "Pencil Sharpener:"

> It has no arms or legs, this tiny nude; yet grip it by the waist, then stir its hips; a dry leaf multiplies, a cold motor starts in the wood.
>
> Revived, still shivering, the pencil sheds itself—and there's a butterfly, teeth, the fragments of a crown.

William Carlos Williams would have been pleased to have conceived of a little poetic machine such as this.

Meyers moves from brief sketches of small objects to brief sketches of a particular landscape. The landscape Meyers captures so well is France, which he was able to visit on an Ingram-Merrill grant. The images found in his sequence should be enough to secure Meyers's reputation as one of the finest imagist poets. Look at these lines:

> When calm, the sea's so blue
> you could paint the sky with it.
> Sometimes, it's a green tablecloth
> laid on the wind.
> —"Ocean"
>
> Villages, like broken pots,
> or baskets of apples,
> scattered on a hillside.

* * * *

> And the light, so much light!
> a harp burning in a glass.
> —"Arrival"

In "Village," a farmer's upright scythe becomes "a tall, one legged bird/ whose long bill the farmer cleans." Later in this poem, Meyers speaks ever so fondly of herbs. In an earlier book, *The Dark Birds* (New York, NY: Doubleday & Co., Inc., 1968), he praises garlic as the "rabbi of condiments/ whose breath is a verb" ("The Garlic"). Here, the herb is endowed with a deserving coruscating culinary finish:

> A market in the street.
> Herbs, those quiet housewives,
> wearing their modest prints,
> were found in the fields at dawn.
> Clods of garlic, the kitchen's diamond,
> hang from every stall.
> Cheese, like the walls of France;
> red peppers with a plastic glow . . .

Meyers ends the poem with a farewell that seems more like a salutation:

> Outdoors, a breeze
> makes all the shrubs
> look sociable.
> White butterflies in a field
> are the frayed handkerchiefs of those
> who didn't finish saying goodbye.

And Meyer's realist's viewpoint insists that while there may be pleasant French villages, there are also Paris slums.

> And here are also filthy streets,
> leprous walls that sunlight

> never touched, smeared with crud,
> battered like garbage cans . . .
> the cracks in a stone
> are a landscape of nerves;
> the air's a perpetual fart
> and even the shadows wear rags.
>   —"Paris"

Compassion for the poor and disconsolate recur throughout Meyers's work, but perhaps nowhere with such sympathy as in these lines, also from "Paris."

> But the buildings of the poor
> divide their bread with everyone.
> At night, each window's a glass of wine
> the darkness drinks as it passes.

Viewing the Arc de Triomphe, Meyers looks through and sees "nothing but grey," and compares triumph to an "abyss/ into which a nation marches." On the 14th of July, "fireworks" are "an empire's crown/ that lasts for a moment," while "a tough guy shows a timid girl/ how to dance in the street." Meyers's juxtaposition of the evanescent light of "empire" and the spontaneity of a seemingly mismatched young couple transcends the pairs of opposites—light and dark, momentary and eternal, brazen and shy. More than a nascent spirituality emerges here.

Recalling a hero's journey, much of the next section deals, thematically, with returning home—though, often the return home seems more perilous than the journey itself. In "The Return," windows are broken, grass has turned brown, and "only a little grey hunchback/ wears the neighborhood like a shawl." Meyers also touches on the helplessness of returning to witness the disintegration of an aging parent.

> There are mouths so cold
> the salmon-colored tongue
> leaps without a sound;
> lonely ditches where a broken dove
> mourns in the rubble of a face.
> Men at the mercy of their parts:
> grime in the skull, despair
> corroding the rainbows in their wires.
> —"Homecoming"

Like Odysseus, Meyers is confronted with agonizing difficulties on his symbolic return home. One of these is the unmitigated distress of a widow. Condolences fall short, and there is no panacea for a widow's grief. If any one poem ever contained a *pathos* similar to that found in some of the paintings of Edward Hopper, this would be it.

> Leaves gnaw at the porch.
> The century, like her family, disappears.
> Life is a movie she's already seen.
> Her cheeks are rose petals
> in the book of better days.
> Wrinkled and powdered and rouged,
> bewildered by others,
> alone wherever she is,
> she opens her purse, she opens a drawer:
> it's twilight—she enters a photograph.
> —"The Widow"

Meyers is not a prodigal son. He is the hero returning from his journey. Upon facing, although not necessarily mastering these difficult situations, he undergoes transcendence and experiences an accrual of grace. In "With Animals," Meyers feels "like the elephant/ enlightened boulder/ held back by a chain," and the last stanza of the poem, "Daybreak," points to new beginnings.

> The sun climbs down from a roof,
> stops by a house and strikes
> its long match on a wall,
>
> takes out a ring of brass keys
> and opens every door.

And yet there is an element of sadness—an affirmation of mortality—in the sequence of ballads that comprise "The Blue Café." By my pure conjecture, these lines from "Images" may have been among the last Meyers was to write when besieged with cancer.

> Hands, twin sisters
> to whom everyone's
> a wrinkle
> that needs to be smoothed,
> a stranger who should be fed.
> Hands, those humble wings
> that make each day
> fly toward its goal;
> at rest, still holding
> the shape of a tool.

A Meyers's poem is carefully constructed, image by image, built into a poetic architecture based on the perpetuity of the eternal image. His poems have the uncanny distinction of seeming handmade, shaped from the elements. His prior profession, picture framer, may account for the way his poetry seems fashioned by a craftsman's loving hands. Bert Meyers's craftsman hands are now "at rest, still holding/ the shape of a tool." And while today readers do have the opportunity to find all of Bert Meyers's poetry among the pages of *In a Dybbuk's Raincoat: Collected Poems,* for many years *The Wild Olive Tree and The Blue Café* was the only place one could discover the blessing of Bert Meyers's poetry—which is something that the entire world both deserved and needed.

THE ART AND NECESSITY OF *FESTSCHRIFT*: *FAIR WARNING: LEO CONNELLAN AND HIS POETRY* AND A REVIEW OF LEO CONNELLAN'S *DEATH IN LOBSTERLAND*

Festschrift (German pronunciation: [ˈfɛstʃrɪft]; plural, Festschriften [ˈfɛstʃrɪftən]) is commonly known as a book that honors a writer, often during that person's lifetime, sometimes not. *Fair Warning: Leo Connellan and His Poetry* (Tokyo, Japan: Printed Matter, 2011), edited by Sheila Murphy and Marilyn Nelson, was both a long labored and much awaited publishing project. Connecticut Poet Laureate Leo Connellan died in 2001, and although this collection of essays and reviews regarding his work was in various stages of being assembled, and then readied for publication, the *Festschrift*, in tribute to him, took nearly a full decade to be fully realized as a published book.

I take delight in the honor of having been invited to contribute a review that I wrote of one of Connellan's books, *Death in Lobsterland* (Fort Kent, Maine: Great Raven Press, 1978), but I am doubly honored since I was also asked to contribute an endorsement for the back cover of the *Festschrift*, which I considered to be a privilege, since many of the contributors to the book included such poets and writers of notoriety as the eminent and perennially charming and magnanimous Richard Wilbur.

Initially, I first met Leo Connellan when I was directing a poetry reading series at The Theater and Space on Orange Street in New Haven, Connecticut some forty years ago. Leo Connellan was enjoying his first real literary success upon his publishing *First Selected Poems* in the University of Pittsburgh Press Poetry Series—and he was then in his late forties or early fifties. He was a man who lost his mother as a child; entertained visions of becoming a writer as a young man, which sprung him from a hardscrabble life in Maine, upon which he would eventually base his big American poems; hitchhiked the country and would go on to write most memorably about the experience, in an historical as well as personal context; could reminisce about seeing Dylan Thomas drink pints of stout in the White Horse Tavern in the East Village; and whose very essence and being, despite being a married man and a father of a daughter, at that time, depended on poetry and the writing of it.

Leo Connellan was only the second Poet Laureate of the State of Connecticut, after the Pulitzer Prize-winning James Merrill. In opposition to Merrill's urbanity and financial wealth as well as his stature in the greater literary community, Leo Connellan was a working man, albeit one who was a salesman in a white collar, and a working man's poet. Although comparisons aside, Leo Connellan worked tirelessly during his years as Poet Laureate of the State of Connecticut in the Poetry-in-the-Schools Program. Whether it was his deep gratitude of his being awarded his new status or his devout love of poetry that mattered, and probably both, his being a proponent of the written word and his teaching students of all ages anywhere from grammar school to high school to college was a passion tantamount to his devotion of writing his own poetry, if not more so.

Leo Connellan's life and his poetry are entwined. His work celebrates the human spirit as well as portraying what the editor of the periodical my review was published in chose as the headline to the piece as "Injustices of the Human Heart." Although Leo Connellan left Maine not long out of his teens, its rocky coast and the calloused fingers and palms of its farmers and fisherman remained in his psyche and became the very ethos of his poetry which today often goes overlooked despite its largesse in the most American of senses—since it resembles, in its metaphysical girth, a symphony by Aaron Copeland or a painting by Edward Hopper. If you seek the American grain, of course you would immediately think of William Carlos Williams and his notion of composition he called the variable foot and of such books of his as *Pictures from Brueghel and Other Poems,* which was the epitome of his shorter lyrical poems as well as the vastness of his four-book narrative poem *Patterson;* whereas, with Leo Connellan his classic shorter poetry is collected in his last book, *The Maine Poems* and his now little appreciated masterpiece was his book-length poem, *Crossing America,* illustrated with woodcuts by one of the great masters of the genre, Michael McCurdy, and issued from the artist's now legendary Penmaen Press.

To augment, and certainly to enlighten, the legacy of the poetry of Leo Connellan and his spirit, I enclose my lengthy back cover endorsement, which was only used in part on the back of the *Festschrift,* and then my review of one of this poet's seminal books, *Death in Lobsterland.*

* * * *

In his poem "On the Eve of Becoming a Father," Leo Connellan writes that he "had been about to hang up" his proverbial "gun," however "the hammer shot one spark into the moon,/ so magnificent, it is beyond me." The poem is from *First Selected Poems* (University of Pittsburgh Press, 1976). That book remains a volume of lasting and memorable poetry, and that is rare for any book in any genre. The author of those poems was only beginning, although well past his mid-forties, he was to eventually write and publish his best work in a series of subsequent books, often by waking at dawn, before going out into the world to make his living as a traveling salesman, to pen his poems that are cut straight from the American grain.

The poetry of Leo Connellan is a poetry of perseverance. He survived the loss of his mother as a child, and, forgoing his having completed a college degree, entered into the arena of American literature, whose territory is often enough overseen only by academics. *However*, his books continue to speak for themselves, and more importantly, not just for poetry, but for America herself. Connellan begins his book-length poem, *Crossing America*, with these autochthonous and memorable lines: "We hitchhiked America. I/ still think of her.//I walk the old streets thinking I/ see her, but never.// New buildings have gone up./ The bartenders who poured roses/ into our glasses are gone./ We are erased."

Although Connellan's poetry has persevered beyond all erasure, like a palimpsest, *Crossing America*, with respect to literary achievement alone, truly belongs next to its fictional and preternatural counterpart, Jack Kerouac's *On the Road*.

I can still see Leo reading his poems aloud, with one hand conducting the line breaks of each verse like a conductor with a baton leading a symphony orchestra, his voice enunciating the last word of each line like a sculptor who has chiseled them out of the granite of the post-WWII American experience. Thankfully, we have his treasure trove of poems of survival: "Amelia, the Mrs. Brooks of my Childhood." "By the Blue Sea;" "Tell Her that I Fell;' and lesser known gems, such as "Blueberry Boy,: finding him, and us, before "the tripup of manhood," on our collective knees "picking/ frantically with expert watered tongue,/ ignorant of what lay out of the woods."

Now, there is a *Festschrift* in his honor that is a veritable celebration of the poetry of Leo Connellan, as it is a tribute to America, and why the work of Leo Connellan is a significant contribution to American literature.

****

A poem is an anonymous gift to an anonymous recipient; and when you're finished with it, it doesn't belong to you anymore, it belongs to someone else.
—KARL SHAPIRO, in a letter to Leo Connellan

LEO CONNELLAN

Leo Connellan is a poet who has weathered a fourteen year silence from writing, a bout with alcoholism, and a number of nine-to-five jobs as a traveling salesman. He portrays his home state of Maine, where the winters can be as harsh as the economy, with verbal crispness, deep empathy, and an active compassion. His poems are often funereal, tragic, and resonant.

"So many of my poems are about Maine because that's where I come from. They're about working men, about the injustices of the human heart," says Connellan, who at the age of fifty has just published his eighth collection of poems, *Death in Lobsterland*.

You don't have to come from Maine to appreciate his work. Nor do you have to be an academic to understand it, although Connellan is an exceptional craftsman. His poems lure you with their lyricism, then snap shut like a lobster trap. Take the poem "Scott Huff," for example:

> Think tonight of sixteen
> year old Scott Huff of
> Maine driving home fell asleep at
> the wheel, his car sprang awake
> from the weight of his foot head on
> into a tree. God, if you need him
> take him asking me to believe in
> you because there are yellow buttercups,
> salmon for my heart in the rivers,
> fresh springs of ice cold water running away.
> You can have all of these back for Scott Huff.

After attending the University of Maine, Connellan took his chances spinning around the country like a chip played on a roulette wheel. For Connellan, Maine would be a place he would always return to, that would draw him back again and again, but New York City proved to be his primary stomping ground from the mid-50s through the early 60s.

When he lived in New York, he would sell carbon paper and typewriter ribbons between 8:00 a.m. and 2:00 p.m., then go the Limelight Café on Sheridan Square to write his poems.

"I made it an atmosphere where I could write," he says. "In that din and over cups of coffee, I realized time was passing me by, and that I didn't have any excuses left for not writing. I embraced it."

"My career as a writer began by what I thought writing might be," Connellan continues. "The trick of writing is simplicity. The thing to do is edit. Once the idea is clear, get rid of excess words. Excess words reveal the writer is bluffing behind nothing to say. I don't rush. The poem will be done when it is. But the minute you have to explain it you're writing prose."

Finally, *Penobscot Poems* was published by New Quarto Editions in 1974. Then a quick succession of books followed— *Another Poet in New York* (Living Poets Press); *First Selected Poems* (University of Pittsburgh Press); *Crossing America* (Penmaen Press); *Seven Short Poems* (Western Maryland College Writers Union); and this year, from Great Raven Press, of Fort Kent, Maine, *Death in Lobsterland*.

"Writing is something you can't help yourself from doing," he says now after his years of struggle. "It is everything to me, and I knew I *could* write if I didn't die from bad luck or from drinking."

Connellan is an elegist, and *Death in Lobsterland* is his best work to date. "It is the book I always wanted to write," he says.

The book contains many long narrative poems such as "By the Blue Sea," "Edwin Coombs," and what just may be the poem he may be most remembered by, "Amelia, Mrs. Brooks of my Old Childhood"—all painful reminiscences knotted like the calloused hands of the fisherman and cannery workers that they both criticize and eulogize.

They are raw and overpowering poems, compelling rereading after rereading. They have so much life compressed in them that they throb like the ache of a lobsterman's hands.

Simultaneous with the publication of *Death in Lobsterland*, a movie has just been released, *Leo Connellan at 50,* and will shortly be aired on public and cable television.

Leo Connellan has succeeded in what he set out to do so many years ago in Rockland, Maine, his hometown, where he feels "it was an accomplishment to be born there, grow up, and leave."

In his work, he fulfills his own poetic credo—writing big American poems that are worth rereading and endowing his readers with a sense that these works of art are in part their own accomplishment.

LYRICAL MATHEMATICS: *THE KINGFISHER'S REIGN* BY JONAS ZDANYS

Prose poetry differs from other forms of poetry the way Jean Cocteau's 1946 classic romantic fantasy, *La Belle et la Bete,* or *Beauty and the Beast,* with its talking wall mirrors and animated candelabras, bears no resemblance to the emotionally charged films of American filmmaker Terrence Maleck, such as the 1973 film, *Badlands.* The former offers the alchemy of the surreal, whereas the latter is dependent on the narrative of the dialogue and brilliant acting. The point is that the difference between the prose poem and any other form of poetry may just be the disparity between what is alchemical and what is magical in any artistic discipline.

Prose poems have their history rooted in the work of Charles Baudelaire and Arthur Rimbaud, who were as responsible for precipitating the genre as Edgar Alan Poe was for initiating the genre of the short story. The prose poems of Jonas Zdanys are alluring and brilliant poetic streams of consciousness, whose strength is more dependent on their being written in sentences and paragraphs than in the polished ladder-like lines of any lyrical or narrative poem. They are perhaps best described as the tie-dyed sunbursts of poetry—often surreal poetic prose structures whose only rule may be that there are truly no rules, but where nothing but lyricism abounds in sentence after unrestrained sentence of at least a full page and not more than two.

The Kingfisher's Reign collects eighty prose poems in the book's four sections: "Icarus Rising;" "The Middle Voice;" "The Outer Gate;" and "The Shadows of Crows in Midwinter." There are twenty poems in each section. Zdanys not only offers a symmetrical arrangement of the poems, but also displays what one of the definitions of the prose poem is, in that it can be a nearly symmetrically arranged lyrical mathematics, as in these sentences from "The Old Hand of the Moon," from the book's last section:

> The black window that reflects the dry ice of the moon framed by the old hand that has no sense that time has passed, that time has passed and our vision is blocked, by the snow when it comes. It is the menace of the moment, a frozen moment, random as the cycle of the seasons, that traces regret with the old hand of the moon that drags itself across the night like the degradation of ice, that melts and refreezes, back and forth, back and forth into glass, when the snow comes, when the snow comes.

It is not only a stream of consciousness that is intrinsic to the prose poem, but specific to prose poems of Zdanys there is a concomitant philosophical essence that blends together—not in a magical way, since the language of his prose poems is not one invested in tricks, but in an alchemical fashion, in that it does turn the lead of his experiences that precipitate the prose poems into the silver and gold of the language of his poetry. One of the most memorable phrases illustrating this attribute is from "Hope," which is also exemplary of the humanistic expression found in the work of work of Zdanys, overall: "hope the square root of doubt." How much poetic verisimilitude is presented here, how much of a lyrical mathematics? It is worth illustrating this in quoting the prose poem in full:

> It was the humming of the water that caught my attention that morning, airy things growing small, the persistent tenderness of tears on her cheek. I had planned nothing that day and felt as if my mouth

> and throat were filled with dust as I kept repeating over and over again that the world is the same as it has always been, gone light then dark as it ages to forgetfulness and dry seed, the solitude of fire. Our arms brush against one another as we pass: hope the square root of doubt, as if the world would end then and there. I remember I had the oddest dream: the face in the mirror, when it smiled, had transparent teeth and its eyes turned to avoid the long white blur of the room.

So what is a lyrical mathematics? I believe it can be described as the balancing of both an asymmetrical and symmetrical aesthetic in language, especially in poetry, and, maybe, even most especially in prose poetry. If the prose poem becomes the vehicle through which to express the formula of the language itself, the stream of consciousness, then Zdanys's "The Invention of Zero" is one of the best examples.

> On the table, wind. The left hand pressed against the outside wall. Footsteps across the cobblestones. The dark rider on a pale bicycle. Wax that will not melt. Blood in the corners of the mouth. The holy fire of night birds healing. The lost salt of living. The small chains of the century fallen to silence. The cold dew on the cross posts of the gate. Statues of mist as the fog lifts. The eyes of women hiding in the dark. The third knock. The sun today set on the wrong horizon: black and white, two and simultaneously one, the double and the contradictory, certainty from uncertainty, a search for what we have not yet lost. And I am everywhere, rising like a sudden shout on the brink of a world in which I play no part. I turn, a shadow between generation and death, the final shape and substance of the narrow orbit of the closing north, the self-intrusion of the assonant

emptiness that betrayed me to dust. Under this hesitant step, in a world cleanly divided, I stand triumphant and immortal at the center, the circumference.

To further the theories and *italicize* the idea of the lyric, which even becomes expansive in the small space the size of a paragraph, is "Icarus Remembers His Lover Dancing," an example of what a prose poem can achieve as *pure song*.

> The look in her eyes each time I enter her, the sound of her breath against my face, the weight of her fingers on my back and arms—these moments of rebirth, faint cries framed by a window dulled by guarded light, a dance in the sky I have waited for all my life. The white ring, the shift of things in the wind she wakes to hear; the mask of desire pulled out of the air and a thousand flowers passing to dust as her legs bear down. I float above the clouds as if to breathe, imitate the calls of other birds. Child of light, I spin from world to world as the grass grows green. I sprawl the bones of a buried life. I rise, I rise.

If this isn't language singing, then how else could the lyric be appropriately exemplified? The sensuality balances with the sinuousness of the language and the images in the prose poem itself. This is also celebratory of all of us as the "Icarus" in our own lives, with our own constructions of wax wings, can be suitably fashioned in the hope that we don't fly too close to the sun; however, it is more of an ode to all of our lovers and to life itself. How beautiful and resonant is the phrase "a thousand flowers passing to dust as her legs bear down;" and how fortunate are we, as readers, to cherish and savor the memorable as poetry as in this prose poem by Zdanys.

This book, as with all the books published by Virtual Artists Collective, as one might nearly expect with a press by that name, is attractively and aesthetically exacting. The size is 8 ½ X 5 ½—making it what old booksellers often term "a book that fits nicely in the hand." Also, replacing back cover endorsements, there is either an entire poem or a stanza from one of the poems in the book, and in the case of this book there is a phrase from one of the prose poems, that clues the reader in to the quality of the poetry inside.

Although the layout of the text is clean and a pleasure to read, there may be an argument in having the right margins of the prose poems justified. If this were done then there should be no doubt in a reader's mind, who might not be familiar with prose poems, that the work is indeed just that: prose poetry and not verse written in lines.

Jonas Zdanys, a bilingual poet, is the author of thirty-nine other books, among them sixteen collections of his own poetry, written in English or in Lithuanian, and twenty volumes of translations of poetry and prose from the Lithuanian. His prolific and qualitative output is nothing less than astounding. What is both astounding and stunning is the alchemy in the poetry of this newest collection, as it crosses over from the realm of just magic to that of Jean Cocteau's talking mirrors and animated candelabras to the cosmic explosions on the screen of Terrence Maleck's 2011 film, *The Tree of Life*. The latter film actually resembles *La Belle et la Bete* in that we are transported by it *first*, and then the real *kick* is that after that what we experience is an actual *transcendence*. Readers will find this same phenomenon occurring when they read the prose poems by Jonas Zdanys in *The Kingfisher's Reign*.

2. Journey to the East
THE WAY OF HAIKU

Since there is so much biographical material contained within the introductions I include here for two major collections of my own haiku, I will attempt to refrain from duplicate anything here that might be included later. However, I do offer that John Barlow, Editor and Publisher of Snapshot Press, of Ormskirk, U. K. and I labored over the publication process of *The Windbreak Pine: New and Uncollected Haiku, 1985-2015* from April 2013 through November 2016. John's editing, especially of the 116 haiku, written over a 30-year period, into a single seasonal tapestry, from spring to winter, is nothing less than remarkable. Although I provided much of the references for the haiku over that span of years, it was John who wove the haiku into the lyric narrative that it is, after my original inklings. For this I offer him my thanks and a deep bow for his yeoman efforts in making the collection what it is, for now and toward a felicitous posterity.

Adele Kenny is a poet, who not unlike myself, works in multiple genres: longer poetry, nonfiction, *and* haiku. She is also a contemporary, and I respect the sense of craft with which she approaches her haiku. When I had learned of the publication of her new book in the spring of 2016, I immediately thought I might review it—and did. It was satisfying for me to do so, and reminded me of the years I was the Book Review Editor of *Modern Haiku*, during the guidance of the inimitable Robert Spiess, who was the strong and equitable presence in making what North American haiku was from the 1960s through the beginning of the 21st-century and his death in 2002. Although seemingly inconsequential, the reviews I wrote of some 90 books in a period between 1985 and 1997, of which I was Book

JOURNEY TO THE EAST

Review Editor officially from 1987 through 1996, filled me with a sense of accomplishing what was *right work*. Jack Kerouac once said that if he had a chance to live his life over again he would have stayed in Lowell, married Maggie Cassidy, and enjoyed a career as a railroad brakeman. During these years, I managed one bookstore, or another, and wrote traditional lyric poetry *and* haiku. For my commute to work and back I carried a tape recorder in my car so that I wouldn't lose lines. Every Sunday, I would transcribe the tape and work the lines I hadn't lost into short lyric and narrative poems as well as haiku. Most Sundays saw me placing a review I had written, or a submission of haiku, in the mail to Bob Spiess. It wasn't a bad life, especially when I am quite aware that there are lives that are much worse. So, my reviewing Adele's book was a kind of Proustian *madeleine*—a touchstone as *mimesis*—which I could live the past through a moment in the present, just by rediscovering the joy of those years I was in touch with Bob Spiess.

My review of John Wills's final haiku collection, *Mountain*, is as much tribute to him as much as it is a critical homage of his work. Among the pioneers in the genre, the haiku of John Wills are prominent examples of American poetry at its best written as haiku in English. His is some of the work that really should be taught in schools, instead of the notion that *anything* written in three lines of a 5-7-5 syllable pattern is what constitutes haiku. Every year during Super Bowl season I cringe hearing *football haiku* being recited on the radio, including NPR of all places. For me to have to listen to such rogue impertinence is akin to Beethoven or Mozart being played on a plastic comb. However, John Wills, and others, were, indeed, literary pioneers in the haiku genre, and their work has held up over decades. Now only if enough people noticed that would make a difference. Although any number of frontline American poets who claim to know what haiku is and to write it competently, in fact, don't know it at all and write what are fatuous three-line poems they themselves call haiku.

THE WAY OF HAIKU

The essay as introduction, "The Poetics of Walking," was written at Fort Juniper, the Robert Francis Homestead, in Cushman, Massachusetts. It was, as I recall, one of the last projects I finished before leaving what was a two-year writing residency there. It is included in *The Silence Between Us: The Selected Haiku of Wally Swist*, published by Brooks Books, in their Goodrich Haiku Masters Series. Any more mention of it than this would take away from the already biographically-rich text.

Ion Codrescu, a Romanian haiku poet and editor, invited me to submit an essay on writing haiku for an anthology celebrating Basho. Ion's letters to me, written in their cursive calligraphy with blue ink, were priceless to receive. However much I appreciated them, I found it constrictive to need to stay within a certain word limit for the essay, and my attempting to stretch to include my themes of what I was avidly reading at the time—the Grail Castle myth as interpreted by the Jungian Robert Johnson, as well as to even make mention of his books regarding the psychology of gender—was an undertaking I may not make today some twenty years later. However, I do believe in framing English haiku against such themes of largesse may, at least, precipitate some readers into thinking of its validity.

As a former bookstore manager, I would shelve William S. Higginson's books regarding *saijiki* in the nature section. The wealth of information alone regarding moths and butterflies should prove surfeit enough for any lepidopterist. Nabokov would have loved this book for that alone. Of any of the reviews I wrote for *Modern Haiku*, these two were ones I felt responsible to include in this book due to the breadth of Higginson's work and its importance—twenty years later. There may never again be a seasonal poetry almanac assembled as assiduously and with such complex references as Bill achieved in his work. These are important contributions to contemporary literature—on any number of levels.

JOURNEY TO THE EAST

Nicholas A. Virgilio was also a pioneer in the haiku genre from the late 1950s until his untimely death in 1989. Nick was an active promoter of haiku, and during a taping of *CBS News Nightwatch* he died of a heart attack. What I remember when I think of Nick is his diligence and perseverance. He came upon haiku after the end of a love affair, and by engaging in writing haiku he not only lifted himself up from the disappointment of that relationship but also became one of the genre's major voices and champions. It is a story worth knowing and repeating to oneself during one's darkest hours. Bravery and courage are not often associated with writers, and certainly not with haiku poets, but these superlatives are indicative of Nick's resilience. These are some reasons why I chose to include the review of his *Selected Haiku*.

As with the preceding chapter, and something I won't be doing for every chapter, I am enclosing some of my own work. The two haiku below are the alpha and omega of the collection of haiku that embrace by *The Windbreak Pine*. May they whet your literary palette for the work celebrating the haiku poets and haiku itself, as well as concepts surrounding it, in the pages that follow.

> spring snow—
> an unopened bud at the end
> of each branch of the dogwood

///

> snowflakes in the wind—
> a slant of light
> on needles of the pine

THE WINDBREAK PINE: AN INTRODUCTION

Nearly ten years ago in my composing an author's preface to *The Silence Between*, I was uncertain where my future in writing haiku might lay. I was at the time living at Fort Juniper, the Robert Francis homestead, in Cushman, Massachusetts, as its poet-in-residence. It would be my last summer there, and finishing *The Silence Between Us* was one of that summer's memorable moments.

The writing that I began over the two years I lived at Fort Juniper took me five more years to finish and polish. These lyric and short narrative poems would constitute a book-length collection entitled *Huang Po and the Dimensions of Love*, which would go on to be selected as the co-winner of the 2011 Crab Orchard Series Open Poetry Competition, chosen by Pulitzer Prize-winning poet Yusef Komunyakaa.

Although I have needed to honor a driving need to produce and craft further collections of poetry since then, in what seems like a relatively short period of time, a series of events that took place in my life in 2008 alerted me to life's finite nature. The spiritual awakening that ensued was one in which I envisioned writing as many as five more books, besides *Huang Po and the Dimensions of Love;* and in my composing poems for these books, I often worked on each book concomitantly. What I did not foresee was my returning to an avid and dedicated practice of writing haiku.

* * * *

I had become seriously interested in haiku in 1973 when I began to practice zazen. My meditation group met in the basement of Yale Divinity School Chapel. Besides Philip Kapleau's *Three Pillars of Zen*, I would also often have Harold G. Henderson's *Introduction To Haiku* in hand. The Doubleday edition of Cor van den Heuvel's *The Haiku Anthology* was such a staple of mine that my copy soon became tattered. It was then that I began trying to write haiku.

In the summer of 1976 I was reading Ippekirō's *Cape Jasmine and Pomegranates*, in a handsome edition published by Cape/Golliard. The 5-7-5 syllabic structure then largely associated with haiku did not attract me, but Ippekirō's "free verse" haiku did. I persevered with my attempts at writing and at that time began to submit work to Robert Spiess, the editor of *Modern Haiku*.

I was frustrated by his rejections of my work, but always found myself encouraged by his comments, such as his indications that I had come "close," perhaps, but "not quite." He sometimes even made suggestions regarding the work I had submitted, but the more I tried the more disillusioned I became with my ever writing successful haiku. What would it be like, I thought, if I could have the good fortune to have even just *one* haiku accepted for publication in *Modern Haiku*?

Finally, in the spring of 1977, I reluctantly tried *Modern Haiku* again. By the autumn of that year I still had not heard back. I thought it time to write a letter to inquire as to what may have happened. Bob, as he was soon fondly to become, who answered with a rapidity that astonished me. Yes, he had finally accepted a haiku of mine, but it was my self-addressed stamped envelope that had proved to be the hang-up.

Bob pointed out that I had placed a small amount of scotch tape on the corner of an old stamp on my return envelope.

THE WINDBREAK PINE

This was against post office rules. Although I had moved in the interim, and had filed a change of address with the post office, the envelope that contained the news of my acceptance into *Modern Haiku* had taken up residence in the "dead letter" office in Boston and was deemed undeliverable. The letter, as Bob enjoyed telling me, was eventually mailed back to *Modern Haiku* because I had scrupulously typed the magazine's address on the top left hand corner of the envelope. Hence, it was not until I wrote Bob to query about the submission that he had a working address for me.

What if I never received Bob's letter of acceptance? Would I have continued to pursue the writing of haiku? Haiku was to become not only such a significant part of my life, but *a way of life* for me over the course of the eleven years that I lived in Haskins' Flats on the outskirts of Cushman, a village of North Amherst, Massachusetts. I have often thought of those years: living in a refurbished barn next to a wetland on the rim of a series of meadows, now a conservation area named Haskins Meadow. That experience provided such inspiration for me that I believe it was tantamount to what "Sweetwater," the name of the farm in eastern Tennessee, provided for John Wills. Concomitant to my living in an idyllic space was my eventual close affiliation with Bob and *Modern Haiku*. Of my several literary friendships and mentorships of import, including the salient relationship I had with Amherst poet Robert Francis, my relationship with Robert Spiess would endure the longest: quite fortuitously for more than two decades.

Many life changes for me in the early eighties prevented much quality writing of any kind, but upon moving to the Haskins' Flats barn in July 1984 I began to steep myself in the nearby meadows, wetlands, and not-too-distant mountains—to breathe it all in, to let it wash over me, and to discipline myself to write down the images emanating from this rich landscape. I renewed my correspondence with Bob and in December 1984 began to submit work to him on a regular basis, continuing for what would be almost fourteen years.

* * * *

In collecting the haiku in *The Windbreak Pine: New and Uncollected Haiku 1985–2015*, it is my intent to augment *The Silence Between Us*, published by Brooks Books in 2005. It is only in the last few years that I have intuited the importance of returning to the practice of writing haiku and to my offering a selection of haiku that was not considered for *The Silence Between Us* at the time of its publication. In also including more recent, and sometimes previously unpublished, haiku in this present volume, my aim has been to create a collection of haiku whose significance is tantamount to that collected in *The Silence Between Us*.

After a break of some eleven years, I returned to writing haiku avidly in 2009. And with my return to writing haiku, I have come full circle. I began writing haiku in a 5-7-5 syllabic pattern before I came upon those haiku of Ippekirō, when I was a young man. And since I began writing haiku again I have returned to writing in a full complement of 17 syllables, although not in the traditional 5-7-5 form. My reasons for doing so stem, in part, to a correspondence with Billy Collins, whom I had hosted when I managed a bookstore at Trinity College. In a letter Billy had written to me, providing me a gracious endorsement for *Huang Po and the Dimensions of Love*, he mentioned, that for him, writing haiku in lines of 5-7-5 syllables gave him "something to push against." Billy acknowledged that I did not write haiku in such a traditional pattern, but he intimated that his practice gave him the necessary rigors that a poet who also wrote longer lyric and short narrative poetry would find engaging.

In using 17 syllables, I am able, often enough, to give myself the leeway for more lyrical lines than are usually associated with

THE WINDBREAK PINE

haiku. This seems especially appropriate given that most of my haiku deal directly with the natural world, with there being inherent song in the images of nature. I also find that using this syllabic parameter offers me the freedom to explore the form more deeply in an imagistic manner, and in doing so it relates more closely to my working in the longer forms of the lyric and narrative poem. Sometimes my *haiku moment* yields a two-page poem, layered with images, and written in a lyric line; and other times, I write 17 syllable haiku, sometimes in lines as unconventional as 3-10-4. Ippekirō is still with me; however, I also have had the felicitous experience of Billy Collins having whispered in my ear.

The more recent haiku in this collection were almost invariably written out of the source of this literary matrix and heritage. Several have since appeared in print, although numerous unpublished haiku, written since 2009, were edited specifically for this volume at the suggestion of John Barlow. Most of these haiku, which we agreed should appear here for the first time, consequently have fewer than seventeen syllables.

The more historic uncollected haiku collected here could all too easily have fallen into remote obscurity had a scrupulous effort not been made in excavating the very best of the nearly forgotten. Their inclusion here is a delight for me, since these haiku are old friends that continue to light up the years and give them validity and substance.

Altogether, *The Windbreak Pine* assembles over one hundred haiku written over the major creative watersheds of a thirty year period, from 1985 to the spring of 2015. An example of my continuing work with the image, it further celebrates the remaining open land in my beloved New England, while honoring green space everywhere. If the image is eternal, as the revolutionary 20th-century psychologist Carl Jung posits, then perhaps an understanding of the ethos behind the 17th-century haiku master Bashō's "learning about the pine from the pine" may assist in saving the planet.

My manifold purpose in collecting the haiku in this book also includes offering a selection of nature poetry that might be appreciated by anyone who opens the covers of *The Windbreak Pine* and begins to read.

* * * *

I had not returned to the Haskins' Flats barn since I left my apartment there in the spring of 1995, although the owners, who have always lived in the barn since the late 1970s, have invited me to visit at some time on numerous occasions. Today, I finally took up my old friends' invitation, and was amazed at the architectural changes that were made to extend their living space into what had once been my late wife's and mine.

The land is not exactly unchanged, since the woods have grown in where there was a back meadow. However, the brook is still visible, if not more so, along with a significant beaver lodge near the bridge that crosses the road. Wild turkeys come down into the back meadow for feed, and I understand deer come for the salt lick that has been placed there. The sign for the meadow, where I would walk Cider, is weathered and illegible; although the significant thing is that it exists at all, especially with all of the development in town. I found myself magnetized by the pull that still exists for me in that hallowed glade.

Although I have driven by before, doing so after having just visited the barn was a travel back in time for me. My yellow Labrador and I walking the land in the meadows and the fields, the curves and meanders of the brook, the woods on the knoll and the ridge, on the other side of which, several miles going back toward town, is Fort Juniper.

THE WINDBREAK PINE

For an hour this afternoon, an important period of time in my life revolved right before my eyes: only 8.8 miles from Haskins' Flats to the farmhouse in South Amherst where I now live, all those years and decades in between. However, in experiencing the present moment, I feel more grounded in having made my visit, as if time, and my life, has broadened and deepened, cut into the earth like Cushman Brook's dog-legs, guiding the rush of the water through its course over the land.

South Amherst, Massachusetts
May 2015

IMAGISTIC PERPETUITY: THE HAIKU OF ADELE KENNY

Not Asking what if is a refreshing book of haiku. I should probably clarify that I have read many of these haiku before, and that I can emphasize that I reveled in reading them *again*. I became acquainted with many of these haiku by having read them either in journals or in previous volumes of Adele Kenny's. However, it is actually nurturing to see these all collected here along with new haiku within a single volume, and a distinguished volume it is.

My overall aesthetic appraisal of the collection, other than its ostensible accomplishment, is that it resonates with what I can term the era the haiku originated from—the 70s, 80s, and 90s—as a golden age of North American haiku. These decades were reflected by what is sometimes referred to as the first wave of haiku poets, and possibly some second wave writers, including the late Nick Virgilio, master of acute perceptions within the haiku moment; Virginia Brady Young, who was expert in representing the layers of images within nature in the haiku form, ever so ingeniously; and Raymond Roseliep, who taught everyone how to look deeper into the ordinariness of our lives and to discover either the *mysterium tremendum* in them or a kind of ribald humor, often with oneself as the subject or object, or both.

We also can't forget the true majesty of Elizabeth Searle Lamb, indeed, as she was dubbed, "the first lady of haiku," and her precision of image and tone, which I wouldn't doubt originated from her being an accomplished harpist and who had played in at least one symphony orchestra.

ADELE KENNY

All that richness comes back to me in reading the haiku in *Not Asking what if*. How can we not forget the inimitable John Wills, who in my mind is, perhaps, the premier American haiku poet, when we read his "a box of nails/ on the shelf in the shed/ the cold." Elements of such classic American haiku resonate within those of Adele Kenny's. Hers may not have been written thirty or forty years ago, or more, but the tones of her haiku echo in a similar demonstrative and memorable way. In her new book we read: "snow in the air--/ the graveyard gate opens/ on rusty hinges," that is reminiscent of Wills. Another haiku of hers that this time recalls the immaculate depths of Father Roseliep, who was also a Catholic priest, reads: "gathering shadows,/ statues/ with broken arms." There is a mysticism that reverberates in this haiku whose spectrum ranges from the alchemical to a treatise written by either Meister Eckhart or Thomas Merton on the benefits of poverty in the life of the spirit.

Two more of my favorites in Adele Kenny's book are: "abbey bells/ muffled by dusk/ as the hills lose shape," which is one of the most lyrically achieved haiku I have ever read, especially with the onomatopoeia of *abbey bells*; and "nightfall:/ the corners of my room/ disappear first," which is such a writer's or poet's haiku in that anyone who has labored long in one's study or over one's desk has had to experience those "corners of my room" become only an evanescent memory as one's day has in working on a revision or a new piece of writing, just to see the perfection you were seeking dissipate into oblivion.

It is also significant for me to see that Adele Kenny, as well as some other haiku poets, have worked successfully in various genres, since she has published books of what haiku poets call "longer poems," as well as prose books regarding creative writing as well as collectibles. Although there is one more haiku, out of a very many in this book that are quotable, which I can't help but mention, as one of my own personal favorites, and that is one that is also reminiscent of Raymond Roseliep, also referred to as "the John Donne of western haiku," who had published several volumes of traditional verse with W. W. Norton & Company in the early sixties only to forego writing "longer poems" and composing only haiku for the last decade, or so, of his life. This haiku reminds me of the one that the American poet, Denise Levertov, who published many books with New Directions, quoted in a blurb on the back of Roseliep's book, *Listen to Light*, published in a handsome edition by Alembic Press in the late 1970s, which reads:

"campfire extinguished/ a woman washing dishes/ in a pan of stars." Adele Kenny's haiku, with its own echo providing equal clarity, is reminiscent of Roseliep's poem as it is concomitantly a fine companion piece: "mountain spring—/ my hands/ fill with stars." Kenny's haiku isn't quite as romantic but it is evocative of the "mountain spring." We can, as readers, feel the coldness of the water she is cupping, before she drinks; taste the fresh water; see a galaxy cupped in her hands. If anything, Kenny's haiku is at least as pure as Roseliep's, if not offering a more elemental clarity—one that is at least as memorable.

Not Asking what if is a book of haiku that can be read for enjoyment and delight. It can also be read as a primer in its own right as to how to craft language into an aesthetic in which haiku can be subtly and providently shaped, whose shape can effortlessly hold itself into an imagistic perpetuity, such as in Adele Kenny's haiku, which could also be described as a "Roseliep," as Father Raymond coined some of his latter haiku, ever so felicitously, "first crickets—/ the pulse/ in my wrist."

Not Asking what if: Haiku—Selected and New by Adele Kenny, published in 2016, is available from Muse-Pie Press, Passaic, New Jersey.

THE WATERSHED OF "JUST AS IT IS": *MOUNTAIN* BY JOHN WILLS

In the mid-seventies, when this reviewer first began to read and study haiku, the work of John Wills became, and remains, a touchstone. The rich simplicity, felt-depth, and the characteristic of *sono mama*, "just as it is," embraced in Wills's haiku poetry not only holds up to but also increases with successive readings. With the publication of *Reed Shadows* in 1987 (Black Moss Press/Burnt Lake Press), two hundred thirty-two of Wills's haiku were presented in a volume carefully edited by Canadian poet and publisher, Rod Willmot. Now with the publication of *Mountain*, issued shortly before Wills's death in September 1993, three hundred nine more of his haiku are made available.

The work of John Wills can easily be placed within the company of our best "nature" poets, such as Wendell Berry, John Haines, Mary Oliver, and Gary Snyder. In fact, this reviewer, who was a bookseller for more than fifteen years (upon the initial writing of this review, however, more than thirty years overall), would represent *Reed Shadows* in both the poetry *and* nature sections.

Yet, as much as an enduring classic as *Reed Shadows* is, *Mountain*, despite all of its highly achieved haiku, is, if only slightly, different. Not unlike Gary Snyder's *Left Out in the Rain* (North Point Press, 1986), that gathers together Snyder's previously "uncollected" poems, *Mountain* appears to do much of the same for John Wills. In this book's foreword, Wills writes that among the haiku collected here "a large number ... were written in the eighties" also "a good number have been gleaned from my journals of the seventies (a few as far back as 1968)."

Snyder's *Left Out in the Rain* does not rival his Pulitzer Prize winning volume, *Turtle Island* (New York, NY: Directions, 1975), but the poems contained in it are of a high caliber, and do contribute to his *oeuvre*. This, too, is true of *Mountain*. The point, in this reviewer's estimation, is that this book of Wills' is a more than competent volume of haiku, but *Reed Shadows* is a masterful one.

What makes *this* collection so important and valuable, though, aside from the competency of the haiku, is an introduction that was originally written for *Reed Shadows* by Cor van den Heuvel. It was not included in that volume due to space limitations. Yet, it is a fortunate decision in that the twenty-one page introduction of van den Heuval's appears here. It is both informative and critically keen, and sheds light of a biographical nature on Willis's life, such as his years living on a farm in eastern Tennessee, called "Sweetwater," with his wife Marlene Wills, now, of course, known as Marlene Mountain, a superior haiku poet in her own right.

At "Sweetwater," Wills wrote a goodly number of the haiku in *Mountain*, as well as the work in *Reed Shadows*. It was here that he almost completely gave himself over to nature, both literally and figuratively, as he tried to make a living from the land—farming, logging, and even raising bonsai. The seven years spent at "Sweetwater" were a watershed for Wills's writing. The farm became to Wills what Walden Pond was to Henry David Thoreau or what Fort Juniper was to Robert Francis. "Sweetwater" was Wills's wellspring of poetic inspiration. And poems, such as these, from *Mountain*, are certainly an *addition* to haiku literature.

    a mountain
    lying out upon
    the water

///

ADELE KENNY

>   dusk
>   and cool mists rising . . .
>   cry of a snipe

///

>   all night like me
>   the cricket unable
>   to sleep

///

>   gathering cress
>   at the water's edge . . .
>   the coolness

Wills was forced to give up his idealistic life style due to financial failure, and his marriage with Marlene Mountain ended in divorce. But the crop of haiku that was harvested year after year, between 1971 and 1978, whether classic, competent, or first-rate are now a part of the genre for as long as the genre lasts. It was quite insightful of Wills to assemble the work contained in *Mountain*, and to self-publish it, as this reviewer suspects it is. Otherwise, these haiku may have been lost to us. Although there have been rare exceptions, such as Vincent Tripi's commendable editing of a book of haiku by the late Charles Dickson, recently published by AHA Books, it is unlikely that any publisher or editor would have either taken the care or interest to issue a posthumous collection of John Wills. Yet, fortunately, we now have Willis' *oeuvre*—the poetry of one of contemporary haiku's most genuine and resonant voices.

>   the pewee
>   keeps telling me
>   his name

JOURNEY TO THE EAST

///

    sweetwater ...
    a song sparrow welcomes
    me home

(Note: Copies of *Reed Shadows*, 1987, 112 pp., paper, flat-spined, are available from Marlene Mountain at $12 ppd. For information about an edition for the public in the future, write to Marlene Mountain, Route 1, Box 475, Hampton, TN 37568. Please enclose a self-addressed postal card.)

THE POETICS OF WALKING

Haiku is a poetic genre that can be defined as the juxtaposition of two or more images that provides insight into nature or human nature. It does not, necessarily, need to be written in lines of five, seven, and five syllables, as it often is in Japan, where haiku poetry originated. There is no exact definition of the English "syllable" in Japanese, except for *onji*, "sound-signs" or "sound-symbols." Also, "syllables" in Japanese are shorter than they are in English. So, seventeen syllables in English can be tediously lengthy in Japanese. The essence of a successful haiku itself is in the experience of an eternal moment, the numinous found in nature, and in the austerity of the juxtaposition of the images themselves, in that experience, without the use of metaphor.

Haiku for me has been a path, a way of life, a vehicle through which I see the world anew daily and newly many times during the day. For me its practice has encouraged me to learn how to *look*, and to paraphrase the American lyric poet Mary Oliver: "the more you look, the more you see." For instance, when I find the first starflower of the season in early May—blooming, as always, beside Canada mayflower—I experience my eyes ranging up the slope in seeing more china-white petals of starflower. And there I see another flower and another. It is in this opening of vision that the best haiku are created.

Haiku is a poetry of consciousness: the tones of Basho's temple bell dissolving among the peonies in the garden, and the resonance of that tolling emanating in the flowers themselves. Haiku is also a poetic, and spiritual, discipline of discovering the epiphany in the commonplace. Since nature, and often human nature, is found outside the walls of our homes and in the outer world, the poetics of haiku, for me, has always meant walking out into nature and having the natural world move through me.

Walking facilitates a kind of psychic *feng-shui*. Either in strolling into a sunlit meadow or hiking a trail up a mountain in the rain, in this "activity on non-action" there is a relinquishing of ego. One's will dissolves into divine will. There is not just the sense, but the experience, of: *all is one*, as medical intuitive, or psycho-spiritual healer, Caroline Myss often recounts in her work regarding healing in relationship to the system of the chakras of our bodies.

It is in walking that the best haiku can be created. The eminent haiku poet Basho walked his *Narrow Road to the Deep North*, and several other poets and writers, practicing in other genres, have too. The Russian poet Vladimir Mayakovsky wrote about this in his book *How Verses Are Made*.

When working out the rhythm and music of one of his poems Mayakovsky would recite the lines of his poem in his mind as he walked the streets of Moscow. The pace of his strides over the cobblestones was in concord to the integral harmony of the poem's evolving of and within itself. The mechanics of the poem would resolve itself through the rhythm of his walking.

In Henry David Thoreau's essay, "On Walking," that remains contemporary through his transcendental use of language, he compares the rhythm of his "strolling" to the equanimity of his life and all of what he experiences in the natural world around him.

The poetics of my own poetry originate in this manner. Over many years, it is in the manner of learning the names of the flora and fauna that present themselves in such an array through each of the seasons on my walks. In this knowledge of being able to name what I see in the natural world precipitates the language in the poems that open themselves to me.

The distinguished mythologist and expert in comparative religion, Joseph Campbell, often referred to the Sioux shaman, Black Elk, and his concept of "Sacred Mountain." Campbell speaks eloquently about that "particular" mountain, and that it need not be the tallest peak in the world, but he refers to it as a "power spot," somewhere you can *look* over the plains. It is a place in nature where you experience oneness with the earth, and refresh yourself with renewed vision.

My "Sacred Mountain," not to mention other "power spots" in and around Amherst, Massachusetts, is Mount Toby, located in nearby Sunderland. Mount Toby is enveloped in a lushness of hardwoods and ferns, and I have seen deer, bear, and porcupine cross its trails.

From the fire tower at the summit, only 1,240 feet at the peak, look north. On a clear day, at two o'clock, you can see Mount Monadnock's granite dome in New Hampshire; at eleven o'clock, Mount Snow's jagged peak is prominent in Vermont; and due west, Mount Greylock's rounded protrusion expresses itself in the distance in the Berkshires, bordering New York's easternmost state line.

It is not only in language that we create a poetics, but through our interaction with nature and its beneficence. It is in looking and looking, then seeing, that we experience what is epiphanal in the commonplace.

Whether it is Basho's travail on his *Narrow Road,* and through his ardor, his opening to the nature around him, or Mayakovsky's working out the rhythms and word-choice in his

JOURNEY TO THE EAST

poems. Whether it is Thoreau's "strolling" to become in touch with himself and in nature itself, or Mary Oliver, like a Johnny Apple-Seed, gifting herself with pencils in the narrows of trees. It is the poetics of walking and *seeing* that allows us to participate in what can be termed as the *ah-ness* of the "haiku moment."

Fort Juniper
The Robert Francis Homestead
Cushman, Massachusetts
August 2005

THE CONCLUSION OF THE GRAIL LEGEND, TROUT FISHING, AND THE ART OF WRITING HAIKU POETRY

The poem concerning the Grail Legend written by Chretien de Troyes, circa the late 13th-century ends abruptly and inconclusively. Various authors attempted to finish the poem, and one of these versions will briefly be discussed here. The version I make reference to is examined at length in a small, but rich, book written by Robert A. Johnson, entitled *He: Understanding Masculine Psychology* (New York, NY: Harper and Row, Perennial Library, 1977), through which the interpretation of the Grail Legend is made use of to plummet the understanding of male mythology. I highly recommend this volume for those who would like to mine the abundance of clues to understanding masculine psychology, and how they might attempt to live through the teachings embodied in the myth presented. Simply, the myth can guide us and make us appreciate the mystery that is central to each of our individual lives. Johnson has also written a companion volume, entitled *She: Understanding Feminine Psychology* (Harper and Row, Perennial Library, 1977) that examines the myth of Amor and Psyche through which feminine mythology is given a locus of understanding, and that also proves to be quite invaluable.

The conclusion of the Grail Legend under discussion commences with the hero, Parsifal, only able to locate the Grail castle "consciously," and then, only when he is both courageous and humble enough, can he enter it. Johnson says, "swashbuckling" will not get him there, but when Parsifal petitions with his heart, he sees the Fisher King there in the castle still in great suffering. It is then that Parsifal finally asks the correct question: "Whom does the Grail serve?" The King is healed as the question is asked, and the Grail is brought forth. The meaning of this, succinctly, is that we are here to serve God, or the Grail.

To take this a step further, as haiku poets, or poets of any kind, when the Fisher King, who always was the Grail King in the first place, makes the statement, "The Grail serves the Grail King," this is quite pertinent and useful for us. Do we not only serve God, as poets, but become one with one with the cosmos? Does this not, in the very least, intimate a state of transcendence? Do we, as poets, not vaguely resemble a Buddhist monk at morning zazen, or a Christian nun raising her eyes upward in her recitation of vespers, when in observation of nature experience an intuitive flash of insight or re-experience that moment in the heat of composition, when the lineaments of time drop away?

Joseph Campbell, the noted mythologist whose learning was of an encyclopedic dimension, explained that our power source was always beside us, flowing as a river might flow, but that in our "modern" world the psychic static that accompanies our day-to-day involvement, with our various responsibilities heaped upon us like weighty sacks, often leaves us bereft of the location of that power? Do we not, as poets, discover for ourselves, but *as* importantly, for readers, perhaps, many years to come, that stones speak, that music emanates from rivers and brooks, and that summer wildflowers are full orchestras of color conducted by the wind? Is this not truly finding the Grail castle, asking the correct question, healing the Grail King, and beholding the Grail? Is this not at least the very beginning of humbly communing with the omniscient universal power?

Although I have stopped trout fishing some years ago, because I so thoroughly enjoy spending my time outdoors with my aging yellow Labrador retriever, named Cider, soon to be eleven this coming spring, I did *attempt* to practice the art of trout fishing, usually with little positive results. I believe my problem was that I had an end-product in mind: to make a gift of a huge rainbow trout to my neighbors, or to reel in dozens of fish, whose sweet meat could be greedily savored by me and my closest friends. In other words, fishing was, when I was able to catch any fish at all, the exclamation, the adrenaline rush, the ego standing up and shouting, "Look at me!"

Those rare instances I did enjoy a good day fishing, I would quietly step along the rocky shore, careful not to cast my reflection, or shadow, over the water. I would cast precisely, into the deepest pool, aware of nothing but the line reeling out from the center of myself. Then, as my hands appeared to act on their own, I reeled in the line, slowly playing a large trout through the sparkling water, the sunlight igniting its many rainbows. Are we, as poets, sometimes not unlike an over-eager fisherman, who wants to compose poetry, but cannot find that powerful river rushing beside us, at all hours, night and day? Or, are we, as poets, sometimes, as well, like the fisherman who discards his ego, and becomes totally aware of the rocks on the shore, who becomes one with the trout swirl beside the boulder in the middle of the river or the brook? Are we, as poets, like the fisherman who makes the intuitively athletic calculation of how much wrist action to put into the cast, so that the fly lands in the pool's center, the fisherman who experiences the "haiku moment" of the splash of the leaping trout, shedding rivulets of water, and, after it is netted, unhooks it, to return it to the river?

Over twenty years ago, in 1973, when I was a young bookseller, I began to seriously practice zazen, and began to read books concerning oriental literature. I always consider this point of my life fortuitous, because this is when I initially discovered Harold Henderson's *An Introduction to Haiku* (Doubleday and Company, 1958) and his *Haiku in English* (New York: NY: Japan Society, 1965). The poem that first spoke to me, and that

JOURNEY TO THE EAST

still remains with me to this day, is Henderson's translation of Basho's "Kare eda ni karasu no tomarikeri aki no dure," or:

> On a withered branch
> a crow has settled . . .
> autumn nightfall

Through what has been an often troubled life, with its personal tragedies, major and minor disappointments, and wrong turns, there is always that "somewhere" on the rutted road of my own poor choosing that Basho's crow appears, perching on a black branch, with the rawness of evening coming on. At this juncture, I am able to summon courage, not unlike Parsifal, to humbly turn, and make my way back to a crossroad, where I can appropriately change my direction, all the time petitioning with my heart for the drawbridge of the Grail Castle to lower. Although it is my spiritual practice that is largely responsible in guiding my life, it is here, at this crossroad, that we have fortuitously met, as we now walk together, writer and reader, more enlightened than before, after having possibly realized the discovery of the Holy Grail of the present from moment to sacred moment.

> mist clears above the ridge
> taking with it
> the wedge of geese

> ///

> the fading glow
> of a field of sunflowers—
> autumn dusk

> ///

> tracks in fresh snow
> a coyote dragging
> its foot

THE INTERNATIONAL *SAIJIKI*: THE LEGACY OF WILLIAM J. HIGGINSON

In *The Haiku Seasons: Poetry of the Natural World*, a book that combines both brevity and depth, as well as enormous erudition, William J. Higginson provides an explanation of the importance of a seasonal element with respect to haiku poetry. Instructive to both newcomers to haiku, as well as those familiar with the genre, Higginson constructs a bridge to the past in offering an historical documentary of haiku literature, and points to the future in his assembling of an international *saijiki* (poetry almanac) that suggests the increasing popularity of haiku worldwide.

With this said, it is discouraging to be aware of the decreasing number of nature haiku being written today, in December 2016, some twenty years after this review was originally written. It seems that with the decline of green space everywhere this ecological disaster is reflected in the diminution of nature haiku, accomplished or not, being composed.

It is naïve of me to even remotely think that anyone reading this critique, and ever so much a commentary, of *The Haiku Seasons*, in my championing of the book, would make a difference. However, I am hoping to make a difference, here and now. Let there be an opening of consciousness regarding the importance and significance of nature writing, and, specifically, haiku everywhere—in that we all don't need to be writers, and certainly not influential or famous ones, but what is necessitated is that we, as a culture, and individually, should be aware of the intrinsic and innate bounty reflected in writing regarding nature, as well as in nature herself, especially in successful haiku, which can augment us in any number of positive and proactive ways.

Beginning Chapter 1, "The Essence of Haiku," Higginson quotes Basho's imperative: "submit to nature, return to nature." Of course, both the binding and transfiguring aspect of the natural world is its seasonal inflection, and through the use of various examples, Higginson italicizes the importance of a compilation of *kigo* (season words) and *kidai* (seasonal topics).

The second of the book's six chapters discusses "The Seasons in Older Japanese Poetry." Here, Higginson relates the classification of the two famous imperial poetry anthologies, the *Kokinshu* (Ancient and Modern Collection) and the earlier *Manyoshu*. These anthologies gather poems written between the eighth and twelfth centuries and largely concern themselves with the natural world, as well as with the theme of "love," two of the major topics in Japanese poetry. Although the poetical form used during this era is tanka, the slightly longer poetic form more conducive to expressing human emotions, and not haiku, the example of how important seasonal references are in Japanese literature is made resonant by the mention of Lady Murasaki's hero, Genji, whose failure to adequately notice the passing seasons meant death.

Chapter 3 covers linked verses. Employing several extensive expositions of various renga, Higginson makes us aware of how the specific use of a seasonal reference can precipitate a depth of association when utilized appropriately. He also explores the growth of *mushin renga*, mainly composed as a diversion, to *haiku renga*, which Basho brought into a literary flowering, and that is now called renku. Also, using many well-chosen examples, both ancient and modern, Higginson explains hokku, haiku, and senryu, in Chapter 4, as well as their derivation from renku, not to mention the importance of evaluating these genres through the context of a *saijiki*.

ADELE KENNY

A comparison of the lunar and Gregorian calendars highlights Chapter 5 in its discussion of "The Haiku Seasons." The difficulty of correlating a seasonal reference to a specific calendar period, even to an exact day, is addressed, and resolved. Also, Higginson explores the problem of gaining a consensus of a uniform seasonal reference geographically, since, for example, different flowers bloom at various times in a range of climates, and he suggest that a dialectic *can be* achieved. Various non-seasonal *saijiki* are mentioned, too, that have been in use, especially recently, most notably, *An Image Saijiki* (*Imeji Saijiki*), edited by Koji Yasui in 1989, only to illustrate that the Japanese themselves have wrestled with the notion of whether a seasonal compilation provides the most thorough method of poetical reference.

Yet, in the book's final chapter, "Towards an International Haikai Almanac," Higginson gives his reason for editing what is ostensibly the first international *saijiki*, that will constitute the second volume of this work, forthcoming shortly from Kodansha International, as putting to rest differences that Japanese haiku poets have, as well as haiku poets from other countries. Does this sound impossible? Well, it is, according to Higginson, and he provides a convincing argument that "whether local, national, or international, a *saijiki* helps us know both ourselves and our place in the world."

This is a project that has been of mammoth proportion, and one that has concerned Higginson enough to not only spend the better part of a decade researching the possibility of an international *saijiki*, but also creating one. Higginson is instrumental in making it possible for a wider appreciation of haiku through his work, and he has helped make haiku a viable and living literary form that can be critically appreciated in academic circles, as well as be an aesthetic practice for everyone, and if *The Haiku Season* is any indication, the volume to follow, *Haiku World*, indeed, *the saijiki* itself, should not only be an international success, but also of inestimable value to those whose lives may be spent, as Higginson writes, "learning and enjoying more about poetry and nature."

* * * *

Haiku World is the long-awaited companion volume to *The Haiku Seasons*, the latter largely being a compact, yet comprehensive, overview of Japanese poetry and its relation to *kigo* (season words) and *kidai* (seasonal topics). *Haiku World* collects over 1,000 poems written by more than 600 poets, representing 50 countries and 25 languages. The poems are arranged by seasonal and nonseasonal topics. Also, contained in the "Index of Topics, Season Words, and Keywords" are 3,600 words and phrases cited in the body of the *saijiki*. Higginson writes that "the *saijiki* index shows the season of each word or phrase as well as its place in the text."

Higginson's goal is to demonstrate "the diversity and unity of the various poetries collectively known as haikai—haiku, senryu, and renku." Many of the poems collected in the volume were sent to Higginson "as a result of a call for poems mailed in January 1994." Also, some of the poems were gathered from his series of articles concerning season words that initially appeared in *Frogpond*, the mouthpiece of The Haiku Society of America.

Five seasonal sections (Spring, Summer, Autumn, Winter, and New Year) are separated into categories: "The Season," "The Heavens," "The Earth," "Humanity," "Observances," "Animals," and "Plants." The all-year (nonseasonal) section similarly includes all of the above, yet beings with "The Year" instead of "Seasons" ("to include phenomena that pervade or characterize a whole year") and "Customs and Religion" instead of "Observances."

Higginson not only includes information of the genus and species of certain phenomena but their occurrence in both northern and southern hemispheres. One of the reasons why *Haiku World* often makes fascinating reading is that the facts regarding season words that Higginson provides is of an encyclopedic nature and reflects both accurate an exhaustive research.

A point worth noting is that Higginson's study of prominent Japanese *saijiki*—such as the *Japan Great Saijiki* or Tohta's *Modern Haiku Saijki*—is evident in the tenor of each entry in that often comprehensive information is offered but nearly always in a succinct manner giving the prose a compact quality.

To the right of each poet's byline appears that poet's country or state as well as an "h," "k," and/or "s" that signifies "hokku," "haiku," and/or "senryu." The distinctions are important to make, Higginson relates, "because for all readers these designations may sort out the differences among hokku, haiku, and senryu, all parts of the haikai genre."

Three essays "interrupt" the body of this *saijiki*. "Butterflies Through the Year" discusses how butterflies can relate to other seasons beside the spring. "On Haze, Mist, Fog" makes the distinction between these "closely related phenomena" in relation to the problem of translation into English from the Japanese. And "Words in International Haikai" investigates the problem of accurately interpreting the correct season words in any given poem.

Higginson began his involvement in the project of assembling this *saijiki* in 1983. With the publication of *Haiku World*, what is clearly evident is that Higginson's project is successful. He writes that "a *saijiki*'s organization of poems by topic rather than by individual authorship conveys a powerful sense of poetry as a group enterprise, a cultural and social phenomena rather than the quirky product of a simple, ego-bound intelligence."

And, I *heartily* agree, yet it is my opinion that more poems than I would like to see included in this book—although nearly always exemplary in exhibiting their specific seasonal element—lack resonance, offer little spiritual felt-depth, and are sometimes, *quirky* in their self-absorption. What has been achieved, though, is that Higginson not only has assembled the first international *saijiki*, but that it is a remarkably comprehensive poetry almanac that represents haikai as a global literary movement. For those interested in serious study of haiku literature, this volume, as well as *The Haiku Seasons*, deserves to be on the same shelf beside the works of R. H. Blythe and Harold G. Henderson. Yet, Higginson points to something beyond just sheer erudition when he writes: "Do not put history, theory, or organization between yourself and Basho's pine tree, but use these and all such books to help you and find the pine tree, so that you may 'learn of the pine' sooner, and more richly."

The Haiku Seasons: Poetry of the Natural World by William J. Higginson, Kodansha International, Distributed by Kodansha America, Inc., 114 Fifth Avenue, New York, NY 10011, 1996, 171pp., paperback, $16.

Haiku World: An International Poetry Almanac, William J. Higginson, Kodansha International, 114 Fifth Avenue, New York, NY 10011, 1996, 407pp., perfectbound in a paper wrapper, $19

WESTERN HAIKU AS AMERICAN POETRY: NICHOLAS A. VIRIGILIO

In his augmented second edition, Nicholas A. Virgilio's *Selected Haiku*, there are over a third more haiku than in the letterpress original, bringing the total up from ninety-one to one hundred and thirty-three. Although this volume is offset rather than set by hand, it is handsomely and professionally produced. This book is an apotheosis of book craft mirroring poetic content— fine poetry printed by the means of high production standards. But content is the primary interest here and Virgilio's haiku are exemplary. The work contained in this book is so well crafted it could be used as a primer for the best haiku poets and beginning students alike. Judging by the poetry in this volume, Virgilio is incontrovertibly a contemporary haiku master.

His use of poetic technique is similar to how a painter uses the primary colors of their palette. Consistently, his haiku embody a skillful use of assonance, caesurae, consonance, alliteration, and even rhyme—skillful because these techniques are used in harmony with the content of each haiku, and focus concentration on the moment itself. And, above all, Virgilio's focus is evident because his eye for the particular combined with his firm grip of technique results is a rare caliber of poetry. These haiku seem to have written themselves.

> the bare maple sways,
> and a tire on a wire cable
> swings in the spring air

///

> the town clock's face
> adds another shade of yellow
> to the afterglow

> ///

> down from the stone bridge
> alone in the darkness:
> the star in the creek

> ///

> the graduation ring
> slips from my finger:
> the midnight river

Yet as graceful as Virgilio's haiku are they are also deep and resonant. To achieve so much in poetry of any kind and with such apparent ease is no small matter. Not only is the essence of the moment recorded in his poetry, but it penetrates our center and an opening takes place, our true self emerges. There is a permeating spirituality to Virgilio's work, and as images are said to be eternal, so are the powerful juxtaposition he constructs.

> lily:
> out of the water . . .
> out of itself

> ///

> after the bell,
> within the silence:
> within myself

Often it is what is left out of these haiku that makes them so successful. Often it is the echo that he instills in the poem that fashions its achievement. Many times it is through the condensation of a complex image into a single word that these haiku gather their potency. And, frequently, it is through his compassion that so successful a brand of haiku is created.

> barking its breath
> into the rat-hole:
> bitter cold

> ///

> approaching autumn:
> the warehouse watchdog's bark
> weakens in the wind

> ///

> over spatterdocks,
> turning at corners or air:
> dragonfly

> ///

> beneath the coffin
> at the edge of the open grave:
> the crushed young grass

There is much to praise in Nicholas A. Virgilio's *Selected Haiku*: the moving sequence "Litany for the Dead," that is laced with social and political overtones; the many haiku that deal with the loss of his brother, Lawrence J. Virgilio, in the Viet Nam War, that are marked by their bitter piquancy of grief; and the searing portrayals he thematically returns to time and again of the prisoners of urban blight and squalor—prostitutes and winos that haunt the inner city. But ultimately what makes Virgilio's haiku so appealing is that beyond any critical considerations his poetry is accessible. If making writing vital and necessary is the active definition of literature is, then Virgilio, over the decades, has distinctly created just that—with his spirit—and for haiku of this quality we should be grateful.

>   my dead brother . . .
>   hearing his laugh
>   in my laughter

>   ///

>   morning sun:
>   my shadow walking
>   swinging its arms

3. Selected Reviews

ESPOUSING A FEW BOOKS I HAVE LOVED

As a self-proclaimed *social* bookseller and bookstore manager over more than thirty years, I invested myself in representing books that mattered and championing both local writers as well as nationally renowned authors. This, I have found, separates me from most poets and writers in that my *raison d'être* wasn't necessarily promoting my own work—although I would carry my own books in the stores I managed and often enough hand-sold them—but it was passionately nurturing active interest in authors and books that might make a difference in people's lives.

When I managed Gallows Hills Bookstore at Trinity College, in Hartford, I had an outstanding student employee, Amy, who was enrolled in a pre-Med program. Once while shelving books in the literature section, she asked me, "If I were to read just one literary work, since I have so little time with my studies in the sciences, what would that be." Immediately, I thought of Lawrence Durrell's *Alexandria Quartet*. I opened the first volume, *Justine,* to the first paragraphs of the novel, written in an intoxicating lyrical prose. Amy read the passage, smiled, and purchased the set of four novels. Some weeks later, I asked Amy how she was enjoying Durrell, and she said, "Oh, Durrell, I am reading him aloud to my roommate every night!" That for me is what actively being engaged in literature is all about. It can be life-changing in some cases, but it often is life-augmenting to discover an author as vital as Lawrence Durrell.

Reviewing was a discipline I enjoyed for several decades. The critical process engaged my left-brain and my analytical mind. Since I am largely an intuitive and use my right-brain in my

SELECTED REVIEWS

creative pursuits every day using the more objective and critical part of my brain was something I found refreshing. The reviews I enclose here are only emblematic of the reviews I wrote for many years. There are just six represented out of probably more than 150 reviews that were published in one form or another—often in journals and in newspapers but also anonymously in the various editing and ghostwriting jobs I have done on a freelance basis.

With this taken into consideration, the reviews included here are done so with great specificity. The John McPhee volume, *Basin and Range*, is not only a book I delighted in reading but also in reviewing; and, furthermore, it was one I enjoyed recommending. Once, I recommended the book to a close friend and colleague who was quite interested in making a career change from retail to *something else*. Characteristically, with his being scrupulous in his choice, since he was in a committed marriage and he and his wife had a young son and daughter. Rich had majored in archeology at university, but never thought he could make a living giving it a go. When I suggested he read *Basin and Range* his eyes lit up and he slowly brought the book closer to his face with his hands as if he had been presented with the key to an enchanted city. After Rich read the book, some months later, he found a job examining soil samples, among other things, in a lab in Connecticut. It was a commute from his home in southwestern Massachusetts, but the last time I heard from him, now several years ago, he was still there, working at a career for which he had not only studied but one in which he found purpose as his life's vision.

The Milosz memoir is one of my favorite books, especially since it exhibits the kind of humility I aspire to myself. *Native Realm* is what Polish Nobel Laureate Czeslaw Milosz (pronounced *Cheswaw Miwash*) calls as his memoir but it is more of a layperson's history of Eastern Europe from the turn of the 20th-century to just after WWII. I can't possibly claim anything close to that in this book, which I have subtitled, *Selected Essays as Literary Memoir*. However, I will always attempt to hold the kind of humility that Milosz exhibits as a beacon to guide my own life.

The review of Robert Penn Warren's *Being Here* is included because I believe he is now unfortunately an overlooked poet and writer, and one in which whose interest should be revivified, especially with respect to his poetry. Few poets can be ascribed to being wise but Penn Warren's poetry is just that. It shines with compassion and wisdom. Also, I wanted to include the review here because I would often see Penn Warren, who was nicknamed "Red Warren," because of the color of his hair, as he walked among students changing classes around noon in front of the Drama School at Yale. Penn Warren was a tall man, and there I would see him, often a head taller than the rest of the swarm students and professors ushering out of a late morning class on their way to lunch or to their dorms. There he was—walking along with large strides, sometimes his head bobbing among the throng, often stepping past people on York Street—providing me with the simple joy of just seeing him.

When President Barack Obama was elected I naively thought that he would institute a 21st-century WPA Program. Or at least I kept on wishing he would. My hope for the country was this was the way we could refashion our infrastructure. Also, perhaps little known by some anyway, writers were employed to write *The Rivers of America* series, which are a set of books regarding the nation's major waterways. Additionally, the WPA guides to each of the 48 states, at that time in the 1930s, were so well researched and written that they are still relevant reading to this day. I looked toward a resurgence in America by what another WPA Program would produce. It is in this spirit I include Malcolm Cowley's classic *Dream of the Golden Mountains*. It is a book that portrays the 1930s as a milieu in which artists and writers banded together as colleagues and

SELECTED REVIEWS

not as competitors, as in the contemporary American literary scene, to march among the coal miners in the strikes for living wages, to proclaim their politics openly for the working men and women as well as for the many jobless Americans in soup lines. It is a grand book that is written in a dignified style that is appropriate for the age it reflects—with verve, integrity, and a voracity for truth.

Another review included here is the one for *Field Work*, a seminal volume of poetry written by Seamus Heaney. When I had finished writing the review, I walked to an USPS mailbox on College Street in New Haven. I had carefully typed the review and needed to enclose a copy of both it and the book to my editors in a self-addressed stamped envelope. As I carried the small package along the street, late on a Sunday evening, I passed George & Harry's, a well-known restaurant on the edge of campus. In the front window was a pannier of oysters, arranged on crushed ice. I stopped to look at the bivalves opened and sparkling in their own juices. Snow began to fall. My mouth watered. Walking to the end of the block where the mailbox was situated at the corner I thought of the first poem in Heaney's book, entitled "Oysters," a perfect poem, one that would become one of my perennially favorite poems. As I turned and walked back toward George & Harry's, I reached into my pocket, pulled out my wallet, and checked to see what money I had, and I thought I might just have enough. Enjoying a serving of oysters and a lime and larger that evening after placing my review of *Field Work* in the mail to my editors is a memory I have truly savored these last forty years—and as Heaney concludes his poem, "I ate the day/ Deliberately, that its tang/ Might quicken me into verb, pure verb."

At a reading I gave in the spring of 2016, with my friend and colleague, Patricia Mottola, which celebrated the launch of our new books, I read a poem from *Invocation* (Beaumont, TX: Lamar University Literary Press, 2015), entitled "Sooey." After the reading

ESPOUSING A FEW BOOKS I HAVE LOVED

there was a Q&A, which I always enjoy, and was asked about literary influences. A writer in their sixties never really wants to admit that they still may be influenced by another poet; however, I offered that I was sometimes influenced, on my best days as a writer, by Seamus Heaney's rhythms and music, which I hear as my own; and cited, for example, a poem I read from the book, entitled, "Sooey," which I include here. Especially in the lines, "just the *oh, yes/* of them a pleasure to observe in their open delight that/ was as sheer of a thing as they were of a weighty heft," I hear Heaney's syntax *and intonation* operative in it as well as the kind of twinkle in his eye in which he imbues certain lines of his poetry, as in importuning that writing this poem was so much work but also so much fun that living such a life is really such a gorgeous thing, indeed.

* * * *

Sooey

The time the drove escaped from their pen from the farm across the road, they moved in a huddle over the lawn,

red-cheeked and pink in their muddied nakedness, cheery in their sanguine abandon, snorting in their anticipation

of their approaching the compost pile beside the barn. They jiggled when they moved, ears cocked,

ruddy-faced, in their collective charge forward together, insouciant in their newfound freedom, just the *oh, yes*

of them a pleasure to observe in their open delight that was as sheer of a thing as they were of a weighty heft.

Gregarious in their gait together in their small herd, they launched themselves forward with an intelligence that seemed to be fertile in their brains, more so, than other

SELECTED REVIEWS

animals, apparently protective of each other as they were

of themselves, seemingly motivated in that they bore
resemblance more to humans, especially in the glib look

on their faces, and that they moved about in the world
not so much at random but that they had intent, a plan

that included one for all and all for one, in their reaching
the kale stems, apple cores, and still-juicy melon rinds

that they so auspiciously found among coffee grounds
in the compost, before their farmer, smiling broadly,

brought them back to the sparseness of their
wooden pens, spattered with a wealth of mud, as tines

of the farmer's pitchfork tickled them from behind,
the lilt of his chanting call of *sooey* the alchemical charm

to bring them home, their snouts turned upwards, mouths
open, congenially returning, squeaking their nasal oinks,

throaty and full, on the run; the beauty in them, seeing
them come; the joy about them, in seeing them go.

* * * *

Including the review of James Merrill's *Mirabell: Books of Number* is a requisite for me. Not only am I, too, drawn into the paranormal, as was Merrill, especially in his poetic masterpiece, *The Changing Light at Sandover* (New York, NY: Athenaeum, 1982), of which *Mirabell* is the first volume, but it is necessary for me to mention my acquaintance with Merrill, which was as felicitous as it was rich. I first met Merrill as a member of Phoenix: The New Haven Poetry Series. We were

ESPOUSING A FEW BOOKS I HAVE LOVED

composed of four members who either loved poetry or had ties to Yale, or both. Our intent was to introduce, or re-introduce, as it were, local and regional poets who we thought deserved more exposure, along with nationally recognized poets who we invited from afar, the latter of which included Donald Hall, Galway Kinnell, Denise Levertov, and, yes, James Merrill.

So, I had met Merrill, briefly, while acting as usher at the doors to the Whitney Library, at the New Haven Historical Society, now called The New Haven Museum. I enjoyed Merrill's inimitable combination of kindness and panache. Secondly, I engendered the courage to phone Merrill after having read *Mirabell*, and had written a draft of my review of the book, initially to ask him particular questions regarding the experience of his using the Ouija board and his exploits into paranormal behavior. After he answered the phone, I wasn't as much tongue-tied, but I was stultified by my own best efforts to pose my questions which would have been somewhat rhetorical, since my answers were really to be found in the text of the poem.

However, Merrill, generously gave me his time and he specifically requested that I send him a copy of the review, when it appeared in print. He even joked with me about my "*panning* the book," as he put it, with the italics all his. The review didn't appear for a while since the venue I published it in was an annual, but I did send a copy along to him, to which he answered in a letter, radiating his appreciation and charm.

The last time I saw Merrill I had delighted in the opportunity of speaking with him, face to face, for a somewhat reasonable amount of time, when I was a book buyer at the Jeffrey Amherst Bookshop in 1982, when Merrill just happened to be attending a reunion at Amherst College that May. Since it was slow in the store at the time, we stood in front of the poetry section for a good fifteen to twenty minutes speaking about his trilogy, poetry in general, and the grandeur of the spring day.

SELECTED REVIEWS

For a man as accomplished and as recognized as James Merrill to have remember meeting me at the reading, recalling my review, and giving me the time of day were all remarkable acts of courtesy but underlying all of that was his integral interest in me as a human being—what was I doing, what was I reading, was I writing and what was it that I was writing.

He made me feel worthy of breathing the same rarefied air as he did, and encouraged me to keep doing so. He offered encouragement and through his affability and his *interest* offered me a kind of lovingkindness and compassion which I have infrequently found since in another mortal. James Merrill is, and was, not only a paramount poet of the 20th-century but was also a extraordinary human being. He didn't necessarily endow me with guidance, as I would find in only a couple of years later through my friendship with Amherst poet Robert Francis, but Merrill did touch me, deeply. His graciousness, not unlike Milosz's humility, is truly worth something to steer by.

Paralleling Merrill's delving into the world of the paranormal, I enclose a poem, initially written in February 2013, and revised in February 2018, when I was still involved in putting one finishing touch after another on the book. The poem, "Windhorse," also portrays the a portal to a world beyond this one, how that world and our present one intersect, on occasion, and how that might provide some uncanny experience and possible insight into our current lives.

* * * *

Windhorse

Slabs of white marble in stacks.
The pictographs carved in them.
Then this thin tablet. My hands

running across the intaglio of a frieze.

Its smoothness in relief.
The celebration of *Bacchus* in honor

of *Equus*.
Unearthing the actual vision of it

in the archeology of dream.
The going to and the digging through

layers of consciousness, as in layers
of earth.

In the city of *Equestrium*.
That is what I heard. The word spoken

as it was spoken.
Workers and trainers

moving here and there, as in a kind
of bas-relief.

Then someone speaking
to me, instructing me with the urgency

in their stentorian voice.
Although I did not

necessarily know the language.
Then the muscular flanks shining,

a chiseled kind of strength.
The natural aesthetic of the uncut mane.

The sheer beauty of it.

SELECTED REVIEWS

    Then putting my foot in the boot

    of the narrow stirrup,
    I inhaled the fragrance of the leather

    before hearing it creak with my weight,
    and I settled into the saddle

    on the breadth of the massive back.
    Before I could even think, the wind

    in my hair, the mane flying.
    Ride, the voice said, and I did—

    in the timeless instant
    before awakening from the dream.

AN ELUCIDATION OF THE SCIENCE OF GEOLOGY: JOHN MCPHEE'S *BASIN AND RANGE*

For many the discussion of geology can be soporific at best, but in John McPhee's *Basin and Range* geology and its tenets become "a fountain of metaphor." It is McPhee's fifteenth book of nonfiction, and it can stand easily next to his other works, such as *Coming into the Country* and *The Pine Barrens*. Unlike the student in a geology class whose best way of memorizing the periods of the Paleozoic Era—Cambrian, Ordovician, Silurian, Devonian, Carboniferous, and Permian—was through a mnemonic such as "cosdecp," the reader of this book will have no such problems. McPhee has written a geology text book for laypeople in which the difficult nomenclature of the science will not confound, but will elicit wonder. It is written in the crisp and clear style that is the stamp of McPhee.

In his geological explicative, McPhee concentrates on the terrain that stretches from eastern Utah to eastern California, known as the Basin and Range. This particular locale is composed of a series of geological features in addition to those that provided the region's name. It is a geologist's paradise. And, as he had done in the past, McPhee hooks up with an authority in the field about which he is writing. In this case it is Kenneth S. Deffeyes, a professor of geology at Princeton University. They choose to travel to the Basin and Range on Interstate 80, which runs from New York to San Francisco, because it is like a journey through Triassic time, between 195 and 230 million years ago, at least as far as rock formations are concerned.

SELECTED REVIEWS

At the onset of the trip, as they approach Hook Mountain in New Jersey, Deffeyes becomes excited by a roadcut where the interstate exposed some oxides of iron and black basalt. After stopping his vehicle and taking out his hand lens, he peers at the rock and finds what he had expected—zeolite crystals. Zeolite (a combination of aluminum, silicon, calcium, and sodium) has the unique quality of absorbing water. It is used in refrigerators to absorb the water that accidentally comes into contact with the Freon. More importantly, it is used in absorbing strontium and cesium, which are contained in radioactive wastes. Deffeyes and McPhee have not yet even reached the craton, or the continental core, that traverses the plains from Ohio to the Rockies, and already they have unearthed what will become a plethora of geological features and information.

After reaching their destination, Deffeyes explains that the fault blocks of the Basin and Range are floating on top of the mantle. When weight is removed it rises higher. For instance, when a landscape erodes, its remains will rise in adjustment, and the older rock lifts upward. This is known as isostatic adjustment. But, as this might suggest, the mantle is not molten. It is solid. Its temperatures vary through its thickness above two thousand feet, and its viscosity floats the crust above it. Deffeyes compares the viscosity of the mantle to the flexibility of piano wire. Under the lid of a piano the wire is taut, but the wire will droop if any weight is placed on it.

Deffeyes's main intent of his expedition to Nevada is to take paleomagnetic samples of sediments in the basins in order to obtain better information of the area and to obtain better information on the formation of the area and to attempt to find out if his theory that silver is extant in tailings left by the miners of the 19th-century is correct. As he explores, Deffeyes continually explains geological phenomena. The Basin and Range, instructs Deffeyes, was once a chaos of volcanic activity. After the volcanism ceased, welded tuff covered the countryside. Erosion did make a modest dent in this volcanic glass, but after 22 million years, sometime in the Late Miocene, it began to break up in crustal blocks and folded and faulted to become what the Basin and Range is today.

In Carlin, Nevada, along the Humboldt River, Deffeyes points out another phenomenon—an angular unconformity. This geological feature is defined as two distinct rock formations that are askew of each other and askew of the earth, but are stuck together just the same. The formations are composed of stratified rock and sedimentary rock that had lain flat under a sea. Now the upper strata are dipping sixty degrees and the lower strata are standing on end. Deffeyes relates that this configuration developed when a mountain range was built up and then destroyed, and then another mountain range rose and was partially destroyed. The rock of the lower level, or Tonka, was lying flat. The first mountain range pushed it and twisted it to approximately its present position: then the range wore away. A sea covered the formation and gradually deposited sediment that slowly contributed to the building of a new mountain range. This, then, lifted the whole formation and rotated it to where it stands now; its lower strata vertical, and its upper strata, or Strathearn, ranging angularly.

To a novice an angular unconformity might seem trivial, but the discovery in the late 18th-century of an angular unconformity by James Hutton, one of the earliest geologists, near Jedburgh, Scotland, proved to be revolutionary. Until Hutton's discovery, the earth was thought to be between five and six thousand years old and sedimentary rock to have been formed at the time of Noah's flood. The prevalent geological theory at the time of Hutton's discovery was neptunism. Neptunists proclaimed that all rock formations, whether igneous, sedimentary, or metamorphic, had been formed out of a global sea. The perpetrator of this theory was Abraham Gottlob Werner, a teacher at Germany's Frieberg Mining Academy. His theory was taken as unquestionable truth even after Hutton's discovery was promulgated.

John Clerk, a friend of Hutton, sketched the discovery. It was a sketch of three worlds: the oldest at the bottom, tilted skyward; the intermediate in the middle, showing unstratified sand; and the youngest at the top, depicting fences, pastures, and a road above the rivercut. Hutton and his followers, who were known as vulcanists or plutonists, knew that it took more than just six thousand years to build an angular unconformity. It was fortunate, also that another friend of Hutton's, John Playfair, compiled his information into a book, *Illustrations of the Huttonian Theory of the Earth*, published in 1802, because Hutton's writing was barely readable, although his theories were brilliant.

These geological finds were in propinquity with the Scottish Enlightenment. Other Scottish geologists and geologists from other countries soon began collecting data too, such as the comparison of corals found under the Old Red Sandstone in Devonshire. These same corals were found in North Britain, as well as in the Old Red Sandstone. It was inferred that these corals of the same maturity that were found in the same rock were of the same age, no matter where the rock was located. So this is how the Devonian Period was named. More discoveries and more inferences added period upon period like layer of rock upon layer of rock. The corals of Europe were on top of the Old Red Sandstone and were judged to be of the same age, and this then became known as the Carboniferous Period. In Russia, the exploration of the Urals unearthed another system of rock and of time, called Permian, in which the fossil story was turned topsy-turvy. The fossils showed higher life forms in greater numbers, but through younger strata these life forms almost vanished, and a great extinction took place, perhaps because of a dying supernova's radiation nearby. To this day, no particular theory of the Permian Extinction wins approval, but it is agreed that most animal and plant life disappeared from the planet at the time, some 230 million years ago, that brought an end to the Paleozoic Era.

It is nearly impossible for the human mind to comprehend such stretches of geological time, or deep time, unless it is put into perspective as David Brower, founder of Friends of the Earth, has done in speeches he has delivered. He asks his listeners to think of the six days of Genesis for what in fact has been four and a half billion years. On Monday and Tuesday the earth was busy with getting itself going. At noon on Tuesday life began and continued to develop for the next four days. At 4:00 p.m. on Saturday the big reptiles had disappeared. Then, at 11:57 p.m. man came into being. At one-fourth of a second before midnight Christ arrived, and at one-fortieth of a second before midnight the Industrial Revolution occurred. As one geologist put it, in this view of deep time "you do not live at all, but in another way you live forever."

A geologist such as Kenneth S. Deffeyes, however, not only researches the history of the earth, but through his vision also illuminates at what stage it is, and toward what end it may be going. In Deffeyes's search for silver in mining tailings, he runs cyanide through what the miners left behind and finds more than a trace of silver, millions of dollars worth of the noble metal that both dentistry and photography depend upon. In his gathering of paleomagnetic samples, he can detect where the earth's magnetic pole was through different eras of geological time, making clearer and "adding polish to chapters of the Basin and Range." Geologists like Deffeyes found in Nevada's Jersey Valley a fibrous zeolite crystal called erionite that causes a lung disease, mesothelioma. In the Basin and Range there are millions of tons of this peculiar zeolite that are relatively passive. However, there were plans, which would have dispersed the erionite. The crystals could have been carried hundreds of miles in the wind if they were disturbed. The Defense

SELECTED REVIEWS

Department changed its mind, in part, because of a few perspicacious geologists like Deffeyes.

Also an expert oceanographer, Deffeyes dredged the rocks on the ocean's bottom off the coast of Oregon, corroborating the theory that the ocean's bottom was spreading out and that it had faulted into blocks similar to the faulting of the Basin and Range, a miniature stratigraphy resembling the land mass between eastern Utah and eastern California. This same faulting opened up what is now the Atlantic Ocean, and Deffeyes stipulates that another such rift will occur in the Basin and Range. Much of Nevada will be underwater. California may well be just an island. "It is just a matter of time," he says.

John McPhee has written a pristine account of geology, geologists, and the importance of the practice of the science. In the past fifty years, the discoveries in geology, such as plate tectonics, have become "as profound as Darwinian evolution, or Newtonian or Einsteinian physics. *Basin and Range* is a small book with many layers of durable information. It not only opens the reader's mind to the earth's history contained within the genealogical registry of rocks, but it is also a pleasure to read. Even when McPhee mentions something that might be considered trite, that in the work of another writer would remain such, as the fact that Deffeyes was a debater on his high school debating team, it sparkles: "He became—as he remained—a forensic marvel, the final syllables and his participles and gerunds ringing like a Buddha's gongs." McPhee has made journalism an art, and he has made geology an understandable science.

POLITICAL MEMOIR AS EASTERN EUROPEAN HISTORY: *NATIVE REALM* BY CZESLAW MILOSZ

An aphorism of Ambrose Bierce's that may be applied to more than a few autobiographies is: "A diary: that part of our life we can talk about without blushing." "But Czeslaw Milosz's *Native Realm* is not strictly an autobiography, and it is certainly not a diary. Milosz, the winner of the 1980 Nobel Prize for Literature, brings his native Eastern Europe into clearer focus in this book, so that the phantasmagorical history of that part of the globe can be put into perspective. However, this burgeons into a much larger venture, because Milosz cinematically interprets the overlapping and colliding events in his life as a journey not only into his own heart but the hearts of a generation of Europeans.

Milosz was born in 1911 in Lithuania, the melting pot of Eastern Europe. In the Middle Ages, the Lithuanians, or "Litwa," as they were called by their neighbors, were considered to be barbarians because of their raids on villages and the practice of their paganism. In order to convert and tame them, the Polish Prince of Mazovia called upon the Teutonic Order of the Knights of the Cross, who made the Litwa swallow Christianity at sword point. This union between Poland and Lithuania provided security against Russia until the late 17th-century under Peter the Great.

In a country whose borders are frequently changed by war, there is usually a conglomerate of peoples, languages, and customs to be found. As for Milosz's native city, the Poles call it Wilno, the Lithuanians say Wilnius, and for the Germans and Byelorurussians it is Wilna. Before World War I, Lithuanian was spoken primarily in the country, whereas in the city either Polish or Yiddish was the common language, with official

SELECTED REVIEWS

decrees appearing in Russian. The religion practiced in Eastern Europe then, as it is now, was predominantly Roman Catholicism, although Jews, Muslims, and Karaites, a Jewish sect that denounces the rabbinical tradition of the Talmud for a strict adherence to the Bible, worshipped freely. However, anti-Semitism was rampant, and Russians who openly practiced Orthodoxy were immediately ostracized from the community.

Because of the diversity of his environment, and his father's position as an engineer, Milosz was spared the destruction of individuality that critics of modern civilization decry. While still young, he accompanied his family to Russia, where his father built roads and bridges. There he witnessed not only the vastness of Russia but also its pre-revolutionary proclivity for industrialization. Artillery divisions paraded the streets, and a new machinery appeared in the fields, bearing the imprint "McCormick, Chicago," while the masses, ill-fed and illiterate, barely comprehended such technology.

Milosz's early memories of Russia are illuminated by candlelit ikons, droshkies, and samovars tipping over on rugged train rides through the Urals. During this time, he experienced his first childhood crush. He could never separate this incident and the Russian Revolution of 1917—the girl he fell in love with was named Lena, and the sound of her name was similar to the chants he remembers hearing in the streets of "Lenin, Lenin." Before the Revolution, the Miloszs experienced little travail, except for the incessant movement and the relentless miles to be traveled that his father's job necessitated, but after the Revolution they were constantly interrogated by the secret police. However, Poland had gained its independence after World War I, and they returned to Wilno.

Almost as soon as they resettled in their native land, though, another war broke out. Poland sent an expeditionary force to regain land that had been seized by the czars, but the attempt ended in failure. The front line shifted to Warsaw, but General Pilsudski defended the city. A peace treaty was signed in 1921, but twenty-five years later, after World War II and the Yalta Conference, Lithuania, overrun by the Russians early in the war, would be formally annexed to the U.S.S.R.

By the time Milosz was entering the eight-year Catholic high school, he was more than used to seeing armies fleeing across the countryside in one direction or the other, and did not think it odd that the boundaries of countries changed from year to year. But there would be peace for nearly two decades, and his attention turned in the direction of the odor of beeswax candles and a white suit for his first communion. In Poland, Roman Catholicism and nationalism are inseparable and for Milosz, this wedding of religion and national pride was difficult to comprehend. He wondered, in his zeal for Roman Catholicism, how the supercilious Polish gentry could be allowed to worship the same god as he did. Only later did Milosz conclude that his efforts to understand such contradictions were not futile.

It was during his school years, however, that Milosz was to meet two men who would shape his life. Later, after reading Thomas Mann's *The Magic Mountain* at the university, he saw how its two main protagonists, the Jesuit Naphta and the humanist Settembrini, reminded him of Hans Castorp, his prefect, and Adolf Rozek, his Latin instructor. At first, Castorp, or Hamster, as he was nicknamed, seemed to Milosz to be a religious fanatic, and Rozek, on the other hand, won his heart with his love for literature, respect for logic, and dapper dress. But in the end Hamster, in Milosz's mind, had given him more than Rozek. He owed the discovery of the basic dualism in all of us to Hamster, and blamed his first unsuccessful attempts in literature on Rozek, whose emphasis on logical structure had stifled inspiration.

At college, Milosz studied law despite his predilection for literature. He came into contact with the concepts of Marxism during these years, but because of his dislike for dogma he did not become a communist then, although most of his fellow intellectuals did. Even at this rather inchoate stage in his life, he thought communism to be a "vulgarized Marxism," and his belief along with Stalin's bloody reign in postwar Europe ultimately forced him to break with his country. Immediately after graduation, he received a scholarship to study literature in Paris, and unhesitatingly spent a happy year there in almost constant company of one of his relatives, Oscar Milosz, a French poet and editor, who published one of Milosz's poems in the influential magazine *Cahiers du Sud* and who assisted him launch his literary career. But all was not idyllic because the fever of Nazism and the shiver of fear it produced in Europe was spreading.

Upon his return to Poland, Milosz experienced the unsettling feeling that afflicted many of his countrymen at that time. It was as though something ghastly were looming, like a specter. And, as his relative, Oscar Milosz, had predicted, it happened—Germany invaded Poland in September 1939. Milosz had been working as a writer for Polish National Radio in Warsaw before this occurrence, but he fled to Wilno, where to his chagrin Stalin had taken over the city. Unwilling to remain in a communist state, he made the dangerous crossing of Poland back to Warsaw, where he became active in the literary underground.

In Nazi-occupied Warsaw, Milosz and the novelist George Andrzewski spearheaded a lively publishing network that kept the remaining inhabitants of the city in touch and in unwavering spirit. He also struck up a friendship with a philosopher, whom he refers to as Tiger, who would be his mentor for many years after the war. Finally, in July 1944, when the artillery fire of the Russians outside the city was heard, the firm belief held by the Poles that Germany would lose the war was confirmed.

However, liberation was not as simple as they had hoped or expected. The Poles, who had sought their own sovereignty and for control over their own country, ironically, found themselves at the mercy of Russian domination. Milosz was offered a position in the diplomatic corps because of his status as a renown poet, and found himself in Washington, D. C., representing the People's Poland. In letters exchanged with Tiger, who was made a professor of philosophy in their native land, they both expressed serious doubts about what they were doing and were tortured by them. In 1951, Milosz went into exile in Paris, while Tiger remained cornered where he was, and died a few years later.

Czeslaw Milosz's *Native Realm* is a tragic account of the machinations of history. But it is a truthful one, and as the book's subtitle suggests, it is a search for "self-definition." If origins and history are obscured or forgotten then it is impossible to understand the present and predict what the future may hold. *Native Realm* is an autobiography that is written with a sensitivity to history that engulfs and permeates life. To the westerner, not familiar with Eastern Europe, Milosz provides a great deal of insight into the people and endows the geographical area with a distinct sense of place, revealing the roots that depict its series of one crisis after another. For the European, and the westerner alike, Milosz has provided an indelible record of the struggle for freedom and dignity seen through the eyes and ears of a global literary son whose historical perspective has become renown in universal proportion.

AGING, IDENTITY, AND TIME: *BEING HERE* BY ROBERT PENN WARREN

At the age of 75, when most poets and writers look back upon their lives and their work, Robert Penn Warren, author of thirty-two books, is not only adding to his already impressive literary *oeuvre* but he is writing stronger, more exacting, and much more gripping poetry than ever before. He is one of the few poets writing today who is able to compose a truly moving narrative poem. It is a feat in itself to write a successful shorter poem—to crystallize experience and language into the diamond of vision—but to keep a longer poem buoyant with this discipline and to hold the reader's attention to the very end, enthralled, is Warren's remarkable genius.

Being Here, his latest book of poetry, is not just an achievement of technical excellence. It is a mature work of the heart. Warren writes about childhood memories, the quest for truth and substance in adulthood, and the questions of conscience that plague everyone. He wrestles with the issues of aging, identity, and time from the position of one who has weathered inclemencies and has "borne the outrageous," but not without coming away with a flash of insight about the cosmos itself. Warren is one of the great metaphysical poets of the 20th-century—always plunging into the cold water of the commonplace in search of truth or beauty and surfacing with reason and uncommon clarity.

Often with a touch of the luminous, Warren concentrates on childhood memories in the book's first section. "October Picnic Long Ago," a poem in italics that casts a sepia light to introduce the work as a whole, is a ballad about a family picnic that takes place in the South, where Warren was born and raised, in the days of horse and buggy. The poem is italicized because it serves as the first of the two brackets for the book. "Passersby on a Snowy Night," the last poem of the book, is the other bracket, giving the book its shape and inherent meaning. The first poem deals with reminiscence and the last one deals with a life's journey through the dark forest of years. The lyric closes on a note not only of understanding of this arduous trip, but also one of compassion:

> We hear the distant friction,
> Then crack of bough burdened with snow,
> And each takes the owl's benediction,
> And each goes the way he will go.

The poems in between reverberate against each other thematically like bells in a carillon. As in "Speleology," a poem about his discovery of a cave when he was a child. Warren continually probes into himself, into different identities that a life embraces, and returns to daylight, having found the lodestone, the inner man, the "heart beating as though to a pulse of darkness and earth." "When Life Begins" recalls his grandfather, a Civil War veteran, whose "curl-tangled" beard was "like skill-carved stone/ with chisel-grooved shadow accenting the white." While sitting at the old man's feet, Warren listened in silent awe to stories of battles and recollections of a long life. He "wondered when life would begin,/ nor knew that, beyond the horizon's heave,/ time crouched, like a great cat, motionless." Again like a carillon of bells, the thematic reverberations of the poems become more life-affirming, joyous, and musical—aging, identity, and time.

"Filling the Night with the Name: Funeral as Local Color" conjures the rich fragrance of rural life as Warren remembers it to have been. A farmer, Mr. Clinch, returns from his wife's funeral with the outlook of "when a thing's gonna be" you better "git used to it fast." Promptly, with his good clothes on, he proceeds to milk his cows at sundown. But upon finishing his chores, he is unable to sleep and sits down to write his son about what has happened, only to find that "no word would come, and sorrow and joy/ all seemed one." At his desk his hears one sound outside his window that pierces the night, and his grief: "whip-o-will," the bird plaintively cries, "whip-o-will."

In "Recollection in Upper Ontario, from Long Before," one of the many stunning narrative poems in the book, Warren explores human fallibility and weakness and the inability to ever really to come to terms with truth. While camping far north "on the Hudson Bay slope" he asks himself "Why do I still wake up and not know?" He is "lost in forests and lakes," but is still disturbed by a recurring dream of an accident he witnessed as a child. The question is whether Old Zack, "pore old white-trash," did or did not push his club-footed wife in front of a train's path while they were scrounging coal near the tracks. Warren recalls seeing Old Mag getting her foot stuck in the switch-V, and remembers Zack's hands out to grab her. Lying in bed, after her pauper's funeral and after running into Zack, who is drunk, he imagines a beautiful scene of the old scoundrel loving his crippled wife with tenderness. But years later he can only think the exact opposite—Zack's murderous rancor directed at the cripple he married. A loon's high-pitched laughter wakes Warren, who wonders what he really did see and what he did not see. But Warren possesses the wisdom to understand that in order to see clearly one must know what clouded vision is and in order to know truth one must know what illusion is.

The next section of *Being Here* deals with the passions, the unraveling of questions, the complicated answers, and strivings of adulthood. Running down a beach, south of San Francisco, as a youth, he is filled with the awesomeness of life. He believes that "you dream that somewhere, somehow, you may embrace/ the world in its fullness and threat." In "Snowshoeing Back to Camp in Gloaming," his past flows backward on a numbing hike through bare trees that are "as though of all deeds unleafed, and/ dead leaves lost are only/ old words forgotten in snowdrifts." Warren experiences the stripping away of the old and the exhilarating flush of the new warming him in the snow. He is affected by his humanness, and, through the evolution of that element in himself, he is able to become warm and to keep warm. As in most of his poems, when he probes for the source, the fires of revelation flame.

In the astuteness of his probing, Warren explores life's reverse aspect, also. The result is sobering as the other can be warming. "Black ruins of arson in the Bronx are whitely/ redeemed" in "Function of Blizzard." The snow falling down on city streets is covering up urban eyesores, if only for a while. It is a forgetting of "three infants locked in a tenement in Harlem," and remembering, paradoxically, that "God's bosom is broad," that soon snow will completely cover the ruins. He hopes that the snow will fall without melting. "Sky," another poem in the middle section of the book, exudes this same quiet human desperation. "We all, have much endured, buckling/ belts, hearts," he writes. But we have survived despite our losses and our fear of losing even more. "What we most fear," Warren concludes, is what "advances on/ tiptoe, breath aromatic." And not only does it sneak up on us but also "its true name is what we never know."

As true of a poet as Warren is, he is also a prophet. In a poem entitled "Truth," tackling the concept straight-on, he states that it is precisely "what you cannot tell." It is something that is shapeless and unclear in strong light or devouring darkness. Truth is history's trick, and "the serpent's joke." He believes truth is what the dead could tell if they were able to converse with the living, for their "accumulated wisdom must be

SELECTED REVIEWS

immense." In another poem, "Trip to California," that exhibits the strength of the last two parts of *Being Here,* Warren follows the savage path of the western movement in U.S. history. Now California waits like a dream come true, but Warren does not forget the bloody injustices that made that dream a reality. The echo of the sound of rifles shot from moving trains into herds of buffalo still resonates in the imagination. Skinners worked off the hides and left the flesh to waste. California dreams, now the diseased facsimile of eastern cities' urban sprawl, are now what they are because they were nurtured by our predecessors with the "dark humus of history or our/ own fate, which blindly blooms, like a flower."

The poetry of Robert Penn Warren transcends the personal and resonates in the particular. He is a poet in complete control of the subtle nuances of language and is receptive to the sublime and tortuous depths of humanity. Through a half century of practicing his craft, Warren offers his readers nothing less than what is an exemplar of clarity of vision in writing poetry that is replete in its compassion as it is quintessentially adept in its virtuosity.

AN ICONIC LITERARY HISTORY OF THE GREAT DEPRESSION: *THE DREAM OF THE GOLDEN MOUNTAINS* BY MALCOLM COWLEY

Three weeks before the Wall Street crash of 1929, Malcolm Cowley started work as a copy editor and proofreader for *The New Republic*, a magazine founded in 1914 as "a weekly journal of opinion." At a time when Hollywood films avoided controversial issues. When radio concerned itself with Amos 'n' Andy skits and brand name advertising; and when most newspapers printed negligible news on their front pages while the glossed-over reports of strikes and the closing of banks were tucked away on their inside pages, *The New Republic* was one of the few sources of in-depth coverage of important topics. From this vantage point, Cowley came face to face with an America in despair. Cowley's position at *The New Republic*, later that of book review editor and reporter, brought him into the whirlwind of social changes sweeping the depression-riddled nation.

Cowley's *The Dream of the Golden Mountains* chronicles the decade of American history when writers marched among the 15,000,000 workers that were out of jobs, striking with the dream "that a City of Man would rise on the other side of disaster." Never before had writers so assiduously and passionately followed the unfolding of historical events. And never before has this turbulent period of literature and history been portrayed with such poignance and clarity.

Densely packed with both fact and personal anecdotes, Cowley's memoir depicts an era fraught with disillusion and dismay. Workers did not know where to turn for help, and the

SELECTED REVIEWS

administration of President Herbert Hoover offered little assistance to those in need. The Smoot-Hawley Tariff, for instance, designed to balance the economy by increasing tariffs on certain imported goods while decreasing tariffs on others, proved an embarrassing failure. Everything seemed to be falling to pieces. There was the sense that something was ending in American society. Poverty-stricken Midwestern farmers found it was cheaper to burn the wheat they could not sell than to buy coal shipped in from the eastern states. Hoovervilles, small cities of unemployed workers living in tarpaper shacks with roofs of tin cans, sprang up in vacant lots.

Americans were in need of an economic and political alternative to a system that had failed them, and for many that answer was communism. Writers, like Edmund Wilson, began expressing this belief, demanding that "communism be taken away from the communists." The more capitalism was scrutinized, the more it seemed illogical. There was a desperate need for a movement in which workers could at least unite spiritually. Communism filled that need.

Under the aegis of novelist Theodore Dreiser, an organization called the National Committee for the Defense of Political Prisoners (NCDPP) took shape. Dreiser, author of the classic novels *Sister Carrie* and *An American Tragedy*, drew together a large group of writers, artists, scientists, teachers, and professional people to join ranks with the workers and to "aid its work."

Cowley, active in the NCDPP as well as in other communist-oriented groups, was among the contingent of writers, including Edmund Wilson, Waldo Frank, Quincy Howe, and Mary Heaton Vorse, who became involved in the Harlan County coal strike in Kentucky. Their intention was to distribute food, hear grievances, and consult with the miners. The miners were paid for each ton of coal produced with script that was worth sixty cents on the dollar and could only be redeemed at the company store. For their situation to be termed unfair would be an understatement. The strike had been a bloodbath, and their families were starving.

At Pineville, Harlan's county seat, the writers' contingent was greeted by machine guns, aimed at them from the courthouse. Arrested and intimidated, they were finally driven out of town, but not before they had handed out some food and spoken with the striking miners. Their presence did not win the strike, but they were able to raise funds for the miners.

Actions such as these taken by writers were not uncommon during the Depression years. Books produced during those years, such as *The Big Money* by John Dos Passos, *Tender is the Night* by F. Scott Fitzgerald, and *To Have and To Have Not* by Ernest Hemingway, dealt with social collapse. There were novels written about the coal, cotton, and lumber strikes, including *Marching! Marching!* by Clea Weatherwax, *To Make My Bread* by Grace Lumpkin, *Gathering Storm* by Myra Page, and *The Land of Plenty* by Robert Cantwell. The poetry of Kenneth Fearing, Alfred Hayes, and Muriel Rukeyser portrayed the cause of the jobless, the oppressed, and the needy.

In 1935 a young playwright, Clifford Odets, read of Hitler's Germany in a report to *The New Masses*. He was so moved that in one evening he wrote a play that was to be produced in over thirty American cities, *Till the Day I Die*. It almost always appeared with another short play by Odets, *Waiting for Lefty*, inspired by a report of the New York City taxi drivers' strike of 1934.

Protests and protest writing were common to the 1930s. The Bonus Expeditionary Force, a group of angry World War I veterans, marched on Washington, for example, in one of the many related incidents. The government had promised them "adjusted compensation certificates," and these certificates were to be redeemed in dollars in 1945. Living on the very edge of starvation, members of the BEF demanded that they be paid immediately, arguing that help was needed sooner than later, that they might not live to see 1945. The Hoover administration reacted harshly. Led by General Douglas MacArthur, a column of infantry routed the BEF, burning their camp on Anacostia Flats near the Capitol and scattering thousand of ex-servicemen and their families across the countryside.

Such government shows of power did not inspire confidence in Americans already doubting the political system who were discontented and confused by it. It was obvious in the election of 1932 that voters wanted a government that would work for them and not against them. In addition to the two major parties, there were candidates representing 23 minor parties. Of these minor parties, the Socialists' candidate for president, Norman Thomas, received the highest number of votes with 885,458. This put the communist candidates, William Z. Foster and John W. Ford, behind them in second place with 103,152 votes. These minor parties were not so much disgraced on election day as abandoned by supporters, for Americans, however, disillusioned, do not like to waste their votes. They like to choose a winner, and the winner was Franklin Delano Roosevelt, a Democrat.

The communist loss in the election of 1932 had little or no effect on organizers and sympathizers, who remained active in the provocation of strikes, hunger marches, and other protests on behalf of the common people. The party actually accomplished a good deal, in spite of political infighting, such as that described by Cowley, for instance, among the League of Professional Groups. The league consisted of various factions, each of which wanted to save the world, each believing emphatically that its own particular ideology was the only way to go about doing so.

Cowley also became critical of the principle underlying proletarian literature that writing should deal only with the struggle of the workers. He often wondered if communists had any interest in the changing of the seasons, making love, or the flight of birds. Cowley thought that a sense of the humane was lacking in communist ideology.

Despite several programs sponsored by Roosevelt's New Deal administration, such as the National Industrial Recovery Act (NIRA), cutting excessive hours on the job for workers and encouraging collective bargaining, and the Civilian Conservation Corps (CCC), creating jobs for the unemployed, many Americans still doubted the capitalist system of government. These people maintained the view that capitalism would eventually die even if improvements in the system were made. Although Cowley continued to remain unflagging in his political activism, he held little respect for this concept, and his preference for communism waned, primarily because of the news of Stalin's bloody tyranny in the Soviet Union.

The Dream of the Golden Mountains is not without moments of personal happiness and tragedy for Cowley. Personal events of consequence include the poet Hart Crane's suicide; Cowley's divorce from his first wife, Peggy; the sound marriage with his second wife, Muriel; and the purchase in 1936 of a barn, which he later remodeled, in Sherman, Connecticut, and in which Cowley lived in for decades. These occurrences play just as large a part for Cowley in the ensuring drama of the 1930s as the political speeches he delivered to the League of Professional Groups in smoky rooms packed with folding chairs.

Malcolm Cowley's memoir of the era of the Great Depression—an era in which literature and politics went hand in hand—is a highly accomplished and informative work, ambitious in scope. It is written with humility, and a compassionate understanding of what transpired. Cowley has written a significant and inspiring book, whose resonance is one of a timeless classic which depicts and delineates a specific era of time—one that portrays the dream of the common man in turbulent times, a dream that shone, lighting up the surrounding darkness.

ELEGY, EPIPHANY, AND SONG: *FIELD WORK* BY SEAMUS HEANEY

Seamus Heaney's poetry is a poetry grounded in elegy, epiphany, and song. It is a poetry that shines. With *Field Work*, his fifth book, he confirms his position as a major poet, on a global level. His voice is not only authentic, confident, and resonant, but its tenor is often sweet. Heaney has listened very closely "to the music of what happens" and had gleaned "the unsaid off the palpable."

In 1972, Heaney quit a teaching position at Queens University in Belfast and left the "troubles" of Northern Ireland. He, his wife, and their three children moved south to Glanmore, County Wicklow, and took up residence there for four years. Heaney had become a spokesman in the north—a political poet obliged to write political poems, someone other than himself with great responsibilities in a milieu of enormous duress. As Belfast had affected Heaney's psyche, Glanmore influenced it in the opposite direction. He farmed, got back into himself, became meditative. Heaney continued to write stirring and trenchant poems after his relocation, but he could not have written *Field Work* if he had accepted the role of spokesman for the northern "troubles."

Heaney's first love is language. But this love of language does not include rhetoric for rhetoric's sake, nor does it show itself off as ornament. The language of Heaney's poems is clean, organic, and precise. There is not a word that does not serve its function. Not only does each of his words perform their appointed task, he also makes sure that they are exacting and necessary. Heaney's gift for the organic in poetry is keenly demonstrated in the opening poem of the book, "Oysters." He does not just recreate the "laying down" of a "a perfect memory/ in the cool of thatch and crockery," but has ingested the moment of "toasting friendship" deeply. By the very nature of food eaten and the special occasion, poetry springs simply from things as they are.

In effect, if the poet, as in Heaney's case, listens and looks carefully enough, the poem is not written but writes itself. And this is true if one has the ear and the eye for both the experience and the craft. In addition to possessing these attributes, Heaney composes a poem so assiduously that it expresses a palpable music. One not only senses the spirit of friendship, one can taste the oysters, and in this particular case, not without his predilection for historical fact:

> Over the Alps, packed deep in hay and snow,
> The Romans hauled their oysters south to Rome:
> I saw damp panniers disgorge
> The frond-lipped, brine-stung
> Glut of privilege
>
> And was angry that my trust could not repose
> In the clear light, like poetry or freedom
> Leaning in from the sea. I ate the day
> Deliberately, that its tang
> Might quicken me all into verb, pure verb.

Heaney's love of language infects his political poems also. In "Sibyl" his tongue moves as "a swung relaxing hinge" when he asks "what will become of us?" On an early morning he meets armored cars on the Toome Road "in convoy, warbling on powerful tyres." A taciturn and stoic young man he met in a pub who disobeyed curfew for the sake of a drink and was killed becomes a "dawn-sniffing revenant," a "plodder through midnight rain." In an elegy for his cousin Colum McCartney, who died in a random sectarian killing, Heaney mournfully concludes that "with rushes that shoot green again, I plait/ green scapulars to wear over your shroud." Heaney's language is not only palpable, but also possesses the magic and power of a gentle touch, a hand on the reader's shoulder, a friendly grip.

Of the several elegiac poems in the book, those written for Sean O'Riada and Robert Lowell are the finest. O'Riada, conductor of the Ulster Orchestra, influential composer, and the main thrust in the recent revival of Irish music, is described by Heaney as "springy, formally suited/ a black stiletto trembling in its mark." He declares that O'Riada "had the *sprezzatura*," and intones that this gifted musician was a "wader of assonance." Even the reader who has never heard the work of Sean O'Riada, or had the pleasure of seeing him conduct the Ulster Orchestra, can almost imagine the keen flavor of his music blossoming in Heaney's vibrating tribute.

"Elegy," addressed to American poet Robert Lowell, "the master elegist/ and welder of English," swells with emotion comparable to that of the Irish Sea. It is woeful and awash with the wreckage of the loss in a storm. The poem depicts a meeting with Lowell, how much his poetry meant to Heaney, and the guidance it provided him. No farewell could be finer or more fitting. It is easily comparable to an elegy of Lowell's, not in a competitive sense, but as an achievement of poetry itself.

The heart of *Field Work*, though, pumps with the fluid "Glanmore Sonnets." They are redolent as a "dark unblown rose," and as refreshing as a "twig-combed breeze." The "Glanmore Sonnets" are verdant pastorals and textured reminiscences of childhood and love. They are rich as fields in harvest and as lush as the fuchsia-colored elderberry.

"The good life could be to cross a field/ and art a paradigm of earth new from the lathe/ of ploughs," says Heaney. The language Heaney has tilled is a wealthy soil. He has caught the wind blowing just right, and the reader takes a deep breath of the delicious coolness of a Glanmore twilight:

> This evening the cuckoo and the corncrake
> (So much, too much) consorted at twilight,
> It was all crepuscular and iambic.
> Out on the field a baby rabbit
> Took his bearings, and I knew the deer
> (I've seen them too from the window of the house,
> Like connoisseurs, inquisitive of air.)
> Were careful under larch and May-green spruce.

These poems are "words entering almost the sense of touch." And touch Heaney does, ever so delicately on memories of his youth in Derry. He is brought back to the first flush of "touching-tongues" in a tree house, and the memory of listening to the ground for the afternoon train that would approach. Heaney feels these ripples still, but now they are trembling through the beating of his heart. The recollections contained in the "Glanmore Sonnets" make the word tender seem even more loving and gentle.

In one of the most striking of the "Glanmore Sonnets," although they are all quite impressive, Heaney tells of a dream in which he and his wife are sleeping in moss with their faces exposed all night to a chill drizzle. Within this dream he dreams of when they first became lovers. While still asleep, Heaney maintains that they were as "pallid as the dripping sapling birches." He compares them to Diarmuid and Grainne, fugitive lovers of Irish legend, "waiting to be found." The last lines of the sonnet are a tribute not only to his wife but also to his sense of poetry's spare beauty and his swarthy sense of language:

> Our first night in that hotel
> When you came with your deliberate kiss
> To raise us towards the lovely and painful
> Covenants of flesh; our separateness;
> The respite in our dewy dreaming faces.

There is such joy in these lines—the satiated and ineffable aftermath of lovers. The first "deliberate kiss" that raised them toward both the contact and the contract of flesh is as inviolable as their "separateness." And their "respite" is such as that on the first morning of the world. These lines are pristine; and, possibly the best among the best in *Field Work*.

In "Polder," a short but poignant love poem, Heaney holds his wife as if he actually had reclaimed a low-lying tract of land from the sea. In the glee of the embrace, he cannot but help but feel "like an old willow" as he stirs "a little" on his "creel of roots." "The Skunk," another highly accomplished work, displays both luminous warmth and affection and, particularly, a sense of humor that is missing from the best of love poems. He is "stirred" by the "sootfall" of his wife's clothes at bedtime, and is reminded of the "mythologized, demythologized" skunk because of her "head-down, tail-up hunt in a bottom drawer/ for the black plunge-line nightdress." "The Otter," on the other hand, an account of Heaney watching his wife swimming, is a poem not only of love but of discovery. His hands are like "plumbed water" as he sees her dipping and splashing in the waves. In obvious adoration, she is his "lithe/ otter of memory/ in the pool of the moment." Emerging back on the shore, she is refreshed, as beautiful as ever; "frisky" and "printing the stones."

SEAMUS HEANEY

The poems of *Field Work* are written with genius. They are crisp, of perfect pitch, and infused with more than just a touch of the everlasting. Heaney has written poetry that toes "the line/ between the tree in leaf and the bare tree." He has accomplished what Oisin Kelly told him "years ago/ in Belfast" in that he has "connived with the chisel/ as if the grain/ remembered what the mallet tapped to know." Heaney has tapped a poetry that reads with an ease, and integral grace, and a natural rhythm, and we as readers will be grateful into perpetuity for his veritable amazement.

SPELLBOUND BY THE SUPERNATURAL: *MIRABELL: BOOKS OF NUMBER* BY JAMES MERRILL

James Merrill's *Mirabell: Books of Number* takes up where *The Book of Ephraim*, a section of his Pulitzer Prize-winning book, *Divine Comedies*, leaves off. For most of us, spending spare evenings toying with a Ouija board would be considered innocuous, but Merrill and longtime partner David Jackson (referred to as JM and DJ in the text) have taken it seriously for more than a quarter century. Through his encounters with the supernatural, Merrill unravels a cosmological detective story in what is one of the most ingenious and masterful long poems ever written.

Merrill is nothing less than a deft craftsman. By using any number of poetic forms infrequently used today, such as terza rima, ode, and sonnet, he achieves a spellbinding narrative through the realm of the occult. Even when the tempo is only slightly more pedestrian, Merrill's poetry is not. Consider this example, as Merrill describes how a portentous addition is made to his household:

> Next comes an evening when the Fisherman's Wife
> Brings home from Boylston Street a 7 x 10
> Chinese carpet, which just fits. A pale
> Field. A Ghostly maize in winter sun.
> The border renders in two shades of tan
> And three intensities of Prussian blue
> Overlapping cloudlets that give way
> To limber, leotarded, blue-eyed bats
> —Symbols of eternity, said the dealer.

JAMES MERRILL

Introduced in full regalia in *Divine Comedies* is the lovable and mischievous spirit named Ephraim, who himself is a dealer, but one of a different sort—since he deals in eternity. Born in Xanthos in A.D. 8, Ephraim ended his short life in "A.D. 36 on CAPRI Throttled/ By the imperial guard for having LOVED/ THE MONSTER'S NEPHEW (sic) CALIGULA." Once again, at the beginning of *Mirabell,* Ephraim is contacted and a connection between heaven and earth is made, but this time hovering close by is a cast of other shadowy forms.

Mirabell, reminiscent of Yeats's dealings with supernatural phenomena, is an actual rendering of the communication between these spirits from the beyond and JM and DJ in the summer of 1976. Not only are previously unknown spirits contacted, but also are friends newly dead who have not yet been cast into another life. Such personages as W. H. Auden and Chester Kallman keep in touch. Also, David Jackson's parents, Matt and Mary, and friends in common, Maria Demertzi Mitsotaki and Marius Bewley, are reached.

The poem's sections are numbered in tenths from zero to nine and nine-tenths. Amid its typeface, sometimes for an entire page at a time, upper case type distinguishes the dialogue of the spirits from that of Merrill's and Jackson's comments and questions. The particular spirits involved, each of whom has a numerical code instead of a name, ask Merrill to continue his work from experiences of the séances held over the Ouija board. There is a request for poems of science, and Merrill's thought is:

    POEMS OF SCIENCE Poems of Science? Ugh.

    The very thought. To squint through those
        still-rimmed
    Glasses of the congenitally slug-
    Pale boy at school, with his precipitates,

SELECTED REVIEWS

> His fruit-flies and his slide rule? Science meant
> Obfuscation, boredom—; which once granted,
> Odd lights came and went inside my head.

The challenge is taken, of course, and Merrill's work is cut out for him. What has been accomplished so far, says one spirit, is but a prologue. The order they have come up with is a tall one—poems of science—but their choice of "scribe" could not have been a better one. Although the spirits do admonish that "ABSOLUTES ARE NOW NEEDED YOU MUST MAKE GOD SCIENCE/ TELL OF POWER MANS IGNORANCE FEARES THE POWER WE ARE/ THAT FEAR STOPS PARADISE WE SPEAK WITHIN THE ATOM."

The spirits, actually fallen angels, inform their mediums, JM and DJ, that the universe is governed by two forces—biology and chaos. God, they say, is biology. Fallen angels, though, in this case are not constituents of evil. They, in fact, voluntarily left the work of chaos, and in doing so, shed their emotions. Losing the ability to feel occurred chronologically in:

> PREHISTORY WE MADE PARABLE & MYTH IN HARD
> BIOLOGICAL TERMS ADAM & EVE ARE IMAGES
> FOR DEVELOPMENTS IN THE VERY NATURE OF MATTER
> A WORLD NEGATIVE & POSITIVE DWELLS IN THE ATOM
> EDEN A STAGE THE EXPULSION THE DRAMA THE MISTAKE
> TO BELIEVE THAT KNOWLEDGE IS EVIL THAT MISTAKE PERSISTS

Essentially, the fallen angels represent the negative force within the atom. God Biology, or God B, as he is cited from now on, is the positive force of the atom. The angels, unlike any that might be imagined, were not "men before mankind." "WE ONCE FLEW/ WE ONCE SOARED," is their response when questioned as to what form they resemble.

Here, the fisherman's wife comes into the picture more vividly, and the pieces of the supernatural puzzle begin to fall into place. "DO YOU IMAGINE THAT CARPET," they ask. The chilling answer is:

> Our bats! The gargoyle faces, the umbrella
> Wings—of course, *of course,* that's how you look!
> A dash of jitters flavors the reply:
> NO WELL PERHAPS JUST A BIT IS IT AN UGLY
>   NOTION

A recurring message communicated by these messengers is that experimentation with the atom must stop; the atom must be brought back to its proper place where God B would feel safer about his creation—heaven. Their advice is to leave the atom alone, and that "THE STRUCTURES NEEDED/ FOR MAN TO GAIN PARADISE ARE MOLECULAR & CAN/ AT LAST BE USED TO BREAK THE CHAIN OF BLIND & WASTEFUL LIVES."

There is enough psychic wattage in *Mirabell: Books of Number* to keep scientists fascinated with the phenomenal data here until electricity is replaced by telepathy. One story, related by the fallen angels, is that of Akhnaton, the Egyptian sun god, and Nefertiti, his princess. Again, like a banner held up by an anti-nuclear protester, the slogan is: "WHAT IS NUCLEAR POWER BUT DESTRUCTION." And what Akhnaton and Nefertiti were forced to face is just that, along with such occurrences as a once fertilizable desert going barren for 1,200 years.

Akhnaton understood light energy and attempted to reproduce it in stone. The dimensions for his pyramids of quartz were exact but not exact enough—the measurements were off one-seventh of a millimeter. "ITS GLOW WAS SEEN IN MINOAN SKIES/ UNDER THEBES TODAY IS THE MELTED LAKE OF HIS JEWEL," reads the report of the spirits of the first nuclear accident.

Merrill is not beyond sprinkling flashes of humor and wit throughout this poem either. When Auden is asked whether or not the talks they are having with these spirits repel him, he answers that he is envious and wishes that during his life on earth he 'COULD HAVE HELD/ HANDS ON TEACUPS."

Veils are continually lifted by the spirits, who seem to be taking turns in their transmissions, until 741, eventually named "Mirabell" only after a peculiar transformation, apparently proves to his superiors that he is best suited for the job. He explains to JM, who is worried about not actually working from his own inspiration, that even Dante received spiritual guidance in the form of transmissions from beyond. A spirit with the numerical code of 80098 masqueraded as a defrocked priest and spoke with Dante for eight years. 741 also delineates that Rimbaud was the ghostwriter of *The Waste Land*. The time was not yet ripe for Rimbaud in the 19th-century, but by the time Eliot arrived on the scene the timing was perfect. So, Rimbaud moved Eliot's hand. In spite of this somewhat inorganic inspiration, Merrill's pen moves better than most. *Mirabell* pours forth in a tidal force of energy and shock wave after shock wave of revelation.

The density of the poem itself is broken up at times with a warmth that is vitally penetrating—as when 741 turns into quite a different being as opposed to his form as a bat. After he has finished lecturing about the nature of love and how mind in its truest form emits a kind of unisexual light, he is censored by nature for attempting to expose too much too soon. Merrill takes on the role of interlocutor by saying: "Let the angels finish/ That sentence, friend. Speak for yourself, not God." Because of this exchange of love and the belief entrusted in 741 by Merrill and Jackson, the spirit is transformed into a peacock. But the event is of a reciprocal nature, since 741 knew that a peacock had the power to please the eyes, so he "TOOK FROM THE FILE/ THE PEACOCK." This is quite an accomplishment in a realm where there are no emotions, no appearances, and only, at best, dark forms.

Later, after suggestions for names are solicited, such as Mehitabel and Methuselah, Mirabell is named, although JM's argument is that he has "so many M's already." Mirabell disputes this, proud of having a name and no longer just having a number:

> INDEED & NOT ACCIDENTALLY M IS AT ONCE OUR
> METHOD & THE MIDPOINT OF OUR ALPHA-
> BET THE SUMMIT
> OF OUR RAINBOW ROOF IN TIMBRE THE
> MILD MERIDIAN
> BLUE OF MUSE & MUSING & MUSIC THE HIGH
> HUM OF MIND

Mirabell continues his lessons as if he were driving his students in preparation for final exams. "A BASIC PRECEPT U WILL NEED TO TAKE ON FAITH: THERE IS/ NO ACCIDENT," he firmly states. Whatever has happened , or will happen has been calculated into the universal plan. And never in whatever does happen can anyone interfere.

In the ten final speeches, Mirabell extrapolates on such subjects as culture and the government of heaven. Merrill and Jackson are told that they have been chosen for "V" work, both an honor and a yeoman's task—this is the work of eternity. By the end of Mirabell's tutoring they are ready to

SELECTED REVIEWS

communicate with an angel of a higher order, who introduces himself as Michael: "I AM A GUARDIAN OF THE LIGHT/ LEAVES THIS FIRST OF THE FIRST OF TWO MEETINGS IN A CYCLE OF/ TWINNED MEETINGS IN A CYCLE OF TWELVE MOONS."

James Merrill has written a work many poets, or novelists for that matter, would not dare to even allow themselves to think of writing—that is if they had the ability to do so. *Mirabell: Books of Number* is an achievement of the stature belonging to that of an Eliot or a Pound. What Merrill had done is to father an oracular testament of the soul. He has written a tour de force of the spirit world. His next book, which is the third and last book in this trilogy, will no doubt be a communion with the angels themselves.

4. Towards an Active Perseverance

A FEATURE ARTICLE THAT MAY HAVE NOT BEEN OTHERWISE WRITTEN

In the winter of 1979, I was surviving a breakup in a romantic relationship with a woman, and as it often is when there is a diminution in an area of one's life, to paraphrase Joseph Campbell, another door opens where you didn't even think another door could possibly exist. Because of my feature writing for the arts section of *The New Haven Advocate*, I was invited by the editors of *Connecticut Artists*, the only state arts magazine at the time, to contribute a cover story for what would be a breakout issue for them. The magazine began as a small press journal, and was published in a 6 x 9 format with a glossy cover. The issue they planned to be published in the autumn of that year would be published in a traditional 8 ½ x 11 magazine format. The subject that I was asked to cover was Rudolf F. Zallinger, the famed muralist of the Peabody Museum at Yale. That was in February. Snow covered the ground. However much cold and vacuity I might have felt in my heart, I put some distance between my emotional state and began to feel the surge of beginning a new writing project.

As a child in the 1950s and 1960s, Zallinger's illustrations of dinosaurs and early man that appeared in *Life Magazine* were iconic to me. To be interviewing the man who probably was somewhat responsible for me winning the science prize in fifth grade and reading college biology textbooks at that time was of a dream-come-true vintage and variety.

Also, I found great pleasure in interviewing artists and writers for the purpose of writing feature articles regarding their lives and the genesis of their craft. Often enough being interviewed for newspaper articles myself, sometimes by colleagues who

TOWARDS AN ACTIVE PERSEVERANCE

wrote for *The New Haven Advocate*, I was chagrined, and on occasion nonplussed, when I was misquoted in a newspaper article. When I conducted interviews, I arranged at least two sittings: one in which I would make extensive notes on a yellow pad, and frame quotes from the conversation with my subject; and then in another sitting I would ask some more questions *and* check my quotes with the subject I interviewed. Sometimes I even scheduled a third sitting in which I could gain more of a personal sketch of the individual I was interviewing, more freely, with more grace and ease. This was also how I developed a lead paragraph, which E. B. White, when writing for *The New Yorker* said that he sometimes took a month to craft. I never had such leisure to take a month to work on my lead, nor such time, but I would take a few days to a week in allowing my lead to develop.

What I wasn't prepared for, as much as I was looking forward to interviewing Rudolf F. Zallinger, was what seemed to be his initial reticence. I phoned him and told him why it was I wished to speak with him and about the magazine's publication which was to be feted with a gala at the New Haven Arts Center, and as much as he was amenable to scheduling a time to meet, I did notice concomitantly a distance in his voice.

When I first visited him, he answered the door bell, and then presently ushered me into the breezeway which quickly led to the garage. To say that he was brusque, at first, was not an incorrect observation. However, I soon learned why he took me to the garage, where he lifted up three large folios, true tomes, from a cardboard box, blowing off the dust from the library buckram of the top volume. I stood there, astounded, as he spoke, "If you are going to interview me, then you are going to have to know something about archeology and anthropology. You may *borrow* these books, which I found helped me in my work on the murals at the Peabody. I will give you three weeks. If by that time you feel you have a

A FEATURE ARTICLE

working knowledge about these subjects, and believe you can ask me intelligent questions about what I have accomplished, then I will agree to speak to you in an interview. If you feel that you aren't able to do that, then I won't be able to sit for you in an interview. Whatever the case may be, do return the books to me within three weeks."

I was no more stunned as if a Zen master had struck me on the shoulders with a *keisaku*, which is used to wake up a monk who had fallen asleep during meditation, or one whose posture had collapsed during a sitting due to leg cramps, numbness, shooting pain, or a combination of all three—as I once had experienced that slap, several times, when I had attended a *seishin*, which is a Zen meditation retreat, often lasting a full weekend and in many cases longer.

Rudolf F. Zallinger placed the folios in my open arms, one by one, and I felt their weight as much as I understood the gravity of the task at hand. I had been openly challenged. Polite as I was as a young man, I verbally accepted the test, and offered that I would phone to set up an appointed interview and to return the books. As much as I felt stretched, I was as much inspired by what was ostensibly a dare. It provoked me and excited me into action at the same time.

For the next three weeks, I studied the books after work from the bookstore in which I worked as assistant manager at the Yale Center for British Art. I had taken an archeology and anthropology course in college, but in studying these volumes, printed on India paper, with their black and white etchings, and two rows of single-spaced 12-point type per page, was a voyage into erudition which made my eyes burn late into the evenings. However much my eyes burned, I felt compelled to educate myself with more than enough backstory to satisfy my new Zen master, Rudolf F. Zallinger. I still felt the slap of his *keisaku*. Years later when I read Joseph Campbell's sharing

TOWARDS AN ACTIVE PERSEVERANCE

of an anecdote regarding a novice who wanted to study with a certain spiritual master and the master relegating him to meditating on a large rock in the forest before he was even allowed to begin his studies later made all the intuitive sense in the world to me. Rudolf F. Zallinger had inflected the same discipline on me as the master had on the prospective spiritual seeker—some experiences in life needed to be earned. I had needed to earn my opportunity in interviewing the artist who painted the dinosaur murals. This was an *enormous* challenge in my life and I dug in, determined not to squander what I knew was an opportunity of *gigantic* proportions—pun intended, indeed.

When I phoned Rudolph F. Zallinger three weeks later to propose to him that I had made diligent reference of the books he leant to me and asked whether he would be willing to sit with me in an interview, I was as surprised as much as I was the first time by his brisk manner and his open challenge to my professionalism as a journalist. He was pleasant, even admiring, as the tone in his voice suggested. I couldn't possibly be sure that I wouldn't have more hurdles to clear to win his confidence in me during the interview sessions but I did feel his approbation toward me for having my having studied the volumes he had leant to me.

The interview, for all intent and purpose, went extremely well. He was animated and at ease with me. I followed that with two more interviews: one to double-check my quotes and one in which I could acquire a personal sketch, to attempt to portray his character as adeptly as I could and in as many specific words as I could. By the end of the interview process, I felt we had reached a level of cordiality of a professor with that of their student. Mutual respect pervaded the air between us.

The article appeared as expected—at a launch for *Connecticut Artists* magazine, which was more like a formal convocation,

A FEATURE ARTICLE

with the mayor in attendance, and a generous offering of wine and *hors d'ouevres*. It was memorable. However, I do recollect feeling more of a vicarious glow for Rudolf F. Zallinger than for myself. I felt that it was his work that was being featured, both with respect to one of the images from one of his paintings, from his *Early Man* series, on the magazine's cover, as well as the feature article presented within. He had given me so much as a youth that in my own small way I was only paying homage to him and his work. and that alone was quite satisfying and fulfilling.

In January 1981, I left New Haven to move to western Massachusetts, and during one of my return trips to visit the city, I had lunch at the Old Heidelberg, now no longer extant, which was on Chapel Street, just beyond the Yale Art & Architecture Building. In having a drink at the bar after my meal, with friends, I struck up a conversation with a gentleman to my left. The conversation lead to what we each did, and he mentioned that he was a painter, and that his father was a painter of some renown. Casually, he offered that his name was Peter Zallinger. With as much ease as had announced his name, I told him mine. He was aghast. So was I. I had been speaking all along to the son of Rudolf F. Zallinger.

Peter had informed me that his father was awarded the prestigious Emery Addison Verrill Medal, named after Yale's first professor of Zoology. He went on to say that his father held this award in the highest esteem, and that it was his feeling that for him it was at least as significant a value for him as was his Pulitzer Prize in painting. Peter stated plainly that his father firmly believed that the awarding of the medal was precipitated by the feature article in *Connecticut Artists*.

I still include my having written "The Varied Career of Rudolf F. Zallinger" on my professional resume, and that it is thought to have been the impetus through which the artist was awarded

TOWARDS AN ACTIVE PERSEVERANCE

with the Emery Addison Verrill Medal. In selecting work that was of subsequent merit for this volume, I discerned that this early piece of mine was still pertinent both for myself and the readers of this book. We all need to begin somewhere, and in my early years as a writer and a freelance journalist being challenged and rising to meet that challenge proved to be an opportunity which I will always remember as being invigorating and life-changing—for both my subject and myself.

A SALUTE TO THE VARIED CAREER OF RUDOLF F. ZALLINGER

In 1943, after eighteen months of researching animal and plant life from the Mesozoic era and working on a *cartoon,* Rudolph F. Zallinger stood on a scaffold to begin sketching a mural in the Peabody Museum's Hall of Dinosaurs. Nearly four decades later, he recalls that moment with distinguished verve and a chuckle. "I remember looking 110 feet down that wall with a stick of charcoal in my hand," says Zallinger fondly, his eyes flashing. "I gulped a couple of times, but after a couple of gulps I started. To avoid hysteria is an orderly procedure."

Orderly procedure has been a way of life for Zallinger, who in 1949 received the Pulitzer Prize in painting for the accomplishments of his "Age of Reptiles" mural located on the east wall of the Great Hall in the Peabody. The mural, completely covering the wall's 110 x 16 feet dimensions, chronicles a period spanning nearly 300 million years of the planet's land life from the late Carboniferous through the Cretaceous periods.

"There is great disorientation in great passages of time," states Zallinger. "When you try to deal with millions of years, it's an inconceivable amount of time," he continues, carefully gesturing with his hands as if they held fine brushes. "For example, if the Empire State Building served as a representation of the entire history of the earth, a block of one foot high would represent the amount of time that human life has existed. Just imagine a piece of parchment or tracing paper at the very top of that block—that would represent recorded history."

TOWARDS AN ACTIVE PERSEVERANCE

Perspective such as this has played an intrinsic role in the recorded history of Rudolf F. Zallinger. Not only has he painted the "Age of Reptiles" mural, but its companion, the "Age of Mammals," stretching 60 feet across the south wall of the Hall of Mammals, and depicting approximately 70 million years of mammal development.

"I had to arm myself," says Zallinger, "and this involved an extraordinary amount of research. I steeped myself in the material, reflecting the knowledge of my colleagues."

Among the colleagues with whom Zallinger consulted in regard to the "Age of Reptiles" mural were, for example, G. Edward Lewis, then Curator of Vertebrate Paleontology, and Dr. George Wieland, one-time Research Associate at the Peabody. Dr. Rowland Brown, a Curator of Paleobotany at the U.S. National Museum, and Dr. Joseph Gregory, also a Curator of Vertebrate Paleobotany, two of the finest scholars in their fields, collaborated with Zallinger on the "Age of Mammals" mural.

From Irkutsk to New Haven

Rudolf F. Zallinger is a quiet soft-spoken man with a sanguine complexion and thick eyebrows. His hair is white, classically proportioned, as if Zeus has combed it with a lightning bolt. Strolling leisurely from his workroom, wearing blue chinos, a pale-knit shirt, and tan casuals, he looks out onto Sleeping Giant State Park through a large picture window in the living room of his tastefully modern home in North Haven. His paintings, perfections in oils and egg tempera, line the walls. Life has not always been such for Zallinger.

On November 12, 1919, Rudolf Franz Zallinger was born in Irkutsk, Siberia. His father, Franz, was an Austrian soldier captured during WWI, and incarcerated in a Russian prison camp. His mother, Marie Koncheravich, was the daughter of a Polish civil engineer working on the Trans-Siberian Railway.

After the war, with the Bolshevik Revolution at its high watermark, release from the country was nearly an impossibility. However, the Zallingers began to forge their way across Russia amidst Bolshevik and Tsarist bloodshed. They were destined for Austria, intending to live with Franz's mother. Their only choice was to travel east via the Trans-Siberian Railway to the port of Vladivostok.

A cattle car, shared by 40 people, and warmed by a potbellied stove, was their home for three months. Travel was slow—bridges had been blow out, derailments were common, military inspection ubiquitous. Then travel slowed to a halt when Rudolph contacted measles. The Zallingers were permitted to leave the train, and the found themselves in Harbin, Manchuria.

While waiting for their son's measles to subside, they learned of the death of Franz's mother in Austria. The Zallingers' plans then abruptly changed; they decided to go to the United States, instead. Franz, an artist, earned the boat fare for the voyage across the Pacific by painting signs. He reached the port of Seattle in 1921. His wife and son joined him two years later.

In Seattle, Rudolph Zallinger began learning art as a child both from his father and private instructors. By the time he was ten he had attended his first life class, and had sold his first painting for $5.00, a fortune, especially at that time, for a child.

At 17, Zallinger, also a serious student of the piano, had to make a decision as to which art form to dedicate himself—music or painting. But his predilection tipped towards pictorial expression, and his intention was to attend art classes at the University of Washington. However, John Butler, an artist from the

TOWARDS AN ACTIVE PERSEVERANCE

East who was teaching a class in Seattle, directed him toward enrolling at Yale. In the autumn of 1939, Zallinger entered Yale University's School of Fine Art to begin his studies, winning merit scholarships every semester after his first.

At the beginning of his senior year, after marrying Jean Day, now the illustrator of dozens of children's books, Zallinger took a job illustrating seaweed for Albert E. Parr, who was a Director of the Peabody at the time. By the end of his senior year, Parr was enough taken by Zallinger's work, and the strong recommendation of Lewis York, then Chair of the Painting Department at the Yale Art School, to assign him the task of painting a mural on one of the walls in the museum.

Zallinger began a crash course in Vertebrate Paleontology and Paleobotany, guided by Carl O. Dunbar, successor to Parr, as Museum Director. "Ideally," says Zallinger, "I felt responsible to accurately state the ultimate knowledge extant up to that time. The research cultivated was a supported progression. There was no great jumping off the end of the pier. I wasn't just putting a decoration on the wall. That would have been a disaster."

After painting the *cartoon*, or the original version of the mural, done to scale, in this case 11 feet long and 16 inches high, one-tenth of the dimensions of the finished mural, Zallinger began what was to become four years of work. Painted in dry fresco and bound to the wall by a solution of casein glue, the mural was finished by June 1947. It was the largest mural ever painted in the field of natural history.

It still is.

A FEATURE ARTICLE

Rich Utilization of Resources

Zallinger moved back to Seattle as a freelance artist in 1950. However, Kenneth MacLeish, Editor of *Life Magazine,* contacted Zallinger in 1952, informing him that the magazine was interested in using his "Age of Reptiles" mural for inclusion in the first of a series of scientific books they intended to publish, *The World We Live In*. He was also offered a commission to portray the evolution of mammals in a painting for eventual publication in the magazine, and publication in a later volume in the science series. *Life* had enhanced the offer by suggesting to present the finished painting to the Peabody Museum, if the Peabody's staff supervised the work. Another mural was in the making. The Peabody, of course, agreed. So did Zallinger.

Given eight months to complete the painting, Zallinger worked arduously to meet the deadline. Refusing to compromise with perfection, his time grew short, and only three-fourths of it was finished within two weeks of the due date. An extension of time was requested, but advertising for the particular issue of *Life* it was to appear in had already been sold.

Alfred Eisenstaedt and his staff of *Life* photographers came to the rescue. By taking a photograph of what Zallinger had already painted, so it could be started in production, another week was gained in which he was able to finish the painting in time.

It was not until 1961 when enough funds could be raised that Zallinger began the "Age of Mammals" mural. And it was not until 1967, on his 46th birthday, that he would actually complete it. Smaller than the first mural, the "Age of Mammals" measures 60 by 6 feet. Still, Zallinger spent as much time painting it as he had spent painting the first—over 7,000 man hours.

Uncompromising in his striving for perfection as in his zeal to move onward to yet other projects, Zallinger began working exclusively for *Life*. He contributed paintings of the tropical rain forest of Surinam, along with his "Age of Mammals" painting, which covered twelve pages, in another scientific book geared for the layperson that *Life* published, *The Wonders of Life on Earth* (1960). In *The Epic of Man* (1961), he painted a series of Cro-Magnon initiation rituals to complete its chapter, "The Dawn of Religion." Appearing in the same text were his paintings recreating Minoan civilization at its glory 3,500 years ago. Zallinger, also during this time, illustrated a series of tableaus from the Russian Revolution.

Travelling to actual historic sites and being able to work with the top authorities in fields such as anthropology and archeology enthralled Zallinger. "That was the real treat," he says, "to work with the finest scholars. Those were the residual benefits. It was very hard work, and eminently worthwhile. If you didn't have the absolute need you'd do things for nothing."

"There isn't anybody in the world who could have undertaken that series," Zallinger states, referring to *The World We Live In* and its subsequent volumes. "*Life* made such a rich utilization of resources. It was the first large science series in American publishing."

"*Life* was coasting in the doldrums of the 1950s ," continues Zallinger, briefly watching a patch of clouds rise toward the summit of Sleeping Giant Mountain. "It was something significant in other than making money. The charts-and-graphs people would lose eight to ten million dollars on the project, but that was accepted as a condition. The profit was almost inestimable—everything went up in geometric progression. *Life* grossed revenues that were greater than all other magazines, radio, and TV put together."

By inestimable profits, Zallinger's concern was not monetary profit for the magazine but profit for the American public: "The charts-and-graphs people sold them short. They couldn't have been more wrong. The American public was more intelligent than they thought. And as a result of that very first mistake, *Life* capitulated. The mantle that they wore so proudly dropped. The American readership will never forgive them."

Despite his criticism, Zallinger believes "to have had a producer like I had in *Life Magazine*, and to accomplish the things I felt I personally had to accomplish is what I am singularly proud of."

Perpetual Realism

"My career has been varied," says Zallinger. One of the interesting things in my life has been this variation. It's been highly stimulating."

Zallinger has been intrigued by the movement of water, and has been painting a series of waterfalls, such as Kent Falls, one of the paintings hanging in his living room. Rudolph F. Zallinger becomes lyrical when speaking of flowing water: "Water is rich and diversified—its movement, changings, and visages are not seasonal but moment to moment affected by atmospheric condition, an environmental shifting. It's an element so diverse, so ephemeral. It has surface and it doesn't have surface. It moves and it doesn't move. It's a reflector of light"

"One begins to deal with it," Zallinger continues, "by definition, like a mirror. It has diversifying facets. It's like a mirror in a fun house. Its movement, flow, and stillness versus the patina of rocks, the carving out over eons of time, is a shared experience."

"The perception of reality," cites Zallinger, "is intriguing in this—in that we mutually share in these perceptions. Some artists reflect a screaming need for linear development. I don't need linear development in terms of my psyche. It mustn't be manifested in my work. I take great joy in doing these diversified things."

Zallinger believes in the "perceptional realism of the approach of art forms." "I teach this," he says, "not objectivity." A professor of drawing and painting at the University of Hartford, as well as being Artist-in-Residence at the Peabody Museum, Zallinger's belief is that "1970s conceptualism is on the wane," but also possesses "an appreciation of all art forms at their best" whether he practices them or not. "It's a question of quality," he says, "to appreciate an accomplished feat in any of these forms is the penultimate."

As for what advice he would give to up and coming artists, Zallinger recommends "manageable control that corresponds to the effort and strain" an artist must put into their craft. "It's variable," he deliberates, "and one can't generalize. But in the case of a painter, hopefully to sell their paintings, dispense them, produce more work. Consequently, they'll be reviewed sufficiently and shown in dealer's galleries."

"There are no overnight successes," he admonishes. "All that's a sham; it doesn't really work that way. If there are overnight successes, it took them twenty years of hard work before they got to be overnight successes."

"Artists have a highly earned following," states Rudolf F. Zallinger, crossing his legs and watching another patch of clouds embark toward the slopes of Sleeping Giant Mountain. "There's nothing earned like what the artist earns in any of the arts," he says with an audible integrity as deep as a pool beneath a waterfall.

5. Reveling in What Is Salvageable
WRITING WHAT AN EDITOR WANTS

My experience for more than three decades was that the copy I submitted to my editors during those years was nearly always accepted, and then when accepted there were only minor changes made to that copy which were marked by the idiosyncrasies that bore the stamp of each particular editor. That was quite fine by me. Normally, I enjoyed working with different editors, and found myself learning something from each one. The one article I wrote toward the end of my freelance career writing for *The New Haven Advocate* was one in which I interviewed a DJ at WYBC because I had thought that his jazz and blues program, intertwined with Afro-American history, deserved a higher profile in the community. There was a new Arts Editor at the newspaper, and she thought the article a bit facile in that it was her supposition that everyone already knew the backstory of the Afro-American saga and she red-penciled my piece and handed it back to me. That was the last time I ever walked into *The Advocate* office again.

Months later I would move some 75 miles north to a semirural town, Monson, that was located more toward central Massachusetts than what is often considered the western part of the Commonwealth. Later, I would move to Amherst, attracted at that time by the notion of living in Emily Dickinson's hometown.

Largely, for some thirty years, I was a bookseller and bookstore manager, as well as an antiquarian cataloger, which was a short-lived career, and one that was not so much for the better but for the worse, since I worked for an individual who was intolerant of even the smallest error in what was the house style, developed after Swann Auction Galleries, in New York, and whose people and management skills were tantamount to his impatience with me. However, in 2008, I left the book business for good, after having managed the general book department at UMass for nearly five years, and although it seemed perilous at first it was for my own long-term benefit. In doing so, I began working as a freelance writer and editor as a means to make a living. Although freelance jobs have been sometimes separated by more months through which I can claim financial comfort, I have made my living by writing and editing, as well as my serendipitous fortune in acquiring philanthropic grants of assistance from granting agencies such as The Author's League Fund, The Carnegie Fund for Authors, and PEN America, of New York City; The Haven Foundation, of Brewer, Maine; and Poets in Need, which awarded me a one-time Philip Whalen Grant for financial assistance.

The freelance writing assignments in the past decade have been both varied and satisfying, never mind their nearly always coming in when I most needed to pay rent and bills. Emissaries from the Moscow Ballet, headquartered in Pittsfield, Massachusetts, phoned me two years after I originally applied for a writing job with them, in April 2012, to ask me if I could assist them in editing and rewriting a new version of *The Great Russian Nutcracker*. I accepted the opportunity and produced copy that I composed in a two-week period that was filled with pure joy. I spent the time infusing the work with lyrical prose, and the book was published in a small folio format, illustrated by a woman who I believe had been a former ballerina and was a rather adept naïve artist who rendered the story boards in a kind of Russian-Polish *tchotchke* style. The volume was published to honor the 25th season of the ballet touring America and was sold at each of their performances that year.

Although I experienced tough sledding through my meager finances over the next couple of years, in October 2013, I landed

WRITING WHAT AN EDITOR WANTS

a job working for a large regional corporation. The job lasted six months and provided me with enough income that I lived for another six months on what I had saved from the salary paid to me. Initially, I was to provide backstory and various articles that concerned retirement in America. To know where your paycheck is coming from, which has infrequently been the case for me over the last few years, is nothing less than liberating. I not only flourished in the work I wrote for my editors at the corporation but also during my own personal writing time. Having the opportunity to be financially responsible was not wasted on me.

At first I thought that I would not include any of the writing I did during this time in this book, since it wasn't literary. However, I actually inculcated the work with a literary tone, not so much because I planned it that way, but because that is how I see the world. Literary references pop up in my mind daily, each day and all day long. So, this wasn't anything of a stretch to me. In discerning what to include in this collection, I finally decided that four of my writing assignments would segue within the other writing collected here.

"Big Data: Uncorking the Genie from the Bottle" was written due to a specific request from one of my editors. Big Data is a metaphor for our time, in the early 21st-century. It's massive ability to collect information on all of us and all of the things that we do can be either darkly Orwellian or used to the best of intentions.

"How We Progress over Time" was another piece that was requested by one of the editors with whom I worked. He wasn't exactly sure what he was asking me to do and I believe he had some trouble attempting to articulate what it was he wanted. At least that is how I came to write this essay regarding pop culture; James Dean, in the part he played as Cal in the film *East of Eden*—and lettuce, as condiment, on a tuna sandwich. After I wrote the piece, the editor basically said, "no, no, not that,

REVELING IN WHAT IS SALVAGEABLE

but this is what I really want you to write for me—a lead into a chapter I am going to compose myself." That is how I came to write the essay, "The Science and Art of Measurement," which discusses measurement and its role in the history of the automotive industry, which also elicits the line, "drive, he said," from Robert Creeley's poem, entitled "I Know a Man." After my writing the essay, the editor, who was not one to proffer praise, said, "You are an expert researcher." I took that from him to be, unquestionably, a compliment.

"The History of Retirement in America" is a long essay that I spent a month researching and writing. As a retiree myself now, and having recently begun collecting Social Security, much of what I wrote in the essay has a significant resonance to me, since when I wrote the piece I wasn't officially semiretired yet. Now with the Trump administration about to begin its reign (as in terror), God only knows what social programs are safe from its manipulation and hackneyed reform. However, I think Woody Guthrie would have enjoyed reading the essay, and just to imagine this possibility makes my having written it worthwhile.

A book was published by the corporation I wrote these four pieces for in the spring of 2015, and although I could only discern my writing among the text of the fashionably published slim volume, I am grateful to have had the job writing and researching for six months. Being mentioned in the acknowledgments also made me smile. The work I did may seem somewhat idiosyncratic but I revel in what I believe is salvageable and what an editor requested that I write, which I believe has made me a better writer today.

BIG DATA: UNCORKING THE GENIE FROM THE BOTTLE

The multifaceted topic of Big Data has been received with amounts of "utter enthusiasm and sincere confusion."[1] Inherently ambiguous due to its largesse, Big Data *connotes* the ability to access enormous pools of structured data, which include datasets with identified labels and locations, and unstructured data, among which consist of qualitative information such as electronic correspondences, audio recordings, and images.

What Big Data then *denotes* is what propels its popularity: endowing businesses, as well as organizations of any kind, to acquire vast amounts of information and then to make use of that with efficiency in a manner to benefit, ideally, both the business, or organization, and the individuals that are its focus.[2] The vision that Big Data offers is similar to Galileo positing in the 17th-century that the earth revolves around the sun—and that in 21st-century information technology the sky is no longer the limit.

Rick Smolan's and Jennifer Erwitt's Big Book on Big Data

A folio refers to a book that is oversized, one that can barely fit on your lap, and Rick Smolan's and Jennifer Erwitt's *The Human Face of Big Data* is such a tome.[3] The volume measures 14 ¼ inches tall and 11 ¼ inches wide; and for all of its 224 pages, it weighs 7 pounds. To some it may initially sound like a techno-book monstrosity; however, the book opens wide,

REVELING IN WHAT IS SALVAGEABLE

much like the breadth of compassion that sometimes can be found in the human heart. The book stands in tribute to an illumination of Big Data—one that is graced with insight and magnitude, if not perspicacity and wisdom its co-authors have invested in it.

"It's like you spent your whole life looking through one eye and all of a sudden you open a second eye. You're not getting more vision. You're getting another dimension," says Smolan. "We have 3D vision for the first time as a species," he is said to have informed his son when the boy asked about Big Data.[4]

Smolan encapsulates Big Data perhaps more accurately, and with the most brevity than anyone has yet, "I'd have remembered quite a bit more, thanks to all-seeing, all-remembering devices that could have turned that little data captured by my fallible human brain into big data capable of analyzing every word and every pattern of our conversation. Whether that's a good or bad, however, is up for debate."[5]

Smolan, who is the visionary behind the *Day in the Life* photography series, is CEO of Against All Odds Productions, which produces large scale photographic projects that blend the art of literary narrative with the science of technology. *Fortune Magazine* selected Against All Odds as "One of the 25 Coolest Companies in America." Several of the company's projects have been featured on the covers of *Fortune Magazine*, *Newsweek*, *Time Magazine*, and *U.S. News & World Report*.[6]

Smolan indicates that Big Data is the "internet-fueled explosion of enormous data sets that can be analyzed for trends and correlations" and that "will soon inundate our daily lives." His prediction is that "not too long from now, we'll all wear devices capable of capturing three-dimensional 'snapshots' of every room we're in, every individual we meet, and every sound we hear to ensure we never forget a person, place, or talking point."[7]

"Literally, you'll have a way able to recreate a room almost like the Holodek on *Star Trek*," Smolan extrapolates. "For almost every moment, it will start being like there really is a time machine where you can step back in time to any moment."

Futuristic vision, or not, Proustian memory[8] is not necessarily always fortuitous, according to Smolan, who with his partner, Jennifer Erwitt, co-published *The Human Face of Big Data*. Smolan's preference is that of "snapshots," which offer themselves as "a silent limited view of a moment in time that symbolizes all this emotion," in opposition to "videos, that offer more information, but are less memorable."[9]

Smolan predicts that "we are going to have auxiliary hard drives to offload our memories, but part of what's nice about being human is the self-deception and the processing of all of it. So it isn't just every moment, but the synthesis of it. We walk away from this meeting we just had and we have a feeling of it, rather than thinking about every second of it."[10]

The truth regarding the mysticism of this kind of visionary techno-speak is that when we are "consciously trying to remember an event and capture it for posterity" that event "decreases what we pick up in the moment [we are living in]."[11] Specific to this idea, Smolan recounts his photographing Robyn Davidson who spent nine months trekking across Australia with her dog and several camels.[12] He suggested that she keep a journal so she could compose a book regarding her journey.

Smolan recalls that Davidson responded by stating, "I can tell you by looking at your eyes what you're thinking about, where you just were, what's happening next, but you're never here with me, in the moment." Smolan continues that, "When she wrote her book two years later, she remembered every line in every conversation we had, every pattern of ants in the sand." When Smolan asked Davidson how she achieved that, she said, "Because I was actually present and you were never here. You were here with your journals, your tape recorder, your cameras, and you were never present in the moment."[13]

In Smolan's and Erwitt's own book, they offer what is a showcase for Big Data and both its affect and appeal, in a human dimension. The volume offers a number of personal cameos, such as Shwetak Patel, computer scientist and entrepreneur, as well as developer of a system in which households may itemize what household appliances require the most energy; and techno-celeb Gordon Bell, whose SenseCam periodically snaps photographs. Also included in the book are photographs regarding Japan's research employing Big Data in predicting earthquakes; technology that can track counterfeit medication in Africa; and what big data uncovered about the patterns of Singaporean taxi drivers.[14]

Smolan believes *The Human Face of Big Data* expresses "numerous positive examples" of its impact; and that his intent is to "spark a global conversation," because he sees "some scary things going on in the world of Big Data, and we need to think about them." Both wise proponent and cautious critic, Smolan admonishes, "It seems like we need to be thinking about who's actually controlling all this information about us and how we get to drive through it." He continues, philosophically, with a great deal of practical sense, "Why is everyone making money off of our data except us?"[15]

The Bigger Deal of Big Data: Chance Favors the Prepared at Black Hills

Tony Ashton, Senior Director of Product Management for workforce planning and analytics for SuccessFactors, Inc., addresses quadrupling his customer base by contracting outside analysts, data scientists, and what he calls "people analytics," which may be on staff, and preparing the company with educational conferences and books regarding Big Data.[16]

"Big data is still the wild, wild west," says Phil Simon, author of *Too Big to Ignore: The Business Case for Big Data*.[17] However, in defining Big Data with an amount of specificity, the term not only refers to the information within a company's records or operations, but also includes a selection of personnel data from its own records and information from competitors in the field, as well as other significant characteristics applied to a distinct refinement of such data for a specified result.[18]

Perhaps what is an ideal example of putting Big Data into action, on a demonstrative utilitarian level, is the case of Black Hills, a Rapid City, South Dakota power-company that acquired a Kansas City, Missouri company, with five utilities, which then not only doubled its workforce but also saw it age into retirement, nearly instantaneously. The inherent problem was replacing experienced and valued retiring workers, including engineers, power-line mechanics, systems operators, and natural gas technicians—each with a skill set that had been developed over a long-tenured working career.[19]

Scrupulously, Black Hills ran a pilot program at one utility to determine its future workforce needs, as a companywide initiative. Workforce analytics were used, as well as other data, to assess what number of employees were about to retire from the utility, voluntarily, within five years, in opposition to projected business growth. Inculcated into the calculations were also data regarding how many job functions needed to be added, changed, or relocated, as well as promotion rates and the time it would take for a bevy of jobs to ramp up to full productivity.[20]

Based on this pilot, Black Hills developed a five-year business plan that delineated their labor needs for all of its businesses, and in each specific location and every individual job. "It has led the company to make a number of changes on how it recruits, hires, and trains, including filling the recruiting pipeline for certain highly technical positions earlier," say Bob Myers, Chief Human Resource Officer at Black Hills.[21]

The social utilitarian proactivity segueing with practiced business acumen is a mixture of sociological boon and economic success story. Black Hills began working in conjunction with technical schools to create training programs to produce a consistent number of entry level jobs each year for a set number of years. In addition, to adequately rationalize the potential skills gap retiring workers would harness Black Hills with by leaving the workforce, they began to offer all employees retirement readiness and financial planning benefits—all employees over age 50, and older, were given the opportunity to work with a company-sponsored certified financial planner.[22]

To optimize future internal labor demand, Black Hills precipitated a management-training program for frontline supervisors and midlevel managerial staff. This was taught by senior managers and included classroom sessions as well as 360-degree feedback and individualized development training. "The company also hired a technical training and safety director and is considering building training centers to do more training on the technical sides of the business," says Myers.[23]

What has culminated for Black Hills, quite efficiently, is that they are automating some processes, with fewer workers. Also, the company shifted from individual workers taking meter readings to automatic ones; and in so doing redeployed some 40 former meter readers into new jobs, while taking opportunities to continue the trend.[24]

"There's an old saying that chance favors the prepared," says Myers. "This is what this is about: How do you develop such an understanding of this that you can prepare well in advance and reap the benefits of being prepared?"²⁵

Making Decisions and Investments: The Big Data Way

In just the span of a few years we have become used to ordering a book online and being able to peruse in advance the menu of that French restaurant we are planning to meet friends at, so can we can practice our pronunciation beforehand. Your smartphone, if you have one, will assist you in copying the recipe for the curried mussels and leek and broccoli quiche, even before you have lifted a fork to your mouth.

However with the new age of smart phone devices and apps, our preferences from whatever practical reference regarding new age spirituality, such as Catherine MacCoun's *On Becoming an Alchemist*,²⁶ that one may desire; to the most recently popular Chick Lit novel that is now available on Amazon.com; to any other unlimited amounts of information, such as traffic reports, disease control and prevention, electrical power usage, and Black Friday shopping trends; is all information that is now tracked by companies and organizations for the sake of data analytics. The results are nearly visionary in proportion from the logistics of business marketing to streamlining corporate protocol to a new grace with respect to advances in medicine and curing the ills of mankind.

In enabling Big Data to work for us and not against us, there needs to be a practiced discernment, which certainly includes the art and science of pulling exacting information from the breadth and depth of what is an incomprehensible amount of material. Sensors installed on a commuter train rounding a curve on its way into a borough of New York City could analyze, or determine, if the speed at which it is traveling is too fast or not, and if it is, to slow the train down to accommodate the calculus of the turn. Terrorism and political violence could be quelled through the use of data analyzed from social network sites across the world. Even the shootings in gang controlled neighborhoods could be mitigated by analyzing data in predicting the site of turf wars and on which city blocks, day or night.

"There's really much more specific and individualized data that is captured through the mobile devices that we all carry around, and it has increased the availability of information in a quantum way," Charles Hess says, the managing partner at Inferential Focus, a consulting firm. "Business intelligence and traditional marketing approaches have been used forever, but this is really significantly different. From our perspective, it's important to recognize that we're in this different capability arena."[27]

"This is an emerging story that is unfolding at the confluence of other major technology trends: faster computers, wireless data and smartphone proliferation, social networking, digital marketing, cloud-based computing, and increasing digitization of almost everything everywhere. All of these major technology themes will continue to propel Big Data, moving forward," says Kyle Weaver, portfolio manager of Fidelity Select IT Services. "Companies involved in everything from storage to analytics are making money now, but we expect the opportunity in the market to continue to grow for many years."[28]

The evolution of winning combinations with respect to Big Data does not guarantee profitability. Simply, just the competition between startups and legacy providers becomes complex because of viability in business models, rapid paced innovation, and the equivocating preferences of customers.[29]

"There may be 20 Silicon Valley companies that are venture-capital funded and have no need to make any money in the short-term" Weaver says. "The demand for this stuff is there. The technology is there. But it remains to be seen how much profit these companies will make."[30]

What is clear is that Big Data has emerged as a trend, and is imminent with respect to it impacting business and how business is transacted; however, what is uncertain, by degrees, is which business technologies and models will be on the cutting-edge. "The technology," says Weaver, "in some ways, is ahead of the cases right now. It is one thing to create the software. It's a whole other thing to change the way people actually make decisions. I think that eventually everyone will be using data-driven analytics because it will help them do their jobs better. But we are still in the early innings."

Big Data's Bolster: The Insight of Long Data

Mathematician and network scientist, Samuel Arbesman, is the person responsible for the phrase Long Data. His intended inflection regarding Long Data is that it represents "datasets that have massive historical sweep" in their application to workforce analytics.[31] Big Data provides analytics normally detailing a point in linear time. Whereas, Long Data offers the distillation of insight from stories that have occurred in deep time, or over a span of time. This facilitates organizations to locate, cull, and interpret data as part of a continuum and its inherent affect and effect in the process culminating in relevant results.[32]

Conceptually powerful, social media sites have introduced the notion of *timeline*. Such timelines are a historical record and offer themselves as visual depictions of personal information, usually on a variety of levels. Tracking information such as this is the view that Long Data provides.[33]

REVELING IN WHAT IS SALVAGEABLE

By developing "employment timelines," Mercer Analytics utilizes the concepts that comprise Long Data and those of timelines, in tandem, over a swath of time, and nominally one of between three to five years. By using the timeline, a data story is revealed through the study of each data point to build upon the occurrences of various events. Per example, Performance Ratings, in a Long Data view, would be interpreted beyond just the current calendar year in order to offer comparison regarding an individual's performance in relation to their ratings in previous years. Included in the result is a visual representation that provides a narrative regarding organizational performance.[34]

Long Data analytics is a spectrum through which organizations can observe trends and acquire the vantage point of "Big Picture" scale. Also, it assists in thwarting reactive, or point in time, decisions. Assimilating employee data, over time, is a concept that is a tool for Human Resource executives and trainers, to learn to master in their transitioning to a more quantitative approach in analyzing employee assessments.

The Necessity of a Haystack for Big Data and the Crusade of Viktor Mayer-Schonberger and Kenneth Cukier Toward an Enlightened Approach to Expand the Future

What does Google, Amazon, Walmart, and the United States government all have in common? You guessed it: they all employ Big Data analysis. Amazon uses customer-driven data based on an individual's previous purchases. Google uses the search data you have accrued to pitch advertisements and launch various products and services. It was revealed recently in *The Guardian* that the National Security Agency collects phone records of millions of Verizon customers in America, "indiscriminately, and in bulk, whether or not they are suspected of any wrongdoing," under court order. Further reports of both *The Guardian* and *The Washington Post* also divulged the Agency's archiving of emails; audio and video conversations; and assorted documents, logins, and photographs from prominent internet companies, such as Apple, Facebook, Google, Microsoft, and Yahoo in their quest to track foreign targets.[35]

The questions resound: Why use the industrial vacuum of Big Data? Why pull up the dirt on a nominal number of terrorists in such an indiscriminate fashion? Jeremy Bash, Chief of Staff to Leon E. Panetta, the former Director of the Central Intelligence Agency (CIA), previously Defense Secretary, said, "If you're looking for a needle in a haystack, you need a haystack."[36]

In *Big Data*,[37] a watershed book that is accessible for the layperson, Viktor Mayer-Schonberger, Professor of Internet Governance and Regulation at the Oxford Internet Institute at Oxford University, and Kenneth Cukier, Data Editor for *The Economist*, posit that "the nature of surveillance" has been transformed.[38]

They write, "In the spirit of Google or Facebook, the new thinking is that people are the sum of their social relationships, online interactions and connections with content. In order to fully investigate an individual, analysts need to look at the widest possible penumbra of data that surrounds the person—not just whom they know, but whom those people know too, and so on."[39]

Mayer-Schonberger and Cukier use the simile of the invention of the Gutenberg printing press to describe the influence Big Data has, and will, have on society, at large. A leitmotif throughout the book is their admonishment that both causality and a keen moral sense need to come to fruition in the application of patterns of Big Data. Also, they reiterate in their book that the accumulation of data is accruing at a rate of more than doubling every other year. The co-authors also point out that as costs of storage become less restrictive, as algorithms become more sophisticated, and as data-crunching techniques, once only a possibility, perhaps, in a suspense novel regarding the exploits of James Bond and his cronies as well as his enemies, now mega-corporations and research laboratories are discovering that these processes are acquired with an uncanny facility.

Already, Big Data has given rise to the founding of a legion of new companies that are involved in having assisted other existing companies to interface in new and proactive ways. Walmart learned, before a hurricane, that the sales of Pop-Tarts, merchandised beside emergency hurricane paraphernalia, increased. So, stores began displaying their stock of Pop-Tarts alongside flashlights and batteries to "make life easier for customers," while concomitantly generating sales. UPS, report Mayer-Schonberger and Cukier, has installed GPS and sensors in order to supervise employees, schedule route itineraries, and to offer maintenance alerts on their vehicles. The co-authors offer a learned predictability themselves, in their stating that Big Data will actively participate in "part of the solution to pressing global problems like addressing climate change, eradicating disease, and fostering governance and economic development."[40]

However, Mayer-Schonberger and Cukier warn straightaway that there is a dark side to Big Data, and offer a perspicacious analysis of the dangers they forecast—especially regarding protecting the somewhat sticky issue of *privacy*, or the phrasing they have adopted, which is: "individual notice and consent, opting out and anonymization." They say, "The ability to capture personal data is often built deep into the tools we use every day, from Web sites to smartphone apps." With the prevalent ways in which data can be accessed, it is often then gathered to be sold to any variety of bidders for further profit.

However, it is a moot point for any individual who wants to have the opportunity to give his or her consent regarding someone *sourcing* that data. Most of the time we have no say with respect to our data being *outsourced*. The co-authors have developed a phrase that is somewhat specific, as well as a bit of an example of exaggerated politeness, straight out of a routine "after Alphonse and Gaston,"[41] with respect to this less than ideal phenomenon of Big Data, as "innovative secondary uses" that weren't even imagined when the data was initially mined.[42] Although in their presentation of the deeper and darker waters of Big Data, they make us aware that there are other colors to the traffic light other than green, for *go,* that we should pay attention to regarding the arc and velocity of this prospective 21st-century tool: yellow, for *caution,* let's slow down; and, *red,* let's think this through.

The Biggest Deals about Bigger Data: The Milliman Perspective

The question arises in speaking with anyone regarding Big Data as to what it exactly is. Even after delineating numerous aspects of the phenomenon, the puzzlement in a listener's face may very well still be apparent. So, what exactly is Big Data? The term remains nebulous for many. Experts and proponents of Big Data offer that the "Big" aspect of the phrase "implies any data where, because of its volume, its management, and analysis is an issue given the current toolsets available."[43] However, one of the current aspects of Big Data is as quickly as it is growing in scope its definition changes in conjunction with its development, and it is necessary to augment its definition, at least at this time, as it evolves.

As hardware and software are developed to harness and facilitate the enormous function and potential that Big Data augurs, "the threshold of Big Data changes, making [its] definition unhelpful."[44] "'Bigger Data,' as in "bigger" than you can effectively deal with using traditional tools,"[45] just might only begin to approximate its expansiveness and its nebula-cloud magnitude.

What can be defined in relation to Big Data, in fact, assists in giving definition to what it is. The terms, for instance, "data science" and "data scientist" are also somewhat new techno-phrases, but in understanding what this terminology means, we can have a deeper and broader comprehension of Big Data. Although the caveat in understanding it is that "data science" can be even more ambiguous than Big Data. However, Drew Conway, considered "a leading expert,"[46] who blogs about "data science," professes the following definition: "the intersection of hacking skills (meaning computer programming skills to manipulate files and implement algorithms, not the skills for breaking into secure systems!), statistics and machine learning knowledge, and subject matter expertise."[47] So, if that is what "data science" encompasses, a "data scientist" is one who functions in extrapolating and managing the "data science."

Specifically, however, "data scientists" employ both "statistical techniques" and "machine learning algorithms"[48] in order to identify data patterns and structures. The toolset is of a parallel nature to that of statisticians, data miners, and predictive modelers.[49] For instance, if you are modulating algorithms and computer rules as a default search in the data you are assimilating to gather "previously unknown and useful relationships in your data, you are then *data mining*.[50]

A *predictive modeler* is someone who may "incorporate these approaches to predict a value or an outcome, given a number of input variables."[51] A "data scientist" runs the applications on large data sets, and writes code specific to software modeled to work on Big Data.[52]

The Drew Conway definition of "data scientist" extends to include practitioners who possess "substantive expertise and deep domain knowledge."[53] In refining the definition further, Conway states that a "data scientist" provides "'motivating questions' (i.e. the important and valuable questions that can be answered with the data) and testing hypotheses."[54] Understanding what the important questions are requires expertise in whatever field in which the individuals work. Often data scientists will use storytelling techniques to effectively communicate the insights from the data to others. Visualization is an important component of communicating with data, as it helps the audience efficiently observe and understand relationships and patterns. While data scientists working in journalism have taken visualization to high levels of sophistication, all data scientists have some familiarity with the principles of design and visual communication with data."[55]

The Open Sesame[56] of Ali Baba and the Future of Big Data

The predictive technology enabling computers to forecast future behaviors of individuals is based on surfacing patterns found in data. It is these patterns themselves that will provide businesses of any persuasion to make informed decisions regarding both risks and opportunities. This is the science that propels Big Data. The results will affect everyone.[57] The metaphor for predictive analysis, then, may be the phrase, "Open Sesame," in attempting to portray its apparently endless capabilities that will lead to any untold amount of financial successes, but also to the potential for a limitless list of advances for the betterment of humankind itself.

However, despite its current use, Big Data is still in a nascent stage of development and growth. The long and short of it is that Big Data is as inscrutable as it is purported to be known. The founder of Predictive Analytics World, former Columbia

REVELING IN WHAT IS SALVAGEABLE

University Professor, Eric Siegel, cites nearly 150 examples of how predictive analytics can be applied in a variety of instances in both business and in life, in his book, *Predictive Analytics*.[58] In it he addresses topics that range across the spectrum of current concerns, such as why early retirement decreases life expectancy—a somewhat shocking phenomenon; how Target is alerted to your being pregnant; and when Hewlett-Packard is able to ascertain whether you are making the decision to quit your job.[59]

Siegel's definition of what predictive analytics are is found in the subtitle of his book: *The Power to Predict Who Will Click, Buy, Lie, or Die.*[60] He propounds, not unlike 19th-century American poet, Walt Whitman, who is also known for using a litany of specific examples, in a colorful fashion and in broad strokes, that "predictive analytics is the technology that learns from data to make predictions about what each individual will do—from thriving and donating to stealing and crashing your car. By doing so, organizations boost the success of marketing, auditing, law-enforcing, medically treating, educating, and even running a political campaign for president."[61] Siegel is describing Big Data as being all-encompassing. Whitman would have loved the idea of Big Data, especially because of his democratic spirit and his propensity for cosmic dimensions.

Also, Siegel posits that the goals of predictive analytics both denotes and connotes prognostication as the atomic alloy that will generate the fusion of, as he indicates, "driving improved decisions, guiding millions of per-person actions." Siegel also speaks to a vision of bettering the field of health care and saving lives, as well as in the sector of law enforcement in reducing crime.[62] With regard to business, Siegel suggests that through the use of predictive analytics businesses will see their risk decrease, their costs lower, and their customer service actually become superlative. He also predicts that predictive analytics will diminish superfluous postal mail and deflect intrusions of spam.[63]

For Siegel, the tipping point of predictive analytics maturing into the technology that it has become occurred due to it inherently heralding a "requisite culture shift."[64] We can think of predictive analytics as having evolved in a right place, right time socio-economic opportunity. Siegel elaborates, "Beyond the technical endeavor of building a predictive model from data, the per-individual predictions it then generates must then be used by the organization, acted upon in order to drive operational activities." His insight also incorporates the idea that "integrating predictive analytics in this way and thereby changing, and improving, 'business as usual' entails an organizational change that doesn't happen with the snap of your fingers."[65]

Siegel also distinguishes the term data mining from that of business intelligence, in that "predictive analytics fits squarely within the broad "data-driven" arena referred by terms like Big Data, data mining, business intelligence, and analytics, without the 'predictive.' The excitement around how much data there is and its potential begs the question, what should we do with it, what's the specific value? The answer to this question is: learn from it how to predict. The thing that makes a direct difference for how organizations operate is prediction."

Also, Siegel differentiates whether predictive analytics deals with correlation or causation. Again, he provides rather exacting delineations within each definition, "Causation is an elusive thing to establish, and you don't necessarily need it in order to predict well. If we see the correlation that early retirees have higher health risks, we'd like to know why—but we don't actually need to know why in order to make use of that information. Instead, early retirement becomes one factor to consider when determining whether to prioritize a patient for additional screening or other preventative-oriented activities."[66]

REVELING IN WHAT IS SALVAGEABLE

In explaining why he refers to data as the world's most available unnatural resource, Siegel cites that "data is certainly a booming resource. 'Unnatural resource' is a play on the well-known phrase 'natural resource'—because, after all, the information on a disk drive, or millions of disk drives, for that matter, would probably be considered artificial rather than part of nature."[67]

Siegel also addresses the dark side of predictive analytics, "as with any marketing, law enforcement, or other activities, the needs and rights of the individual become part of the equation. With any activities that operate en masse across many people, there is always the risk to lose site of the individuals. It is critical to increase public understanding of what predictive analytics is, how it is being used, and a sense of how it works in order to inform discussions, debates, and legislative action."

In addition, Siegel discusses the consistency in the development of sophisticated algorithms and whether these formidable tools will lead to making creativity or serendipity obsolete. "I strongly believe," Siegel embellishes, "this powerful tool helps the world and elevates human activity. Predictive analytics helps tweak existing operations—it is a paradigm shift but it does not create new paradigm shifts like the iPod. Running things more intelligently and rendering operations more effective and efficient (e.g. decreasing junk mail and spam) only opens up additional resources and opportunities that in turn foster continued human creativity. There's nothing there to disincentivize human creativity, and I don't see entrepreneurs and scientists to slow down any time soon."[68]

Notes

1. Government Business Council (GBC) and Research Manager, Dana Grinshpan, "Retirement Saving's Big Data Problem-Promising Practices-Management, http://www.govexec.com/excellence/promising-pracices/2012/09/retirment.
2. Ibid.
3. Rick Smolan and Jennifer Erwitt, *The Human Face of Big Data*, Sausalito, CA: Against All Odds Productions, 2012.
4. Bianca Bosker, "Rick Smolan On What Big Data Is Dong To Us (And What It Looks Like)," "Tech," *Huffington Post*, http://www.huffingtonpost.com/2012/09/25/rick-smolan-the-human-face, November 14, 2013.
5. Ibid.
6. en.wikipedia.org/wiki/Rick_Smolan.
7. Bianca Bosker, "Rick Smolan On What Big Data Is Dong To Us (And What It Looks Like)."
8. Marcel Proust (1871-1922), author of an iconic early 20th century set of novels, written in a series of seven books, known for their sense of timelessness with respect to human memory; specifically as "involuntary memory," that pervades everyday life and evokes recollections of the past without our conscious effort. The work, entitled *À la recherché du temps perdu*, and recently translated into English as *In Search of Lost Time*, is perhaps better known in an earlier English translation as *Remembrance of Things Past*; and was originally published in seven volumes, between 1913 and 1927, beginning with *Du cote de Chez Swann*, or *Swann's Way*. See en.wikipedia.org/wiki/In_Search_of_Lost_Time.
9. Bianca Bosker, "Rick Smolan On What Big Data Is Dong To Us (And What It Looks Like)."
10. Ibid.
11. Ibid.
12. Robyn Davidson, *Tracks: A Woman's Solo Trek across 1,700 Miles of Australian Outback*, New York, NY: Vintage Books/Random House, 1995; Republished, as Tracks, London, U.K.: Bloomsbury Publishing, PLC, 2013.
13. Bianca Bosker, "Rick Smolan On What Big Data Is Dong To Us (And What It Looks Like)."

14. Ibid.
15. Ibid.
16. Michelle V. Rafter, "Big Data, Bigger Deal," http://www.workforce.com/articleds/big-data-bigger-deal, November 20, 2013.
17. Phil Simon, *Too Big to Ignore: The Business Case for Big Data*, Hoboken, NJ: Wiley and SAS Business Series (Book 72), 2013.
18. Michelle V. Rafter, "Big Data, Bigger Deal."
19. Ibid.
20. Ibid.
21. Ibid.
22. Ibid.
23. Ibid.
24. Ibid.
25. Ibid.
26. Catherine MacCoun, *On Becoming an Alchemist: A Guide for the Modern Magician*, Boston, MA: Trumpeter Books/Shambhala Publications, Inc., Distributed by Random House, Inc., 2008.
27. "Big Data—Big Opportunities?" https://www.fidelity.com/viewpoints/investing-ideas/big-data.
28. Ibid.
29. Ibid.
30. Ibid.
31. "'Big Data' May Not Hold All the Answers for HR," http://www.mercrer.com/pages/1523795.
32. Ibid.
33. Ibid.
34. Ibid.
35. Michiko Kakutani, "Watched by the Web: Surveillance Is Reborn: 'Big Data' by Victor Mayer-Schonberger and Kenneth Cukier," *The New York Times*, http:www.nytimes.com/2013/06/11/books/big-data-by-viktor-mayer-schonberger, June 11, 2013.
36. Ibid.
37. Viktor Mayer-Schonberger and Kenneth Cukier, *Big Data: A Revolution that Will Transform How We Live, Work, and Think*, Boston, MA & New York, NY: Houghton Mifflin Harcourt, 2013.

38. Michiko Kakutani, "Watched by the Web: Surveillance Is Reborn: 'Big Data' by Victor Mayer-Schonberger and Kenneth Cukier."
39. Ibid.
40. Ibid.
41. "After Alphonse and Gaston" refers to the characters in the pioneering newspaper comic strip of American illustrator and cartoonist Frederick Burr Opper (1857-1937), Alphonse and Gaston, in which he displayed the characteristic of excessive politeness of his two humorous protagonists who were often presented uttering the phrases "after you, my dear Gaston" and "after you, my dear Alphonse." See www.merriam-webster.com/dictionary/Alphonse%20and%20Gaston.
42. Michiko Kakutani, "Watched by the Web: Surveillance Is Reborn: 'Big Data' by Victor Mayer-Schonberger and Kenneth Cukier."
43. Milliman Insight, "Why Big Data Is a Big Deal," http://www.milliman.com/insight/2013/Why-big-data-is-a-big-deal/, originally published in Insurance ERM, August 6, 2013.
44. Ibid.
45. Ibid.
46. Ibid.
47. Ibid.
48. Ibid.
49. Ibid.
50. Ibid.
51. Ibid.
52. Ibid.
53. Ibid.
54. Ibid.
55. Ibid.
56. Ali Baba, a character from the folk tale *Ali Baba and the Forty Thieves*, is collected in the classic children's book, *One Thousand and One Nights*. This story was added to the collection by Antoine Galland in the 18th century. It is one of the best known of the tales, also known as *Arabian Nights*, and has been widely annotated, or vetted, especially for children, where the more violent facets of the story are expurgated. In the story, Ali Baba, a poor woodcutter, discovers the secret of a thieves' den, which is entered only by speaking the phrase "Open Sesame." The thieves

learn this, and try to kill Ali Baba. However, Ali Baba's faithful slave, a girl named Morgiana, foils their plots to murder him and saves the day. In a show of his appreciation, Ali Baba gives his son to her in marriage and keeps the secret of the treasure. See en.wikipedia.org/wiki/Ali_Baba.
57. Ned Smith, "Predictive Analytics Unlocks Big Data," *Business News Daily*, Tech Media Network, April 12, 2013.
58. Eric Siegel, *Predictive Analytics: The Power to Predict Who Will Click, Buy, Lie or Die*, Hoboken, NJ: John Wiley & Sons, 2013.
59. Ned Smith, "Predictive Analytics Unlocks Big Data."
60. Eric Siegel, *Predictive Analytics: The Power to Predict Who Will Click, Buy, Lie or Die*.
61. Ned Smith, "Predictive Analytics Unlocks Big Data."
62. Ibid.
63. Ibid.
64. Ibid.
65. Ibid.
66. Ibid.
67. Ibid.
68. Ibid.

HOW WE PROGRESS OVER TIME IN CONJUNCTION WITH HOW WE ARE AFFECTED BY THE EVOLUTION OF TECHNOLOGY—OR WHAT CONSTITUTES THE FOUNDATION FOR A MEASURE OF SUCCESS RELEVANT TO POP CULTURE

We can actually discover a matrix of cultural progress, and a measure of success relevant to pop culture, often in what is in front of our very eyes. It could even be the red and white checkered tablecloth that we might remember in a favorite restaurant when we were still in our late teens, waiting for what you might have considered to be the best tuna sandwich served on whole wheat bread with lettuce, as you were dreaming of becoming a writer and reading John Steinbeck's[1] classic novel, *East of Eden*.[2] Sometimes the most insightful moments in life occur from some of the simplest events—such as that lettuce in the sandwich and the quest of the characters in Steinbeck's biblical story who strive toward the perfection of refrigeration so that they can ship California lettuce by freight to all points east.

However, if we take the foundation of this matrix in the genesis of our progression over time, in how technological developments affect us through their becoming more efficient, then by taking lettuce as an example is a relatively profound touchstone, since its transportation transcends just shipping ordinary produce to becoming the vehicle for literature, film, and our daily lives—including being one of the main condiments on a sandwich eaten by an aspiring young writer over a red and white checkered tablecloth, which in one hand held the tuna and lettuce and in the other a copy of *East of Eden*.

REVELING IN WHAT IS SALVAGEABLE

The scope of this particular novel of Steinbeck's is vast and multigenerational; however, what is tantamount to its brilliance of plot and theme, that are carried on the shoulders of what are memorable characters, is that the work was also adapted into a film, which actually makes *East of Eden* an iconic part of American cinema and pop culture. This is due, primarily, to the magnetic performance and celluloid presence of method actor,[3] and young rebel, James Dean. He would only make barely a handful of movies before his tragic death in a car accident—some six months after his having starred in this film and after its only having been released.

Since lettuce is what is initially functionary as the focus of discussion here, and what is actually of more significance even than Steinbeck's gift for writing mesmerizing and masterful fiction, is the magnitude of the film and how lettuce is of such importance that it could be a co-star in the film, along with youthful and handsome James Dean,[4] who plays the haunted younger brother, Cal, who engages in a familial dispute, and his romantic counterpart, an alluring and heartbreakingly beautiful Julie Harris, who portrays the character Abra.

Dean's magnetism nearly eclipsed film idol Marlon Brando's[5] popularity at that time. With this aspect of personal mystique and the new CinemaScope[6] close-ups and the magnified and brightened "WarnerColor" images, the film displays, even to this day, a certain catalyst for innovation—which may be one of the reasons why the film may act as a working definition as to what makes a classic, and that is getting back to what the word matrix is indicative of, in that it offers an ageless quality of youthful verve and newness that never relents in its aura combining to offer a combination of charisma, glamour, romance, and charm.

However, it is necessary to get back to the lettuce and the unfolding drama that fuels the film, and the original book,

HOW WE PROGRESS OVER TIME

with an intensity that is found in all human quests, in improving any process that not only fosters the progress of humanity but that furthers technological efficiency, whether it be fresh salad in winter, or Louis Pasteur[7] ensuring the providence of the simple act of drinking a glass of milk, or Jonas Salk[8] who persevered to develop the first inactivated vaccine for polio. As Dan Willmott writes in a review of the film,[9] also introducing the character of Cal's older brother, Aron, played by Richard Davalos,[10] when a "scheme to refrigerate rail cars to ship lettuce farther east fails (the ice melts too fast), Cal sees an opening to win—or perhaps to buy—his father's love."

The film, and the book it is based on, takes part in the rich agricultural area of Salinas, California and the verdant San Fernando Valley. In a film in which what might arguably offer as its leitmotif the maintenance of lettuce in adequate refrigeration to be consumed by the population east of the Mississippi, there is also the bitter sibling rivalry between Cal and Aron, that Steinbeck intended as a parallel to the biblical story of Cain and Abel,[11] although one brother doesn't in fact murder the other. So, lettuce, in fact, becomes more than just a condiment on a memorable tuna sandwich in a favorite luncheonette in the fiction of one's youth.

What is essential here is how we are drawn to champion Cal's father, Adam (played by the inimitable Raymond Massey),[12] who envisions what is revolutionary—the shipping of lettuce to destinations east during the outset of World War I, from the fertile basin of the valley of Central California. Both in the book and in the film, when an initial attempt to ship the lettuce fails, and the fresh crop withers during its shipping by freight due to the ice used to preserve it having melted, we, as moviegoers, or, initially, as readers, feel the heartache of the Trask family, through which further develops the plot and the theme and increases the arc of the drama. Who would have thought there would be so much at stake in what we very well take for granted in what is considered to be a common ingredient in salads? Or with respect to such a simple condiment, that is often added to a sandwich, what only had been lettuce has now become a large part of the reason of why it may have been designated, by John Steinbeck, to become so intentionally memorable in the first place—because it is something we often overlook, and don't see, that is before our very eyes?

Of course refrigeration and refrigerated rail cars have long been perfected, so the lettuce we use for our consumption is an element that has, indeed, become an active part of our daily lives. However, as Don Willmott cites in his movie review of *East of Eden*, "the movie is as exciting a drama as you're ever likely to see, and ultimately it's the unforgettable [James]Dean that makes it so."

In another review, written for the MUBI website,[13] the reviewer provides a rather insightful and perceptive understanding of the ramifications of the film, once again, which functions on such a high level due to the refrigeration of lettuce for market: "[Director, Elia] Kazan[14] fashioned a classic with *East Of Eden*, ranking with his very best work, full of empathetic and appropriate touches that allows Dean's intensity to work. The visual style is more poetic than some of Kazan's other films, and there are real John Ford style touches in some of the moments the camera chooses to dwell on, such as a shot with Dean and an American flag flying in the background, and a clutch of red, white and blue balloons escaping over the town spire during the war parade. The look of the color and tone of the film is beautiful, expertly helmed by veteran silent era cinematographer Ted D. McCord, who also shot the excellent John Huston location piece, *The Treasure of The Sierra Madre*,[15] and some of the field working sequences in *East Of Eden* anticipate [Director, Terrance] Malick's masterful *Days Of Heaven*[16] in their expansiveness and lavish poetic cinema. James Dean's wonderful performance as Cal was posthumously nominated for Best

Actor, and it captured the zeitgeist with disaffected Eisenhower youth in a similar way to how Elvis Presley tapped into it in the same year. Dean's second feature, *Rebel Without A Cause*,[17] with Kazan's friend Director Nicholas Ray was released shortly after his death and its success no doubt helped further build his legend as the avatar of '50's teen angst, his untimely death pushing him into the deified legend class."

So, life is dignified by societal trends and the improvements through the ages which complement our existence. From what is small, we can be offered the insight into what is large; and in benefitting from being able to see what is large, we can see what is conspicuously small. The genesis of technology is a constant that continues to influence our lives and how we live it, even as it might start with a few leaves of lettuce adding some nourishment and culinary gravitas, as well as garnish, to a tuna sandwich for an aspiring writer who sat in a favorite luncheonette, named *Wendy's*, reading a memorable novel, that was also turned into an iconic film. As the imaginary camera shot dissolves on the sandwich held in one hand, and the book in the other, the lens is held over that red and white red checkered tablecloth, sprinkled with bread crumbs, and perhaps a stray bit of dislodged lettuce leaf, that provides a matrix for this story, and possibly for just about any other.

Notes

1. John [Ernst] Steinbeck, Jr. (1902–1968) was an American writer, primarily known for the Pulitzer Prize-winning novel, *The Grapes of Wrath* (1939); a saga of biblical proportion, *East of Eden* (1952); and the heart-rendering novella, *Of Mice and Men* (1937). Steinbeck authored twenty-seven books, including sixteen novels, six non-fiction books, and five collections of short stories. He was the recipient of the Nobel Prize for Literature in 1962. See en.wikipedia.org/wiki/John_Steinbeck.

2. *East of Eden* is a novel by Nobel Prize winner John Steinbeck, published by Viking Press in September 1952. It is often described as Steinbeck's most ambitious novel. *East of Eden* portrays the intricate details of two families, the Trasks and the Hamiltons, and their interwoven mythologies. Originally, the novel was addressed to Steinbeck's young sons, Thom and John (each at the time being just 6½ and 4½ years old, respectively). Initially, and perhaps idealistically, Steinbeck wanted to offer the images of his beloved Salinas Valley for his sons, in the perpetuity of detail—its sights, sounds, fragrances, and colors. See en.wikipedia.org/wiki/East of Eden (novel).
3. Method acting, with respect to the dramatic arts, constitutes a group of techniques actors employ to create the thoughts and feelings within themselves of the characters they develop, which result in dramatic and lifelike performances. Though not all Method actors use the same approach, the "Method" refers to the vehicle of teaching the actor's craft, which was created by Constantin Stanislavski, through which he, and others, were able to transmit and to teach concepts of acting to their students. Later, Stanislavski's method of teaching acting was adapted by the eminent Lee Strasberg in the instruction of American actors. Strasberg's view of Method emphasized the art and practice of connecting viscerally to a particular character's persona—through the actor's own emotions and memories. "The Stanislavski System," as it is known, was the foundation of Lee Strasberg's technique. Rigorous adherents of Strasberg's own acting technique are now commonly known as "Method Actors," although the "Method," itself, makes reference to Stanislavski's original system.
4. James [Byron] Dean (1931–1955) was an American actor, who also became a cultural icon of teenage disillusionment, especially as expressed in the title of one of his most celebrated films, *Rebel Without a Cause* (1955), in which he starred as troubled Los Angeles teenager, Jim Stark. His only other two defining roles that launched him into his stardom were in his dramatic portrayal of the sensitive loner, Cal Trask, in *East of Eden* (1955); and as the enigmatic and flippant ranch hand, Jett Rink, in *Giant* (1956). Dean's enduring fame and popularity rest entirely on his performances in just these three films, which were all leading

roles. His premature and tragic death, at the age of 24, in a car crash, has provided the additional mystique that has perpetuated his legendary persona as an American icon. See en.wikipedia.org/wiki/James Dean.
5. Marlon Brando, Jr. (1924–2004) was a renowned actor of the American screen and stage. He was critically praised and lauded for bringing a striking realism to film acting, and is widely considered to be one of the most superb movie actors of all time. See en.wikipedia.org/wiki/Marlon Brando.
6. CinemaScope was an anamorphic lens series developed for shooting wide screen movies from 1953 to 1967. Its invention, in 1953, by the president of 20th Century-Fox Spyros P. Skouras, marked the beginning of the modern anamorphic film, or simply stated, an improved technique of shooting a film in a widescreen format, both in principal photography and movie projection. See en.wikipedia.org/wiki/CinemaScope.
7. Louis Pasteur (1822–1895), a French chemist and microbiologist who is renowned for his discoveries of the basic principles of vaccination, microbial fermentation, and pasteurization, a process of removing the bacteria from milk, that is named after him. He is remembered for his significant breakthroughs in the causes and preventions of diseases, and his many discoveries have resulted in the saving countless lives, ever since. See en.wikipedia.org/wiki/Louis_Pasteur.
8. Jonas Edward Salk (1914–1995) was an American medical researcher and virologist who made the discovery and developed the first successful inactivated (meaning that the bacteria are dead) polio vaccine, which bears his name, "The Salk Vaccine." See en.wikipedia.org/wiki/Jonas Salk.
9. Don Willmott, "East of Eden Movie Review." See www.contactmusic.com › James Dean.
10. Richard Davalos is an American actor born in New York City in 1930, of Finnish and Spanish descent. He starred in *East of Eden* (1955), as James Dean's brother, Aron, and portrayed the convict Blind Dick in *Cool Hand Luke* (1967). He also won the Theatre World Award for his performance in an Arthur Miller play, *A Memory of Two Mondays* in 1955. See en.wikipedia.org/wiki/Richard_Davalos.

11. Cain and Abel were, according to the Book of Genesis, the two sons of Adam and Eve. Cain is ascribed to have been a crop farmer, and his younger brother Abel was said to be a shepherd. Cain has the distinction of being the first human born, and Abel as being the first human to die. Cain committed the world's first murder by killing his brother. Exegeses of Genesis 4, by ancient and modern commentators, have consistently interrupted the motives to have been jealousy and anger. See en.wikipedia.org/wiki/Cain_and_Abel.
12. Raymond [Hart] Massey (1896 – 1983) was a Canadian-American actor of repute, who also starred in *Arsenic and Old Lace* and *The Fountainhead*. See en.wikipedia.org/wiki/Raymond_Massey.
13. "Adam Raised a Cal," purportedly written by someone writing under the pseudonym, "Musycks," MUBI, September 21, 2012. See mubi.com/reviews/27278.
14. Elia Kazan (1909–2003), a Greek-American director, producer, writer and actor, was described by *The New York Times* as "one of the most honored and influential directors in Broadway and Hollywood history." See en.wikipedia.org/wiki/Elia_Kazan.
15. *The Treasure of the Sierra Madre* is a 1948 American adventure film written and directed by the legendary and visionary director John Huston. The film is an adaptation of B. Traven's 1927 novel of the same title, that regards two financially desperate Americans, Fred C. Dobbs (Humphrey Bogart) and Bob Curtin (Tim Holt), who, during the 1920s, join an initially reluctant aging miner Howard (Walter Huston, the director's father) in Mexico to prospect for gold. See en.wikipedia.org/.../The_Treasure_of_the_Sierra_Madre_.
16. *Days of Heaven*, a 1978 film written and directed by Terrence Malick, stars Richard Gere, Brooke Adams, Sam Shepard, and Linda Manz. See en.wikipedia.org/wiki/Days_of_Heaven.
17. *Rebel Without a Cause*, a 1955 American dramatic film regarding emotionally disenfranchised suburban, middle-class teenagers was directed by Nicholas Ray. The film offered both social commentary and an alternative vision to previous films that depicted delinquents in urban slum environments, since the film's characters were represented as being middle class. See en.wikipedia.org/wiki/Rebel_Without_a_Cause.

THE SCIENCE AND ART OF MEASUREMENT

> "Length is measured as much by how long
> it is as by how often it comes up short."
> —LAOZI, *The Daodejing*[1]

Measurement.

Our world, in fact, our universe, revolves around many concepts; however, what may be the most significant aspect of living, on all and any level is: *measurement*.

We *measure* everything—not because we choose large over small, or even short over long. It is because we need to: *measure*. We do so in order to live: simply and daily. We *measure* ourselves to be able to appropriately purchase clothes and shoes; we *measure* to develop the most technologically advanced automobiles. *Measurement* is indeed a science, but it is also an art. The eminent Emeritus Professor of History of Science, Robert M. Palter,[2] who apprenticed himself, as a young scientist, with Robert Oppenheimer and his other colleagues in the Manhattan Project in developing the atomic bomb, during World War II, also wrote a well-respected voluminous tome regarding the literature of fruit.[3] In both projects, one of incalculable estimations of *measurements* in splitting the atom, and the other in not so much the *measure* of each fruit itself, but the *measure* of resonance of each example from literature that honors various fruits themselves, Palter needed to exercise being a master of *measurement*—both in science and art, which given only a modicum of thought induces the conclusion that *measurement*, taken as the inveterate and exacting practice that it is, is both a *science* and an *art*. Such attributes can be said of very few things that influence our lives, and to such a degree, as *measurement* does, itself.

So, what about measurement—the American poet and writer, Robert Creeley,[4] fashioned a phrase that not only fueled an entire culture, or ethos, but also can possibly be said to contain, in its three words, both our heritage, in a 20th-century epigram, and upon its closure, also an epithet of these early years of the 21st-century. Heritage and epigram because those were the keys that started the engine of the automobile and epithet and key to the future since we, as a global culture, now find it necessary to develop an automobile that is fueled and maintained by something other than gas and oil. Those words referred to are from a poem written by Creeley, entitled "I Know a Man,"[5] the words themselves are: "drive, he said."[6] After turning on the ignition of a car, if we think *"drive, he said,"*[7] those three words, when uttered, can propel the engines of industry; improve our lives and our labors; insure our safe arrival and ensure our lives, so that we can actualize the operative happiness that we not only seek but, both individually and as a culture, are also aware of through our intuitive capacities that we can actively ascertain and actualize.

So, what about measurement—how is this pertinent to how measurements are made? Bill Roberson's recent article[8] is seminal not only regarding the *measured* differences between a 1913 Ford Model T and a 2013 Tesla Model S, but also the *measure* of our society—where it has been and where it is going.

Roberson offers that rare balance of providing both insightful vision and hard fact in this article. He writes, "while electric vehicles today seem like something from a science fiction future, the truth is they're old as cars themselves."[9]

"Today," Roberson continues, "the petroleum-based infrastructure and fueling of cars (*and most other things*)[10] is just another part of our daily reality. But thanks to the fluctuating prices and political volatility, oil is also akin to a sleeping dragon we all tiptoe around, inevitably, the dragon stirs whenever there's a terrorist attack, stock market quake, international conflict or another face-off in the interminably convulsive Middle East. The oil dragon belches fire, making gas prices drop or soar, the latter more often than not."[11]

Roberson's prose is an example of how *clear thinking* produces *seamless writing*. An impressive exhibition of this is his memorable sentence, which if you may remember anything from his article, is: "Today, we'd call the Model T the automobile industry's killer App."[12]

He continues, "Back then it was just a better way to get outta Dodge, and for many people then, just like today, the lure of easy travel was irresistible. We know how it turned out, Ford sold *millions*[13] of Model Ts. Sorry. As the car's popularity increased, so did the related industries surrounding it, including gas stations, auto repair businesses, and the like. Eventually, city planners turned cities into car-friendly grids and multi-lane highways replaced dirt roads. The car became a status symbol, an item both central to human culture, and a transportation reality we take for granted."[14]

Roberson nearly makes it sound as if one substituted the idea, or the word, for automobile, instead, for that of anything else that everything he relates automobiles to holds a similar resonance, as well as influence and outreach, as does just about any other concept which you can possibly think?

Doesn't it? Well, but what about *measurement?*

REVELING IN WHAT IS SALVAGEABLE

For Good Measure: The World of the Model T
and the Universe of the Tesla Model S
(85kw Performance Version)

Roberson has high regard for the Model T, because of how its development opened up the world in such a way that it would never be the same again, but also his apt criticisms of this early automobile are as sharp as they are humorous, "Once started (never easy), the Model T is almost hysterically complicated and dangerous to pilot. Drivers need to watch where they are going while simultaneously doing the hand jive and tap dancing, it makes cell-chatting teen drivers look like paragons of focused, safe driving."[15]

Now, we move on to specific measurement. Roberson specifies, "Under the hood (or cowl, in this case), a 2.9-litre inline-four cylinder engine with a single, cantankerous carburetor develops 22 horsepower, which when you think about it from a time and power context, was simply amazing since most people were getting around on one or two horsepower at the most—because they used actual horses. Having over 20 stallions stuffed under the flimsy metal hood of the Model T must have been like buying a whole horse ranch for the back-then price of $550 ($14,000 today). And you only had to feed it gas, oil, and parts now and again."[16]

What else Roberson makes apparent in his article is how he *parallels* various aspects of the Model T, and actually engenders it in its being a true vehicle, for a working metaphor of where we were *culturally* in 1913—as we might do the same with the Tesla, or for that matter what retirement platform or package we might subscribe to now, since there was little, as we have come to know, historically, for aging workers to depend on back then.

"Walk up to it and the door handles emerge from their flush position in anticipation of your arrival," writers Roberson astutely about the Tesla Model S, "sit down in the sculpted seats and a giant 17-inch vertical touch screen in the center of the dash beckons with maps, endless settings, energy reports, ride controls, cellular-based Internet, a backup camera and more, all in split screen if you'd like. There are no keys to turn, no button to push to start it up. Step on the brake and the elegant driver's display spools up quickly, then pull the little lever by the wheel to "D," and the Tesla Model S is ready to drive. No warming up. No shift linkage. No drama."[17]

Remember, *"drive he said."*[18]

Roberson relays his delight and appreciation of the Tesla Model S with such verve that we might associate the fit of one's hands into luxury leather gloves or our feet to a pair shoes designed by *Gucci*, "In decades of driving, I've never been in a car that spoke so loudly of the future as the Tesla Model S. It's just impressive from any angle, both visually and of course, technologically. And to think this is only a second-generation car for the upstart automaker headed by Elon Musk,[19] founder of PayPal, SpaceX, and other ventures. Technically, it's a first-associate generation car since the Roadster was based on a Lotus Elise platform while the Model S is a clean-sheet design."[20]

Roberson's descriptions are not only keen but they are also examples of his ability to elicit *measurements*, both metaphorical as well as factual, "A glass-smooth electric motor the size of a big watermelon sits spinning between the rear wheels, propelling nearly two and half tons of weight with a single gear and over 400 horsepower. There is no throb of the engine in the steering wheel, no low-level buzz through any surface in the car. Talk normally. Enjoy the ride—just buckle up and hold on."[21]

This sounds like a little more *"drive he said,*[22]*"* with the reference being, once again, a reflection of who we are, culturally, in comparison, or *parallel* to the Eros of the automobile industry, and its *measurements*.

REVELING IN WHAT IS SALVAGEABLE

How Elon Musk Augmented *Measurement* in His *Changing the Equation*[23] and How *Everyone Is Chasing the Model S*[24]

Bill Roberson is an adept practioner of the epigram, and not just any epigram, they are epigrammatic phrases that you will recall, much later on, after reading his article. He writes, "Just as the Model T changed the way we think about horses, the Model S is also changing the way we think about cars."[25]

Roberson not only provides an intriguing report regarding the Model S but also frames the information he relays within the context of a larger whole, "The car is so tremendously good at this stage of its development cycle [because it] is a credit to Mr. Musk's engineering prowess and his able employees. But years from now, history will show it shifted the proverbial paradigm just as the Model T did in the early 20th-century."[26]

When you read, or hear, that someone, or something, is responsible for influencing *paradigm shifts*, watch out, and listen—because *this is big stuff*. Roberson takes off from here, like a smoothly-functioning basketball team exhibiting the science, and art, of a fast break, that, let's say, finishes spectacularly, with an orchestrated alley oop pass, and a powerful behind-the-back dunk, "Hopefully, Tesla's Superchargers will light a fire under carmakers, politicians, city planners, and transportation departments to get chargers in place to fuel the growing number of electric cars. Once the charging network hits critical mass—which is when EV[27] owners of electric cars can essentially drive anywhere and charge up quickly—electric car ownership numbers will carve heavily into those gas-powered cars. Eventually, it will be goodbye gasoline, at least for personal cars."[28]

Roberson adds, "When it costs a fiver (or much less) to charge up your EV and 10 times that much to do the same distance on gas, the party is already over. Liquid fuel will still be needed to power trucks, trains, jet planes, and other large vehicles, but even in those industries, change is in the wind. Electrical power, especially when combined with solar collection systems, could push down demand for liquid fuel in those segments as time goes on."[29]

In indicating just how much the Model S "has blown apart the confines of vehicle design,"[30] as Roberson so adroitly puts it, he further suggests that "about the only thing past and future cars will have in common is four tires and a steering wheel. Beyond that, everything is up for a rethink when it comes to electric vehicles."[31]

Roberson gives another big *for instance*, "The Model S moves the fuel supply—sheets of batteries—to the bottom of the car, lowering the center of gravity in ways a gas-powered car can't even hope to. The power plant, with power outputs above 400hp and 400lb-feet of torque from a standstill, is tiny compared to what a gas engine would require in size, complexity and liquid fuel for the same performance. In the Tesla, it drives the back wheels, but in the future Model X, Tesla has hinted that an all-wheel drive system will be available. It may come to a new iteration of the Model S, as well."[32]

Written in almost a whisper of a sentence itself, Roberson confides, "It's the silence of the car that immediately impresses."[33] His espousal of the Model S may be presented with attentiveness to the writer's craft; however, it is grounded in avid detail of the car's features themselves. He describes the "all-wheel steering [that is] on par with experimental vehicles that don't need to parallel park; they just rolled sideways into the spot. Such a system allows a turning circle the size of the car itself. An experimental EV by DLRde called the ROboMobile is a taste of what's to come."[34]

Continuing almost lyrically on the design of the Model S, Roberson writes, "In terms of physical design, carmakers are no longer tied to the concepts of hoods and trunks. The Model S features two

REVELING IN WHAT IS SALVAGEABLE

trunks, one front (the "frunk") because there's no engine there, and a traditional hatch out back. Yes, I know VW did this in the past but the Model S takes it to another level and eventually, it will be the norm. While BMW's new i8 stole the show at Frankfurt in 2013, the real breakthrough beemer[35] was the i3, with its carbon-reinforced plastic space frame, suicide doors, cartoon wheels, and grille-less grille. The i3 shows that BMW gets it, that the possibilities are pretty much endless when it comes to what's possible in EV vehicle design as move forward under electric power. The Model S has given carmakers license to think very radically again, instead of having to work around the same old form factors that have been with us since the Model T."[36]

Roberson quotes Model S owner Steve Ou, who, as he writes, "summarized the future of vehicle technology when he said the Model S is essentially 'a computer on wheels.'"[37] Roberson continues, "The Tesla allows give and take over the 3G cell network, and cars capable of interplay with 4G LTE[38] are coming on line soon. Even people who are only tech savvy can usually update their smartphone, computer, or smart TV/appliance with a firmware update, apps, and new OS. It will be the same for cars very soon, especially for electric vehicles. Beyond that, controlling the car with other connected information nodes, such as Google Glass, show how serious tech companies are about getting into the computerized car."[39]

Roberson specifies further, "As fabulous as the tech 17-inch screen in the Model S is, it's a 128K Mac in terms of EV car computer evolution. Expect rapid, meteoric advances as cars become just as connected as phones, let alone the symbiosis they will share with our addicting pocket computers. Pandora and other common entertainment apps are pointing the way to a day when updating your ABS system and battery-efficiency programming is a download away. The downside: Malware."[40]

Another epigrammatic phrase that Roberson may have coined in relation to the Tesla Model S is: "There are no keys to turn, no button to push to start it."⁴¹ Roberson predicts, "History will show the Model S is the Model T of our time. Both were designed by men driven by their visions. Both changed the course of mobility history. The present-day automobile traces back to a spindly little runabout that braved muddy roads and set the world on a trajectory of oil dependency. The future automobile will trace back to the Model S, which made it possible to slip those shackles and drive at high speed into a cleaner, smarter, and less expensive era of personal transportation."⁴²

"Twenty-five years from now," Roberson posits, "when you get into your fully autonomous Tesla and videoconference on your way to . . . wherever, just remember that the sleek sedan from the start of the century that [now] seems like an antique was the second coming of the car."⁴³

Notes

1. The quote is taken from the second verse of new interpretation of *The Daodejing* by David Breeden, Steven Schroeder, and Wally Swist (Lamar University Press, 2015), originally composed by the sage Laozi, circa the 6th century B.C.E. *The Daodejing* is considered to be a perennial book of wisdom and of how to live one's life through the practice of an elemental spirituality, of placing oneself in harmony with nature. This translation is from a new version of *The Daodejing* that was published by Lamar University Press, of Beaumont, Texas, in January 2015. This note is made by both the author of this introductory chapter, as well as one of the interpreters of this new version of Laozi, along with Steven Schroeder, a Professor of Philosophy, of Chicago, Illinois, and Unitarian Minister, David Breeden, who holds a Ph.D. in Divinity, of Minneapolis, Minnesota.
2. Robert Palter was the Dana Professor Emeritus of Science from Trinity College, in Hartford, Connecticut. He also taught at the University of Texas. He is a graduate of the both Columbia University and the University of Chicago, where he obtained his Ph.D. The author of this essay provided this note. See also www.amazon.com/Duchess-Malfis-Apricots.../1570034176.

3. Robert Palter, *The Duchess of Malfi's Apricots and Other Literary Fruit*, Columbia, SC: University of South Carolina Press, 2002.
4. Robert Creeley was an eminent American poet and writer (1926-2006) who also taught at Black Mountain College, a progressive liberal arts college, in Asheville, North Carolina, and the State University of New York (SUNY), at Buffalo.
5. Robert Creeley, excerpted from "I Know a Man," from *Selected Poems of Robert Creeley*, Berkeley, CA: The Regents of the University of California Press, 1991.
6. Ibid.
7. Ibid.
8. Bill Roberson, "From Hand Cranking to Charging: Why Tesla's Model S Is the Model of Our Time," Digital Trends, September 14, 2013. See www.digitaltrends.com.
9. Ibid.
10. The italics given here are inflected by the author of this essay for the purposes of evincing another example of how the ethos of the automobile industry parallels other aspects of our lives in the 21st century.
11. Bill Roberson, "From Hand Cranking to Charging: Why Tesla's Model S Is the Model of Our Time," *Digital Trends*.
12. Ibid.
13. The italics here is indicated by Bill Roberson, the author of the article from which the quote is referenced.
14. Bill Roberson, "From Hand Cranking to Charging: Why Tesla's Model S Is the Model of Our Time," *Digital Trends*.
15. Ibid.
16. Ibid.
17. Ibid.
18. Robert Creeley, excerpted from "I Know a Man," from *Selected Poems of Robert Creeley*, Berkeley, CA: The Regents of the University of California Press, 1991.
19. Elon Musk (born 28 June 1971,) a South African-born Canadian-American, is a business magnate, investor, and inventor. This modern Renaissance man is currently the CEO and CTO of SpaceX and CEO and Chief Product Architect of Tesla Motors. If this is not enough to insure his fame, he also founded SpaceX and PayPal. See en.wikipedia.org/wiki/Elon_Musk.

HOW WE PROGRESS OVER TIME

20. Bill Roberson, "From Hand Cranking to Charging: Why Tesla's Model S Is the Model of Our Time," *Digital Trends*.
21. Ibid.
22. Robert Creeley, excerpted from *Selected Poems of Robert Creeley*, Berkeley, CA: The Regents of the University of California Press, 1991.
23. Bill Roberson, "From Hand Cranking to Charging: Why Tesla's Model S Is the Model of Our Time," *Digital Trends*.
24. Ibid.
25. Ibid.
26. Ibid.
27. The abbreviation EV means "electric vehicle" in relation to "electric vehicle owners." The author of this essay provided this note. However, please also see en.wikipedia.org/wiki/EV.
28. Bill Roberson, "From Hand Cranking to Charging: Why Tesla's Model S Is the Model of Our Time," *Digital Trends*.
29. Ibid.
30. Ibid.
31. Ibid.
32. Ibid.
33. Ibid.
34. Ibid.
35. This is a name for a motorcycle by the manufacturer BMW. It is often enough confused with bimmer, which is also the name for cars by the same manufacturer. For instance, the BMW R 1200 C is a beemer. See www.urbandictionary.com/define.php?term=beemer.
36. Bill Roberson, "From Hand Cranking to Charging: Why Tesla's Model S Is the Model of Our Time," *Digital Trends*.
37. Ibid.
38. LTE is an acronym for Long Term Evolution. It is marketed as 4G LTE, which is a standard for wireless communication of high-speed data for data terminals and mobile phones. See http://en.wikipedia.org/wiki/4G_LTE.
39. Bill Roberson, "From Hand Cranking to Charging: Why Tesla's Model S Is the Model of Our Time," *Digital Trends*.
40. Ibid.
41. Ibid.
42. Ibid.
43. Ibid.

THE HISTORY OF RETIREMENT IN AMERICA: EPILOGUE TO THE AMERICAN DREAM, A SOCIO-ECONOMIC AND POLITICAL RETROSPECTIVE

Ice Floes, Patricide, and Shakespeare

If we are to envisage the plight of the elderly in American society, we also need to briefly examine the seeds of the treatment of aging elders against the vast backdrop of global history itself. There clearly appears to be a struggle from tribal culture, such as some of the Eskimo peoples who would set their elderly and infirmed on an ice floe which would drift slowly out to sea, to medieval European society in which the population of the elderly grew to such numbers that their having accrued wealth and property precipitated a trend in patricide by their middle-aged sons who were impatient to acquire their inheritances. The latter, at least, may have provided the arc of drama and a historic theme for a playwright such as Shakespeare; however, the task of any society adapting a proactively plausible and viable plan in taking care of their aging and elderly has offered its challenges throughout world history.

Cotton Mather and William Osler

Puritan cause célèbre Cotton Mather[1] is known for his stoking the proverbial fires for witch trials but is also, to his credit, one of the first to recommend enforced retirement for the elderly in 17th-century New England. His admonitions included, "Be so wise as to disappear of your own Accord." As lacking in felicity as his words may have sounded, his meaning was at more than just tinged with positive intent: "Be glad of dismission... Be pleased with the Retirement which you are dismissed into."

Perhaps not entirely without Mather's doing, the earliest form of retirement in America was in direct result to the occasion when a Plymouth colonist was wounded in battle while fighting Native Americans in defense of their colony. The injured combatant would receive a pension and this would then assist in the support of the colonist and his family. This was predicated upon the wounded veteran being unable to perform manual labor due to the seriousness of his injuries. These pensions were funded in a way that we may think that is in keeping with the ascetic notion of Puritanism itself, with the pensioner performing the tax collections himself.

Historically leapfrogging forward to the 20th-century, renowned physician William Osler,[2] in giving the 1905 valedictory address at Johns Hopkins Hospital, would, somewhat inadvertently, encourage the case for retirement by offering a scientific rationale for it as well as making it economically attractive. Osler, who had been the hospital's physician-in-chief, noted that the years between 25 and 40 are "15 years of plenty" in a worker's career. Osler's denotation specifies that this span of years is "the anabolic or constructive period" in the production of a worker's life. Although Osler himself was getting on, he suggested that workers between the ages 40 and 60 were not as productive, or creative, and were tolerated in the work force more often than not. He even went on to indicate that workers in later life were "useless;" and to further connote that, he suggested that if they were to colloquially be "put out to pasture," that may be the kindest act society could actively pursue.

Otto von Bismarck and the Notion of a Specified Retirement Age

In 1881, German Emperor, William the First,[3] wrote a letter to his Parliament in which he made the historic political proposal that ". . . . those who are disabled from work by age and invalidity have a well-grounded claim to care from the state." In 1889, German Chancellor, Otto von Bismarck, nicknamed "The Iron Chancellor," designed what was to be the first national social insurance program for the elderly; however this was more of a stroke of brilliant brinksmanship than earnest good will. Bismarck posited that a pension be paid to unemployed Germans over the age of 65 to polarize the nascent Marxists who were positioning themselves to overtake Europe. His brinksmanship was as covert as it was utilitarian in its own right. Nearly no one lived to be 65, or over, at this time. Miracle drugs, such as penicillin, were two generations beyond invention.[4] With his strategizing, Bismarck placated the Marxists, and, unintentionally, set an arbitrary retirement age, at least conceptually. It so happened to be that Bismarck himself was 74.

Although Bismarck is often credited with setting the age requirement for retirement, the age demarcation for the retirement program in Germany was first set at 70. It wasn't until 1916, some 27 years later that the age of 65 was established for retirement, which was 18 years after the death of Bismarck.[5]

Anthony Trollope and *The Fixed Period*

An idiosyncratic and curious work of fiction in the *oeuvre* of British novelist Anthony Trollope is his early dystopian and futuristic novel, *The Fixed Period*.[6] Written in 1882, while Trollope, at 66, himself was advancing in age, the novel is his most satirical. Although more than likely apocryphal, but legend just the same, it is purported that Trollope laid claim that his book was not fiction at all but factual story. What was true, however, was that he wrote the book during the bleak months of one winter—when his ruminations were turned toward the novel's main character, President Neverbend, a New Zealander, who leads an elite group of colonists on an island freed from British sovereignty and on which they set up a new government in the year 1980. One of the most salient principles of their society is that there is forced euthanasia at the age of 67 by the state. Ironically, 67 was the age Trollope was approaching. As with most Victorian classics, there is a heroic *denouement*, and in *The Fixed Period*, after the law of forced life termination is abolished in various acts of valor, President Neverbend is brought to England, where, in his liberation, he composes his memoir, which in turn comprises the novel, *The Fixed Period*, itself.

Written nearly 70 years before George Orwell's *1984*, Trollope's novel is unique in that it not only addresses a futuristic world but also specifically directs its focus on its older citizens. Perhaps the only failure in Trollope's creative process is that he did not offer an imaginative solution to what society can do to insure quality of life to the aging and the elderly.

What Is Retirement and What Is Its Evolution in America?

American philosopher, William James, author of his classic study, *The Varieties of Religious Experience*, published in 1902, whose philosophical writings are associated with the school of pragmatism, posited that words are influential in how we think and it is in how we think which produces our actions. A useful tautology here is: negative thoughts precipitate negative actions; positive thoughts evoke positive action. If we put this axiom to use in exploring the word "retirement," and what it means, or is intended to, then we can discern what we mean by the word is not what the word itself means.[7] The question simply put is do human beings desire to or discover enjoyment entering the phase of their lives in which they either decide to quit working for a living or need to leave the workplace because of their no longer being able to keep pace with their professions because of their age or infirmity?

Preeminent crusader for social change, Eleanor Roosevelt, addressed retirees in this manner, in 1934: "Old people love their own things even more than young people do. It means so much to sit in the same chair you sat in for a great many years."[8] As true as this may be, few, if any, individuals look forward to an unproductive life perpetuating itself into old age after their having left the workforce. At a conference organized by the Corning Company in 1951, the question of whether retirement could be made more popular was debated. Santha Rama Rau, expert in Eastern and Western culture, observed that Americans are apparently ill-equipped to be able to access enjoyment in their leisure.[9]

Although the wealthy discovered the joys of leisure with little effort, by 1910 Florida began to become the palatial retirement haven for the middle class. Between 1921 and 1930, golf courses tripled in the United States. Technology, with the invention of television, in the 1950s, facilitated watching films and sporting events. Americans proved that they were up to moving forward with panache after exiting the hubbub of the marketplace, while still actively taking part in and contributing to its economy.[10]

The Aging of Americans

T. S. Eliot, in his poem, "The Love Song of J. Alfred Prufrock," wrote that: "I grow old . . . I grow old . . . / I shall wear the bottoms of my trousers rolled."[11] In 1850, when the life expectancy, at birth, averaged 38 years, and 28 more years for those who were fortunate to live to be 40, the sheer notion of retirement was something of an unfathomable lark.[12]

Industrial centers in the Northeast and Midwest became magnets for employment for indigenous American citizens and immigrants, especially toward the end of the 19th-century. Industry drew a whole new generation off and away from the farms and agricultural work for jobs such as the one described in Theodore Dreiser's novel, *Sister Carrie*:

> The firm of Speigelheim & Co., makers of boys' caps, occupied one floor of the building, fifty feet in width and some eighty-feet in depth. It was a place rather dingily lighted, the darkest portions having incandescent lights, filled with machines and work benches. At the latter labored quite a company of girls and some men. The former were drabby-looking creatures, stained in face with oil and dust, clad in thin, shapeless, cotton dresses and shod with more or less worn shoes.[13]

There was no tacit respite for workers at the time, regarding age, since there were no retirement plans to accompany working on the farm and benefits to the laborers in industry were limited. At the turn of the 20th-century, life expectancy was about 49 years, at birth, and 12 more years for the fittest who lived to the age of 60.[14]

Societal benefits were the mean: workers who labored in a particular industry bonded, as did workers of the same immigrant group, or nationality, and mutual benevolence were both fortunate and common. Workers who left the labor force due to old age or infirmity could actually depend on the generosity of church, friends, and neighbors. Charity, at that time, was an unwritten rule.

The Joanna Short and Augustana College Studies

In the 21st-century, individuals are not only retiring from the work force, unlike earlier eras, but also doing so at a younger age. The statistics in 1850 reveal that 76% of men aged 65 or older were still employed.[15] In successive decades in the 20th-century, 1950 statistics show that 47% of those men aged 65 or older were still employed in the workplace and that in 2000 just 17.5% were still actively employed.[16]

The studies produced by Joanna Short and Augustana College are invaluable for their accumulation of significant data, and establishes not only how difficult life was for workers but also that the workers who could no longer function in the workplace, due to age or injury, found themselves placed in a perilous position. If a worker, and especially industrial workers, did not have the luxury of children who could take care of them for whatever time they may have before dying, then something worse than death awaited them—poverty and homelessness in the form of death in life on the street. However, farmers and agricultural workers, Short and College illustrate, worked to an older age. Furthermore, their reasoning for the increase of retirees throughout the 20th-century is attributed to higher earnings which lead to worker's improvement in an ability to save.[17]

What is salient about the Short and College studies is their ability to concretize statistical studies in a relevant manner for both an economic, or qualitative analysis, and a historical, or qualitative, analysis, such as in a quote from the article, below.

> Over the period from 1890 to 1990, economic growth has led to nearly an eightfold increase in real gross domestic product (GDP) per capita. In 1890, GDP per capita was $3,430 (in 1996 dollars), which is comparable to the levels of production in Morocco or Jamaica today. In 1990, real GDP per capita was $26,889. On average, Americans today enjoy a standard of living commensurate with eight times the income of Americans living a century ago. More

income has made it possible to save for an extended retirement.[18]

People retire earlier because they are able to afford to. The expansion of the workforce paying into Social Security was largely responsible for this. The other side of the swing of the pendulum in the tautology of this economic equation is that it requires more personal savings, as well as wise investments, to retire with less risk at 65.

More Short and College, Goldin's Gender Economics, and Costa's Quantitative Research

The Short and College study on the history of retirement bases its findings nearly entirely on the employment behaviors of men—permanent departures from the labor force in old age is uncommon for women.[19] Other landmark research, such as that accomplished by Claudia Goldin,[20] posits that "even as late as 1940, most young working women exited the labor force on marriage, and only a small minority would return." With the onset of WWII, employment of married women grew exponentially, with current statistical evidence pointing to retirement patterns between men and women now nearly the same.[21]

What the Short and College economic study also portrays is a trend in living arrangements of the men that retired in the 19th-century in comparison with those in the 20th-century. What the study proved was that a rise in independence of retired men increased in the modern era. Earlier, almost 50% of retirees lived with children or relatives. Currently, less than 95% of retired men live independent of family or progeny. Again, rising income is an apparent explanation of the mega-trend away from co-residence. The Goldin study also suggests that the preference of the elderly is to nearly always live independently; however, it is only recently that this possibility has been realized due to having a means in which to accomplish it.[22]

Empirical considerations, including age, disability, and pension, are directly relevant to an individual's retirement. Contextually within an individual model, the trends in retirement can be observed and offer an explanation in its rise. Disability alone is shown to increase retirement today but even more so in previous eras. Although disability rates are unlikely to be the only reason for increased retirement rates since health care improvements have been made to such a significant degree to facilitate a healthier population overall.[23] The renowned socio-economic study of Dora Costa,[24] *The Evolution of Retirement: An American Economic History, 1880-1990*, which provides substantial quantitative research, exhorts that chronic health conditions prevailed for the elderly who were born in the 19th-century as opposed to those who were at least slightly more fortunate to be born in the 20th-century.[25]

From Early Pensions to the Establishing of Social Security

With military and civil service pensions becoming more available to workers between 1875 and 1934, this benefit also developed into a new and important, and in the very least, residual source of income for the elderly. Private firms also began offering pensions, of which The American Express Company was the first to develop the first formal pension plan. In the late 19th-century, railroads were among the largest employers of workers to begin providing pensions to workers, and the Pennsylvania Railroad was entirely employer-funded.[26] Service of 30 years was required and there was a mandatory retirement age of 70. The scheme of employers was to reduce the less productive and older employees in their labor force and to achieve this in the most humanely acceptable fashion. In the favor of workers themselves, the 1926 Revenue Act excluded the current taxation from all income earned in pension trusts, which as a result provided added impetus for employers to provide pensions. Large employers, by 1930, had adopted pension plans that covered 20% of industrial workers; and by 1928, over a dozen unions paid benefits through the establishing of pension plans. Typically, these pensions also benefitted those members of craft unions that were employed by smaller employers who did not offer pensions.[27]

Despite the financial windstorms of the Great Depression, most private pensions survived intact. However, pension plans funded as 'pay as you go' programs were the exceptions for financial survival. Funded through current earnings, instead of accrued reserves, a significant enough percentage of union pensions were financed in this manner in the 1930s—and they failed. The struggling railroad pensions, thanks to the strength of political allies, were protected by government takeover in 1937.[28]

Designed to extend pension benefits to workers not covered by any plan whatsoever, the Social Security system was created in 1935. Consisting of two programs, The Social Security Act offers Old Age Assistance (OAA) and Old Age Insurance (OAI). OAA was initiated to provide federal matching funds to financially support state old age pensions. This provided motivation to develop pension programs or to increase benefits by many states. By 1950, 22% of the population of 65 and over was the recipient of OAA benefits, which proved to be the high watermark of the OAA program; however, the OAI program became liberalized, and thus began to dominate Social Security itself.[29]

OAI, administered by the federal government, is subsidized by payroll taxes. Those eligible for benefits are retirees—and later, survivors and dependents of both the retired and disabled—had paid into the program; and the program remained relatively small until 1950. Coverage after this date was extended to include agricultural and domestic workers, which increased average benefits by 77%. The Social Security Act of 1965 was amended to include Medicare to provide the elderly with health insurance, which continued to expand in the late 1960s and 1970s, and is the primary source for retirement income for most retirees today.[30]

Short and College Summary

What the current retirement pattern offers is a resourced self-financed leisure class, which is constituted of a range of class structures that has evolved, sometimes in a painstakingly slow fashion, over more than the last century. What actualizes itself as a historically significant rise in retirement is seen through the lens of economic historians as occurring through an upswing in the labor market and increased pension income. Workers now primarily choose their own time of exiting the labor force, instead of their being forced out through either their own obsolescence or infirmity. Also, decline in agricultural jobs, consistent improvements in medical technology, and because of our rapidly expanding techno-centric world, the cost of enjoying leisure activities is made more affordable to a mass audience in quite an egalitarian fashion. In addition, increases in the income of the younger population enable this segment of society to begin planning for their own retirement and old age. For those individuals retiring today, men and women, equitably so, often enough have more options to save and plan for their lives after leaving their working careers, independently of living with their children.[31]

Boomers Booming

The post-War World II generation, known in media hype as Baby Boomers, born between 1946 and 1964, had redefined, in a socially revolutionary fashion, *the art of retirement*. If retirement can be connoted as an art, this generation has had the imaginative ethos to create active lives after their leaving their employment careers.

A study conducted in 2000 for the Association of American Retired People (AARP)—founded in 1958 by Ethel Percy

Andrus, Ph.D., a retired educator from California, and based in Washington, D.C.—through The Roper Starch Worldwide Survey, concluded that the following percentages of Boomers planned not to retire but to remain in the workplace:[32]

> 30% desired to work part-time, however not out of necessity;
> 25% desired to work part-time for both enjoyment and to supplement their income;
> 23% discerned that they needed to work due to financial obligations;
> and 9% did not desire retirement whatsoever, but wanted to continue working in their current professions.[33]

The late Betty Friedan, activist and author, best known for her feminist socio-political classic, *The Feminine Mystique,*[34] as well as the founder and first president of the National Organization for Women (NOW), continued to teach at Cornell University and to write well into her 80s. Lillian Carter, mother of President Jimmy Carter, spent two years in India as a member of the Peace Corp at 84. The inimitable modern avatar of bodybuilders and guru of fitness impresarios, Jack LaLane, spent his 92nd birthday promoting a newly-designed food juicer of own his invention and to sign copies of two newly published cookbooks, *Celebrating 90-plus Years of Healthy Living* and *Cooking with Jack: Eat Right and You Can't Go Wrong,* in New York's Times Square.

Founder and CEO of Harmon International Industries, Inc., Sidney Harmon, was quoted in the October 2006 issue of *AARP*, in response to a question from the *Washington Post* that this pioneer of the high fidelity industry didn't need to be replaced with a more youthful successor and that his intent was "to retire in 25 years." The Springfield, Massachusetts native, Theodore Geisel (1904-1991), better known as Dr. Seuss, the iconic and prolific children's book author, responsible for instilling

REVELING IN WHAT IS SALVAGEABLE

a sense of whimsy in generations of children, has distilled the ethos of the modern retiree, perhaps in the most efficient manner possible, in his bestselling book, *Oh, the Places You'll Go*,[35] a book actually meant for adults, and one that is often given as either a graduation or retirement gift:

> You have brains in your head. You have feet in your shoes.
> You can steer yourself any direction you choose.
> You're on your own. And you know what you know.
> And YOU are the guy (or gal) who'll decide where to go.[36]

The Future of Social Security According to Schreiber: Financial Realism

Despite the proactive psychological approach to retirement in America, economists and politicians alike, from blue states and red states, and every increment in between, are aware that retirement needs to be righted if it is to be fully realized by Americans of every class and other than career academics, business professionals, and those of the wealthy upper class. Sylvester J. Schreiber, Ph.D. in Economics from the University of Notre Dame, and former member of the Board of Directors of the Pension Research Council at the Wharton School of the University of Pennsylvania from 1995 to 2000, has written a landmark book that addresses the flies in the ointment and the trolls under the bridge in retirement theory, entitled *The Predictable Surprise: The Unraveling of the U.S. Retirement System*.[37]

Schreiber's recounting of Social Security points to the actuarial value of early participants in the program being worth considerably more due to lifetime contributions to their earnings; whereas most American workers today cannot count on, with any certainty, an equitable return on their investment. In short, Social Security and Medicare, as well as employer-sponsored programs, all appear to be propped up on precarious financial foundations. A succession of American presidents has attempted to refurbish the shaky architecture of the system to little or no avail.[38] Today, ideologically speaking, we have the polarized hard right of the Koch Brothers and the social mores of a progressive politician, such as Bernie Sanders, Senator of the State of Vermont, squaring off against each other not in the give and take of proactive political dialogue but hip-deep in the verbal war of a mud-spattered dialectic.

President Franklin D. Roosevelt envisioned the accrual of Social Security contributions, from both workers and employers, resulting in financial security after a career spanning decades. Ideally, every generation of beneficiaries of the plan could expect to reap benefits equivalent to an equitable value of contributions including interest. However, as Schrieber illustrates, the implementation of Social Security was originally a political compromise. Lawmakers jury-rigged the program into a pay-as-you-go funding platform when it was initially beginning, then used most of the initial contributions of those early workers to pay full-career benefits to the first retirees.[39] What resulted is that Social Security offered generous returns to the initial waves of generations of retirees; however, the new millennium generation, at this point, without readjustments to the system, will see less value on their financial contributions.[40]

What has kept the financial retirement platform in balance are traditional employer-sponsored pension plans, which have revitalized retirement security for workers in America. Despite these gains in economic equilibrium, political dilettantism has often enough undermined both sponsorship and plan funding. This has precipitated employers to capitulate on their support of traditional pensions nearly unilaterally. Concomitantly, the preponderant concern of workers who have subscribed to defined contribution plans, such as 401Ks, may not be financially viable enough to provide benefits to workers through the span of long retirements, despite the popularity of such programs.[41]

REVELING IN WHAT IS SALVAGEABLE

The Predictable Surprise by Sylvester J. Schrieber offers both a descriptive account of the quantitative and historical development of employer pensions and government-sponsored programs in direct correlation to their evolution and how they have affected American workers.[42]

The Schrieber Theory of Social Security Ineptitude

Initially, FDR, and his supporters, in their inimitable pro-worker WPA[43] spirit, intended to circumnavigate the poverty, due to unemployment, most Americans at the time were in, which was, as they saw it, "the necessity of going deeply into debt" in the government's funding of Social Security.[44] Although, FDR believed it would not be fair to place the burden of unfunded obligations on future Congresses which would then need to become competitive in their attempt to stretch limited government resources. FDR's belief also incorporated the vision of an egalitarian retirement program that was predicated on benefits substantiated on "insurance principles;" and that it would be inappropriate to pay workers less than the value of what they contributed into the program themselves.[45]

The crucial argument that lost out was the long-term funding for Social Security. Contingent on FDR's initial intent and notion of the breadth of the plan itself, the long-term funding aspect of Social Security was repeatedly defeated in policy and political battles. What the catalyst proved to be for debate was that FDR favored the paying of full benefits to retirees who had contributed to the system and another political faction directly opposed this—the GOP. Despite FDR's financial stipulations, Social Security, in appearance, seemed to be take care of itself for decades. However, the Baby Boom generation, and the changing population demographic, inherently altered the 'pay-as-you-go' rationale and made it susceptible due to its necessitating escalating costs. Presidents Ronald Reagan, Bill Clinton, and George H.

W. Bush all admonished that the system was approaching critical mass—although each one was stopped short of providing resolve to the situation due to political firestorms.[46]

The deduction Schrieber also makes is that although employer pensions operate in a different nature than government financing what is sacrificed, with respect to lasting solvency and a short-term conceptualization, is a dissonant echo found also in the history of Social Security itself. The reasoning is that rather than allow employers to fund their plans with cogent long-term ramifications, policymakers continually selected to limit tax expenditures, even though laws were passed as protection to pension participants from unfunded, or underfunded, pensions promised by sponsoring employers. With funding tightening into knots, most employers opted to invest their benefit dollars on defined contribution plans with more predictable and steadier funding obligations.[47]

A Tom Sawyer or Billy the Kid Approach for America's Retirement Future: More of the Same?

In referring to Social Security and Medicare in 2009, President Barack Obama addressed the issue proactively, "This, by the way, is where some very difficult issues of sacrifice, responsibility, and duty are going to come in because what we have done is kick this can down the road, and we are now at the end of the road." Schrieber acknowledges, as well as endorses, this sentiment; however, rebalancing the vessel of Social Security and making it seaworthy is what is required in a political climate that is divisive and, at times, hostile to the presentation of socio-political cogency.[48]

Countering President Obama's inclinations are Republican Representative from Wisconsin Paul Ryan's budget, called "Path to Prosperity," which demands making Social Security available for 21st-century participants but one in which also falls short of making any specific revisions whatsoever, except that he strongly recommends also cutting entitlements such as these to achieve a balanced budget. Although, in his pitch of "Path to Prosperity," Ryan does challenge what is a dysfunctional Congress to cooperate in fashioning reforms in the Social Security system, as is.

This augurs what Schrieber offers as both President Obama and Representative Ryan as "employing a Tom Sawyer strategy for painting the fence—they are trying to get somebody else to do the work."[49] According to Schrieber, the Pension Benefit Guaranty Corporation (PBGC), that reported an unfunded obligation of $20 billion in its single-employer insurance plan in 2010, which was an increase of $500 million over the previous year, thus placing the PBGC in "an insurance death spiral," whose remaining plan participants will likely make claims that far supersede their premiums.[50]

Schrieber indicates, with refreshing innovational thinking and proactive resolve, that redirecting sunken program costs could be mitigated by directing low-risk plan sponsors to affected industries, including airlines and steel. Schrieber also suggests a $2 a head airline tax be placed on tickets for all flights through the continental United States to as not only a partial remedy but as the beginning of a new conceptual approach to the solving the problem.[51]

In addition, Schrieber recommends moderating excise taxes on pension reversions. Employers who withdraw funds, under current law, from an overfunded plan are made subject to punitive excise taxes.[52] Such excise taxes discourage sponsors from accruing reserves, in excess, during the time of booming markets; although, factually, pensions also become underfunded when there is a market failure. What Schrieber posits is that the incentives, as they remain today, actually work against the stability of long-term funding.[53]

Schrieber makes the argument that annuities could not only be made more attractive to retirees but also the acquisition of them could be facilitated. This proposal would involve purchasing an annuity on an installment basis, and this then would eliminate timing risks that workers incur in their needing to wait until retirement for their annuities to mature.[54] Another belief Schrieber espouses is that he suggests workers delay their retirement and that there be a commission established to examine the possibilities of current employer pensions to forge a future that is based on a more rational approach.[55]

Winston Churchill exhorted that "you can always count on Americans to do the right thing—after they have tried everything else." Sylvester Schrieber admonishes policymakers and politicians to both a call to action and to demonstrate prudence:

> ... although they have a blind spot about the program's function as one piece in the larger system, and they have ignored options for modernizing the benefit structure ... there is a glaring lack of knowledge about plan operations, the incentives affecting them and their outcomes. Until policymakers treat this component of the retirement system as something other than a revenue loss, we can expect our history of bad policy to continue. They are pretending to be Tom Sawyer but are really more like Billy the Kid, trying to get their opponents to draw first so they can slay them in the next political street fight.[56]

Some Keys to Social Security History

FDR signed the Social Security Act into law on August 14, 1935. That is a significant sentence. The intent of the legislation was to assist working Americans, who were often enough at that time unemployed, in supplementing personal retirement savings but not to replace it. To ensure that American workers were equipped with the basic living necessities during their retirement years, because they were unable to save enough due to a broken economy, the intention of Federal legislators was to return income tax dollars to provide Americans with a modicum of comfort during retirement at the expense of the U.S. government. This singular positive intention has been the precipitant of policymakers and politicians throughout history—and not just the last century and a half of American history. Marcus Tullius Cicero attempted to address the issue, not without an amount of axiomatic elegance, in 55 B.C.E.

> The national budget must be balanced. Public debt must be reduced. The arrogance of authorities must be moderated and controlled. Payments to foreign governments must be reduced if this nation doesn't want to go bankrupt. People must again learn to work instead of living on public assistance.

To a fault, Cicero appears to be in legion with conservative twin pillars Speaker of the House John Boehner, Congressman from Ohio, and Kentucky Senator Mitch McConnell.

However, returning to the keys of Social Security history, FDR made two promises: to ensure that funds for the system would be available, and that while he lived no American would pay income tax on Social Security Benefits. FDR was better than good on his word. In 1983, Congress finally broke the second promise that was made. If an individual has an income of $25,000 and is single, or a combined income, if married, they will pay income tax on 50% of their Social Security Benefit. The algorithm becomes only more usurious if an individual has an income of $34,000, if single, or of an income of $44,000, if married, they will then pay income tax on 85% on their Social Security Benefit.[57]

With working Americans paying Social Security Tax, as well as those receiving benefits with income over thresholds of what they may earn, the U.S. government becomes the recipient of covering both sides of the proverbial street. However, this also cuts into budgets of senior citizens trying to keep up with bills and inflation, which stretches the already thin fabric of their so-called safety net that legislators originally created with positive intentions.[58]

As retirees earn income to better support themselves through their retirement years, the probability they will pay income on their Social Security Benefits rises. While this is oxymoronic—an individual's motivation to earn more being negated to at least some degree by being docked in another area of their finances—it is significant to be aware that distributions from traditional IRAs are also taxed as "ordinary income."[59] This unfortunate formula for the retiree then can be posited as writing itself as the increases in one's taxable income can, or does, equate to an increase in the tax on your Social Security Benefits.

The Employment Retirement Income Securities Act (ERISA)

In 1974, Congress passed The Employment Retirement Income Securities Act (ERISA) as legislation—delineating the beginning of the modern era where many of American workers have invested in contributing to retirement plans for the last 30 years and more. From the fertile ground of the landmark legislation of ERISA grew a bumper crop of company-sponsored retirement plans, such as IRAs; 401(k)s; 403(b) plans, used by educators; and nearly every other operative and qualified retirement plan.[60] The legislative design of ERISA was to precipitate Americans to prepare for their own retirement, so as to be less dependent on Social Security—and it has largely succeeded.

ERISA encouraged working Americans several incentives to save, offering more of a classic win-win strategy, in which:

> participants could deduct contributions on their yearly taxes;
> all gains were tax deferred;
> retirement accounts were exempt from creditors;
> and company employees contributed through payroll deductions, which actually facilitated saving money, or, axiomatically, funds that you don't access is money saved.

Although American workers found such retirement enticement irresistible, and went on to save millions of dollars in IRAs and other retirement plans similar to it, there was a caveat. These accounts could become an unforeseen tax prison.[61] IRAs, 401(k)s, and other retirement platforms, for many employees represent the bulk of their retirement savings. However, in an employee making systematic, tax deductible contributions during an employment career, when that employee turns 70 ½, systematic, fully taxable withdrawals are made as well. A cumulative balance in such a retirement account that has accrued to possibly three times the amount deposited over the employee's employment career is not at all uncommon. What this establishes, however, is that such compound interest can balloon tax-deductible contributions into substantial, and taxable, IRS "nest eggs." The underside of IRAs, and plans such as these, can leave the American worker on the other side of the equal sign in an equation in which tax incentives should have added up to a positive; although, by saving tax on the *seed*, tax is owed on the *crop*.[62]

Georgetown University Law Center Study

Of the several salient sources of information regarding economic retirement history in America, Georgetown University

THE HISTORY OF RETIREMENT IN AMERICA

Law Center's timeline,[63] posted online in 2010, is a sterling example in the scholarship of retirement legislation and company-funded programs, and how they evolved. It is an unequivocal font of fact and factoid. For the purposes of presenting the more significant progressions in development for the sake of intelligent discussion, the following dates and historical data are indisputably relevant, as well as offering both a cornucopia and wellspring for further reference. The abbreviated timeline presented here, based on the research of Georgetown University Law Center, is offered for the purpose of providing a cogent outline of retirement policies and legislation, so that both their principles and history can be fully understood to promote overall clarity regarding the subject and for more of an adept grasp of it for future research.

1875 The first private pension company in the United States is established by The American Express Company to insure stability to a career-oriented workforce.[64]

Late 19th century Nearly 75% of males over 65 are still working. For males over 65 who are not working, they are typically disabled.[65]

1913 The first Federal income tax law is enacted by Congress.

1919 Covering approximately 15% of America's wage and salary workers, over 300 private pensions are operative.[66] This is largely attributed to the intent of employers to draw workers, reduce turnover, and "more [humanely] remove older, less productive employees."[67]

1926 Trust income originating from pension plans in the form of an employee's taxable income is exempted by The Revenue Act of 1926. What the act also establishes is that pension plans must be created for the *exclusive* benefit of "some" or all employees.

REVELING IN WHAT IS SALVAGEABLE

1935 Social Security is enacted. Age 65 is established as the normal retirement age. At the time the legislation is passed, the belief that most American workers will not live long after retirement is largely held by policymakers and politicians. Social Security Benefits were initially meant to serve retirees for only a minimal amount of time.[68]

1935 Life expectancy is about 60 years, at birth; individuals who reach age 65 can expect to live on an average of another 12 years.

1939 Just 6% of Americans pay income tax.[69]

1940 4.1 million, or 15% of all private sector workers are covered by a pension plan.[70] As with Social Security, these plans are instituted with the operative intention that the employers will be paying workers benefits for a minimal number of years before their death.

1942 To freeze wages, in an attempt to restrict wartime inflation, The Wage and Salary Act of 1942 is passed.

1945 Almost 75% of American workers now pay income taxes. Tax deferral of pension income is made more attractive to the population at large because of this.[71]

1950 9.8 million workers, or 25% of all private sector workers are covered by a pension plan.[72]

1956 The Social Security Act is amended to provide women with the opportunity to elect early reduced benefits at age 62; full retirement benefits remain available for women retiring at age 65.[73]

1960 18.7 million workers, or 41% of all private sector workers, are covered by a pension plan.[74]

1961 The Social Security Act is amended to provide men with the opportunity to elect reduced benefits as it did with women in 1956; with the same stipulations of early reduced benefits at age 62 and full retirement at age 65.[75]

1967 The Age Discrimination in Employment Act (ADEA) is passed as legislation. The Act prohibits age discrimination for American workers who are age 40, or older, and under age 65. ADEA does not prohibit discrimination against workers over 65, since it also does not limit any mandatory retirement.

1970 26.3 million workers, or 45% of all private sector workers are covered by a pension plan.[76]

1974 The Employee Retirement Income Security Act of 1974 (ERISA) is passed as legislation. It is significant because it requires more disclosures with respect to a plan for participants and the U.S. government. This includes a summary plan description, material modification notices, annual reports, and the provision of a statement of the participant's accrued benefits upon request.

1978 ADEA is amended to prohibit discrimination against American workers up to age 70; the law does not prohibit discrimination against workers over age 70, since it does not limit mandatory retirement either.

1980 35.9 million workers, or 46% of all private sector workers, are covered by a pension plan.[77]

1986 ADEA is amended to prohibit discrimination against any American worker age 40, or older, without an age ceiling. The legislation also includes prohibition on mandatory retirement, except for tenured faculty members.

1994 ADEA is amended to prohibit mandatory retirement for tenured faculty members.

1996 Just 8% of all American workers are currently involved in physically demanding jobs.

1996　The Small Business Job Protection Act is passed as legislation. SBJPA is intended to encourage a *simplified* retirement savings platform for small businesses (established as those with under 100 employees) as an alternative to qualified 401(k) plans. Essentially, the Act requires the employer to make matching contributions of up to 3% of compensation to attempt to promote a more equitable employer sponsored pension plan.

1999　40.1 million workers in the private sector, and 60.4 million workers in the private sector, are covered by defined pension plans in America.[78]

2000　The Social Security Act is amended to eliminate an earnings ceiling for individuals who have reached standard retirement age.

2006　Life expectancy is age 74 for men and age 79 for women. Men who Reach the age of 65 can expect to live until age 81; women who reach the age of 65 can expect to live until age 84.

Retirement: Partly Fact, Partly Fiction, or a Financial Contradiction?

A recent Employee Benefit Research Study cites that increasing numbers of American elders are grinding out their retirement years in poverty.[79] Retirees below the poverty line have been increasing steadily since 2005, and those succumbing to poverty as they age and spend down their savings is occurring at an alarming rate.[80] Not unlike Garrison Keillor, when he offers a transition from a sketch that ends with at least one of the characters in a compromising situation, and he cues the Guy's All-star Shoe Band up for a rendition of the upbeat commercial jingle, "Bebop-A-Reebop Rhubarb Pie,' which is purported to offer a panacea to anyone wilting from the stress of being challenged by whatever it is that seems to be indomitable, a little humor can go a long way. The great vaudevillian and American humorist, George Burns, who continued to work until after his turning 100 years of age, commented on his quitting performing with this one-liner: "Retirement at 65 is ridiculous. When I was 65, I still had pimples."

Wherever both socio-economic critics and pundits place the financial security of retirement in America, we can find some solace, as a society as a whole, that there has been a progressive approach, largely, toward making various retirement programs secure for elders. It is only recently, and for the first time American history, that we have had a greater population of citizens over 65 than under 18.[81] An estimated 80% of America's wealth is possessed by retirees and "empty-nesters," who also own the proclivity to vote more often than many younger citizens, as well as doing so in their own best interests.[82]

However, those statistics can be as obfuscating as elucidating. A recent Consumer Education Services, Inc. (CESI) Debt Solutions survey revealed that 56% of American retirees were under financial obligations of outstanding debt upon retirement. Retirement, purportedly, is not defined by debt, but by ability to afford even a modest lifestyle of comfort, even if it may mean psychological freedom from concern and worry regarding personal finances. Also, pragmatically, living on a fixed income and having to pay off outstanding debts is not the most optimal of financial situations to lower oneself into. However, most American workers who select to retire do so with their accounts in the red.[83]

Even more inauspicious is that an increasing percentage of retirees are going bankrupt. A recent University of Michigan study cited that Americans age 55 and older now compromise 20% of all bankruptcies in the country. In 2001, this number was just 12%. However, between 1991 and 2007, Americans filing for bankruptcy between the ages of 65 to 74 escalated exponentially to an astronomical 178%.[84] To put it mildly, these current trends are alarming.

Despite these calculations, many American elders under financial duress do not decide to retire. A recent AARP survey of Boomers categorically found that 40% owned a "work until I drop" philosophy—not because this is their choice, but because it is what is necessary for their financial survival.[85]

A study, entitled "The Impact of Deferring Retirement Age on Retirement Income Adequacy," exhibits the trend that nearly all Americans surveyed needed to work longer than they had anticipated. Released in June 2011, the study indicates that most American workers will *need* to work well into their 70s *and* 80s to even afford to retire. The word *Dickensian* holds an unfortunate, but an appropriate, darkly foreboding resonance here.[86]

Regarding the speculative question of inflation, journalist Robert Powell, perhaps spoke the most eloquently about it in a *Marketwatch* article, dated March 7, 2011, when he addressed the issue of inflation as "one of the most insidious risks Americans will face in retirement." Powell also posits that even though those moving toward retirement have witnessed, first-hand, the dismay of negative effects of inflation that they may unwittingly not be calculating for in their retirement plans, even if these same individuals, on the cusp of retirement, remember when gasoline was only a dollar a gallon, or less. The Society of American Actuaries published a study that reads, in part, "Compared to other planning activities, only 72% of pre-retirees and 55% of retirees are calculating the effects of inflation on their retirement planning."[87]

The Epilogue to the American Dream[88]

Americans before the Civil War were not viewed as negatively as they are today. Elders were venerated for their wisdom and experience. They were even given preferable seats in the front pews in church. With the advancement of technology, to the delight and benefits of many worldwide, our societal vision and humanistic capabilities for compassion appears, often enough, to have diminished in direct correlation to the advancement of modern inventions. Circa 1910, the current new business theory, of "scientific management," was developed, and gave rise to a profession of "efficiency experts," whose worldview of social Darwinism—a.k.a. political and economic "survival of the fittest"—which then precipitated the market branding that a highly efficient society would give rise to the most powerful one. *Labor productivity* is a phrase that still remains electric as a buzzword.[89]

In a great sense older American workers are still finding themselves in the Chaplinesque situation, as in the film *Modern Times*,[90] of needing to get out of the way of not so much labor-saving technology, but the sometimes heartless ideologies that unfortunately become part and parcel of policymakers and politicians who want to balance budgets but are out of touch with elders who may find themselves wandering the streets if their safety net of Social Security entitlements are cut.

However, retirement in America has become established, after the economic and political struggles of the past century and a half and up until today, as not only as a cherished institution but also as an inalienable human right borne out of the sweat of a lifetime of labor and not at all originating from a fallacious or ostentatious posturing toward entitlement. The institution of retirement in America is the result of honoring a life not just well lived but one that has been fashioned from an individual's work and contributions to forging a living and, more than likely, supporting and raising a family en route. Retirement has never been any grand bargain but an evolution of ideas and legislation more so on a level of ideological courage and progressive intention more than any other.

REVELING IN WHAT IS SALVAGEABLE

Sociologists have coined the term *discouragement* to theorize the concept of aging as a process whereby elders *naturally* withdraw from society in preparation for death,[91] actually echoing Anthony Trollope's fictional ideas he purported in his 19th-century novel, *The Fixed Period*, as well as earlier tribal peoples dispensing of their elderly in any number of untimely ways. However, the positive and proactive associations that hold sway regarding retirement has completely become assimilated by the American psyche. Elders have come to love the idea. Essentially, retirement in America is here to stay—and to evolve and to further become both an entitled and non-entitled benefit for all, as the human right that it has been honored as. Retirement has become a rite of passage and it keeps becoming and developing as such into human ritual.

A further aspect of work that we can hardly stand to miss is that workers do tend to retire from jobs when they can because those jobs, however sustaining they may be, on at least a financial level, may not be sustainable for the individual's spirit or the soul. We can think of the poignant pyscho-social observations of French philosopher, and mystic, Simone Weil in her chronicling working life in a factory as a parallel here. As the trends indicate, more and more Americans of retirement age are working longer due to their augmenting their lives with second, third, and fourth careers that may be more attractive to them individually than their forebears had similar occasion, or opportunity, to gainfully pursue. Although 17th-century Americans are often enough castigated for their Puritanical habits, their lives reflected a fundamental truth: work *is* life. If the question is posited to anyone out of work for any length of time, they very well may answer with a similar axiom—based on experience.

However, despite any philosophical theorizing, retirement is heir apparent to the central idea of labor in the first place. It is a natural rhythm, and one that has been fluid over centuries

THE HISTORY OF RETIREMENT IN AMERICA

of human history: work *and* rest; sun up *and* sun down. Synergy is a word that has become somewhat prevalent in modern usage and means "the interaction of multiple elements in a system to produce an effect different from or greater than the sum of their individual effects."[92] There is a synergy in the rhythms of work; and there is synergy in the wisdom of retirement. The two can be complementary. In fact, they are. Prudence and wisdom can be the byproducts of such synergy. This then can result in active humanity and compassion.

In a society that offers signs of health and that supports the life-affirming pursuits of its citizens, young and old, the *synergy* inflected regarding who works and for how long should be based on an answer that is equitable and proactive for everyone, which is one that is also copacetic, on all levels. Our true inalienable rights, elementally, as humans, is to engage in work and for those of us that are too old, or infirmed, then, it is in harmony with our biological rhythms to *disengage* from the workforce and be valued by society, in the very least, with more than a modicum of esteem. It is this *synergy* that would make for the true definition of the word itself: for the world of business and the nation's economy to be in harmony with and to honor the labor and eventual needs of the American worker—and for that to be the basis of true productivity and commerce.

Notes

1. Mary-Lou Weisman, "The History of Retirement, From Early Man to A.A.R.P.," *The New York Times*, March 21, 1999.
2. Ibid.
3. Official Social Security Website, http://ss.gov/history/age65.html.
4. Weisman, "The History of Retirement, From Early Man to A.A.R.P."
5. Official Social Security Website.
6. Graham Handley, "The Fixed Period: An Introduction" http://www.victorianweb.org//authors/trollope/tsociety/fixed.html.

7. The Five O'Clock Club, "The Changing Face of Retirement: A Perspective," www.fiveoclockclub.com/publications/PDF/GoodLifeSample.pdf.
8. Weisman, "The History of Retirement, From Early Man to A.A.R.P."
9. Ibid.
10. Ibid.
11. T. S. Eliot, *The Waste Land and Other Poems*, Harcourt, Brace, Jovanovich, 1934.
12. William J. Wiatrowski, "Changing Retirement Age: Ups and Downs," *Monthly Labor Review*, 2001.
13. Theodore Dreiser, *Sister Carrie*, Houghton Mifflin Company, 1959.
14. Wiatrowski, "Changing Retirement Age: Ups and Downs."
15. Joanna Short and Augustana College, "The History of Retirement in the Modern Age" http:///www.saveandconquer.com/history-of-retirement-in-us/.
16. Ibid.
17. Ibid.
18. Ibid.
19. Joanna Short and Augustana College, "Economic History of Retirement in the United States." http://eh.net/encyclopedia/article/short.retirement.history.us.
20. Claudia Goldin, *Understanding the Gender Gap: An Economic History of American Women*, New York: Oxford University Press, 1990.
21. Ibid.
22. Joanna Short and Augusta College, "Economic History of Retirement in the United States."
23. Ibid.
24. Dora Costa, *The Evolution of Retirement: An American Economic History, 1880-1990*, Chicago: University of Chicago Press, 1998. Winner of the 1998 Paul A. Samuelson Award given by the Teachers Insurance and Annuity Association-College Retirement Equities Fund (TIAA-CREF), Dora Costa's study elucidates why various factors underlie the correlatives between increasing life expectancy and retirement of men over 64 through the use of statistical and demographic concepts. Costa's quantitative approach

reveals how rising incomes and retirement, specific employment and disease, employment prospects of older workers, elderly living arrangements, the development of retirement lifestyles, and the shifting political plate tectonics of pensions and policymakers affect the evolution and history of retirement.

25. Ibid.
26. U.S. Department of Labor, "United States and Canadian Pensions before 1930: A Historical Perspective," *Trends in Pensions*, Vol. 2, 1992, pp. 34-45.
27. Joanna Short and Augusta College, "Economic History of Retirement in the United States."
28. Ibid.
29. Ibid.
30. Ibid.
31. Ibid.
32. "The Changing Face of Retirement," The Five O'Clock Club.
33. Ibid.
34. *The Feminine Mystique*, New York: NY, W. W. Norton & Company, 1963.
35. Ibid.
36. Dr. Seuss (Theodore Geisel), *Oh, The Places You'll Go*, New York, NY: Random House, 1990.
37. Sylvester J. Schrieber, *The Predictable Surprise: The Unraveling of the U.S. Retirement System*, New York, NY: Oxford University Press, 2012.
38. Towers Watson, "The History of American Retirement and Future Social Security Reform," http://www.twoerswatson.com/en/Insights/Newsletters/Americas/Insider/2012An-American Ret...
39. Ibid.
40. Ibid.
41. Ibid.
42. Ibid.
43. The Works Progress Administration, founded in 1935, then renamed in 1939, as the Work Projects Administration (WPA), was seminal to the development of FDR's ambitious vision of his New Deal program. The WPA employed millions of unemployed people—often unskilled men—to carry out public works projects. However, it

was also a demonstrative socio-economic tool in its employment of artists and writers in projects such as the illustrating and writing of what came to be known as the WPA Guides to each of the current 48 states and to another series of books that also celebrated America in its waterways in The Rivers of America series. Although many of these titles are now out of print, and have become collector's items, the information contained in these books is not only still highly pertinent but also ostensibly relevant to this day, which is an ongoing testament to the quality of the work the artists and writers accomplished, many of whom either were or became well-known. The WPA was, perhaps, one of the most successful socially-responsible work programs ever designed and legislated in history. See Malcolm Cowley, *The Dream of the Golden Mountains: Remembering the 1930s*, New York: Viking, 1980.

44. Schrieber, *The Predictable Surprise: The Unraveling of the U.S. Retirement System.*
45. Ibid.
46. Ibid.
47. Towers Watson, "The History of American Retirement and Future Social Security Reform," http://www.twoerswatson.com/en/Insights/Newsletters/Americas/Insider/2012An-American Ret...
48. Ibid.
49. Schrieber, *The Predictable Surprise: The Unraveling of the U.S. Retirement System.*
50. Ibid.
51. Ibid.
52. Towers Watson, "The History of American Retirement and Future Social Security Reform," http://www.twoerswatson.com/en/Insights/Newsletters/Americas/Insider/2012An-American Ret...
53. Ibid.
54. *The Predictable Surprise: The Unraveling of the U.S. Retirement System*, Schrieber.
55. Ibid.
56. Ibid.
57. "A Brief History of Retirement Plans in America: Keys to the IRA Kingdom," http://www.keystotheirakingdom.colm/blog/?p+230.

58. Ibid.
59. Ibid.
60. Ibid.
61. Ibid.
62. Ibid.
63. Georgetown University Law Center, "A Timeline of the Evolution of Retirement in the United States: Workplace Flexibility, 2010, http://scholarship.law.gerogetown.edu/legal/50.
64. Steven McCourt, *Defined Benefit and Defined Contribution Plans: A History, Market Overview, and Comparative Analysis*, 43 Benefits and Compensation Digest, 2006, http://www.ifebp.org/PDF/webexclusive/06feb.pdf.
65. Steven A. Sass, *The Promise of Private Pensions, The First Hundred Years*, at 9, 1997.
66. Ibid.
67. Joanna Short, *Economic History of Retirement in the United States*, Eh.Net Encyclopedia, Robert Whaples, Ed., 2002, http://eh.net/encyclopedia/article/short.retirement/hsitory.us.
68. There are two reasons age 65 was chosen as the age at which Social Security would begin. The first is that the few private pension plans existed then used 65 as a retirement age. The second is 50% of the 30 state pension systems then used 65 as a retirement age while the other 50% used age 70. See *Social Security Online, History, Frequently Asked Questions: The Origins of the Retirement Age in Social Security*. Also, another scholar posits that age 65 was chosen because policymakers contemporary to that era believed that workers experienced at least a slight decrease in mental and physical abilities. See Dora Costa, *The Evolution of Retirement, an American Economic History, 1880-1890*, at 11-12, 1998.
69. Steven A. Sass, *The Promise of Private Pensions, The First Hundred Years*, p.54.
70. Employee Benefits Research Institute, *History of Pension Plans*. http://www.ebri.org/publications/facts/index.dfm?fa+0398afact.
71. Steven A. Sass, *The Promise of Private Pensions, The First Hundred Years*, p.118.
72. Employee Benefits Research Institute, *History of Pension Plans*.

73. A legislative compromise was struck allowing for early reduced benefits rather than full retirement benefits at an earlier age. For a full discussion of this debate see Kathryn Moore, *Raising the Social Security Retirement Ages: Weighing the Costs and Balances*, 33 Ariz. St. L. J. 543, 549-50, Summer 2001.
74. Employee Benefits Research Institute, *History of Pension Plans*.
75. The primary justification of lowering the retirement age to 62 was that making benefits available would be of assistance to older workers who might be challenged in finding new employment if they were to lose their jobs. See Kathryn Moore, *Raising the Social Security Retirement Ages: Weighing the Costs and Balances*.
76. Employee Benefits Research Institute, *History of Pension Plans*.
77. Ibid.
78. Employee Benefits Research Institute, *The U.S. Retirement Income System*, April 2005, http://www.ebri.org/pdf/publications/facts/0405fact.pdf.
79. Peter Grandich, "Retirement Means Poverty for Many," *Resource Investor*, June 1, 2012, http://www.resourceinvestor.com/2012/06/01/retirement-means-poverty-for-many?page=3.
80. Ibid.
81. Ibid.
82. Ibid.
83. Ibid.
84. Ibid.
85. Ibid.
86. Ibid.
87. Ibid.
88. MelP, "A Brief History of Retirement in America," October 18, 2009, http://www.thenexthill.com/a-brief-history-of-retirement-in-america-part-1.htm.
89. Ibid.
90. The 1936 film comedy starring in and written by Charlie Chaplin, as the character known as "the Little Tramp" is both iconic and timeless. *Modern Times* (United Artists, 1936) was selected as a "culturally significant" film by the Library of Congress in 1989. Also, it was considered to be a historic film of social significance and chosen for preservation in the United States National Film

Registry. In 2003, *Modern Times* was screened "out of competition," an honor bestowed to the film at that year's Cannes Film Festival.
91. MelP, "A Brief History of Retirement in America."
92. Wikipedia, en.wikipedia.org/wiki/Synergy.

6. Biographical Literary Monograph
THE FRIENDSHIP OF ROBERT FRANCIS AND ROBERT FROST

When I introduced renowned woodblock artist Barry Moser at Trinity College, in Hartford, in October 2000 to celebrate the publication of *The Holy Bible: King James Version/The Pennyroyal Caxton Bible* (Viking, 1999), I spoke of the time I visited the Amherst poet, Robert Francis, and after returning from a trip into town to the local Rexall Pharmacy for certain prescriptions Robert needed, how we found a box of author's copies of *The Trouble with God*, a letterpress volume bound in boards and published by Moser's Pennyroyal Press, had been placed on the stone stoop. I mentioned how Robert requested that I read a chapter a week to him, as bands of sunlight streamed through the west windows in his living room those Monday afternoons during the autumn of 1984.

After finishing reading one chapter aloud, Robert leaned back in his rocking chair and quietly exclaimed, "I could sure think when I was a young man." The book contained some rather deep theological essays which were previously published in *The Christian Science Monitor* that Francis wrote during the 1950s. It is no light reading and the *thinking* Francis refers to is as crisp and clear as the writing is. When I had known Francis, he was suffering from age-related Macular degeneration (AMD), so I would read to him, open his mail; drive him into town check the electric meter by lifting the trapdoor in the galley kitchen, brushing away the resident fearsome-looking black house spiders there and their webs; and look up words he had saved all week so he could frame those definitions in his mind—colloquialisms such as *hogwash* or *monkeyshines*.

BIOGRAPHICAL LITERARY MONOGRAPH

Monday afternoons were the scheduled times for our visits. When I first brought my yellow Labrador, named Cider, Robert asked me to tie her up outside to one of the two posts on the stone porch stoop. It didn't take him very long to realize she was a well-behaved. She knew the visit was special, so she would lay in front of me with her chin on one of my boots, and Robert always enjoyed it when we all knew it was time to go, and she would begin to thump the rudder of her tail on the pine floor.

In 1986, when I was the manager and lead buyer (which included going to antiquarian book auctions) at the Globe Bookstore on Pleasant Street in Northampton, Massachusetts—no longer extant but at the time one of *the* literary bookstores in the area and a kind of Mecca for the *intelligentsia* since the likes of artist and sculptor Leonard Baskin visited multiple times per week—I was the co-director of *Readers and Writers Live!*, an author event series. During our first season, I asked Robert if he would be willing to read in the series. I didn't even give a thought to his ostensibly being blind, although he would surprise me, on occasion, and pick up a dust ball on the floor in the sunlight from his resident rocking chair. However, with the assistance of his literary trustees, he prepared a twenty-minute program. In fact, Robert had memorized the poem he was to read over a period of six months. When he read in October 1986 to a packed house at the Schoolhouse Commons Building in Northampton, it was no ordinary event. It was to be Robert's last reading. I had the occasion to both introduce him and to record the reading. That recording is collected in the Jones Library Special Collections in downtown Amherst.

An anecdote emblematic of my many glorious Monday afternoons spent in Robert's company at Fort Juniper, the nickname for Robert's cottage, built on a rise and away from the berm of Market Hill Road in Cushman, a village of Amherst, is one that regards coffee and Robert's Yankee *thrift*. A couple of weeks before the reading, Robert asked me if we would be serving coffee at the reading. Politely, I replied that I thought we might. Although I knew we had plans to offer wine, crackers, and cheese. Then Robert asked me to go to the large hutch which was situated to the right of the front door, to look into a certain drawer, and to open the cigar box contained in it. When I did so, I saw a plethora of shiny white plastic teaspoons. Robert suggested that we use them at the reading when serving coffee. It was his small contribution to the event—other than himself, his voice, and his poetry.

I brought the plastic spoons home and washed each one, dutifully brought them to reading, and although I made sure to have some coffee available, don't believe anyone had any, since the wine, crackers, and cheese were consumed in a flash by the sizeable audience that attended the event. Afterwards, I returned the plastic spoons to Robert's, stored them back into the cigar box in the drawer in the hutch, but could not quite let go of the idea of Robert's assemblage of plastic spoons.

Some years later, I found out that Robert had a special room upstairs at the Jones Library where the librarians would allow Robert to write on a daily basis. I have seen the room. It overlooks the main intersection in town and the brick building that was once a hat factory when Emily Dickson was alive, which now houses the offices of Blair, Cutting, and Smith upstairs and, where there was once the Rexall Pharmacy, there is now a Subway Sandwich Shop. It is a quiet and a cozy space. Certainly this is where some of the hushed stillness and unobtrusive goodness of some of Robert's poems were composed there. However, and this is key with respect to those plastic spoons, here is where the thoughtful Jones Library librarians, at the time, would serve Robert a cup of coffee every morning. And, yes, Robert saved every one of those plastic spoons—a testament to his Yankee thrift and the mystery unveiled as to the abundance, many years later, of all of those plastic spoons in

BIOGRAPHICAL LITERARY MONOGRAPH

the cigar box (Robert never smoked by the way), which eventually made it the final poetry reading of his career, without their ever being used. I will forever be bemused by this episode of the plastic spoons. It makes me smile every time I think about them and about Robert's prudence and frugality.

After Robert's death in July 1987, upon his wishes, and through the efforts of his literary trustees, Fort Juniper was offered as a writer's or artist's residency. First the sills of the cottage would need to be repaired, but beginning in 1990, Fort Juniper was offered to a writer or artist every year from September 1st to August 31st. Sometimes a resident was given a second year. The first guest of Fort Juniper who was awarded a residency was poet Jack Gilbert. Some of the other residents have included not only poets but dancers, musicians, and painters. Although I never thought I would become a resident for any number of reasons, I was awarded a residency in September 1998, only to need to rescind my residency due to my being offered at job at Trinity College, and a daily commute to Hartford from Amherst, especially in winter was out of the question.

When I left Fort Juniper in December 1998, part of me palpably rued my departure, another part of me looked forward to a new adventure. By 2001, I assessed I had enough of urban living, although I grew as a writer, in leaps and bounds through my return to Connecticut, largely by my affiliation with the Sunken Garden Poetry Festival, which is held at the Hill-Stead Museum, in Farmington. It was there I especially relished working with gifted high school students in preparing them for their reading in the festival in The Night of Fresh Voices Program, which I served as mentor and teacher for three summers.

Spontaneously, I met both Jack Gilbert and Linda Gregg at a *soiree* held by mutual friends. I had already known them both. In speaking with Linda, who was the second resident of Fort Juniper, she suggested that I request another residency, and to petition the major trustee, poet Henry Lyman, who lived in Northampton. As Linda's voice whispered in my ear that evening, I fortuitously heard her voice whispering to me once again in the spring of 2003, and taking that as a sign, I contacted Henry Lyman, who informed me that there was an opening at Fort Juniper that coming September, but reminded me that I had left the last time I was there, and that convincing the other trustees might take some doing. However, Henry phoned me back in a couple of weeks and informed me that I had been accepted *again*, and that I was welcome to begin my residency in September.

I not only reveled in my year there but was also awarded a second year, so that I resided at Fort Juniper from September 2003 through August 2005. My stay was richly productive since I composed what was later to become nearly all of the poems in my collection of poetry, *Huang Po and the Dimensions of Love,* which was selected by Pulitzer Prize-winning poet Yusef Komunyakaa for the 2011 Crab Orchard Series Open Poetry Competition, and which was published by Southern Illinois University Press. Although I first wrote much of the work at Fort Juniper from 2003-2005, I spent another several years honing and revising the manuscript to what it was to finally become. In all, I spent seven years working on the collection of 62 poems, including the sequencing of the poems, which was key to the success of the book as a whole, since they are segued together, without section breaks, much like what W. S. Merwin accomplishes in his books, where the poems are juxtaposed one after another like wood in a parquet floor.

When I refer to Fort Juniper in polite conversation, I normally refer to it as a cottage, but in my poems I call it a cabin. It is, indeed, small: a galley kitchen, bathroom with a soapstone shower, bedroom, and dining area/living room, which includes a hearth and fireplace. My friendship with Robert Francis, those memories of my visiting him, and my own living at Fort

BIOGRAPHICAL LITERARY MONOGRAPH

Juniper are all watershed years in my life. They are inimitable touchstones and without them I wouldn't be the writer I am today. Tantamount to that, knowing Robert Francis and my experience of living at Fort Juniper has become such a part of me that I have been able to bring all of that forward, along with me—since the years I knew Robert and had lived at Fort Juniper as one of its residents. Where I live now, and have lived since my residency at Robert's cottage, in a refurbished farmhouse in South Amherst for the last dozen years, along a stretch of protected farmland, is an extension of my creative life that I so richly mined at Fort Juniper.

My most significant years as a writer were precipitated by the Fort Juniper experience, what I refer to as its stony Thomas Merton-like solitude; an ascetic life which included the bite of the frigid winter mornings there, warmed only by propane heat that issued from slats in the kitchen stove; the delicious coolness during summer days beneath the canopy of the tall trunks in the surrounding grove of white pine. Fort Juniper will always be one of my favorite homes. I love where I live now—the quiet of the farm flats broken by the moaning of the black Angus across the road during rutting season; the snowflakes falling over the open expanse of the south meadow, and Long Mountain, the easternmost promontory of the Holyoke Range, in the near distance; the windbreak of white pine on the northern edge of the property with their ragged green branches having been shapeshifted by miles and miles of wind.

However, I directly owe much of my mature writing life to Robert Francis and Fort Juniper. The essay I enclose here was precipitated by my being invited to deliver a lecture at the Frost Farm in Derry, New Hampshire in August 2002. Upon first writing the essay, I had been asked to connect my affiliation with that of Robert Francis and his friendship with Robert Frost. I read the result of that writing in the Frost barn during one of the hottest days that summer to a rather loyal, but

THE FRIENDSHIP OF ROBERT FRANCIS AND ROBERT FROST

small, audience: loyal because only one person left, and they apologized for doing so, because they had something previously scheduled; and small because there may have been no more than two dozen ardent admirers of poetry, and largely of Robert Frost, that sweated through my delivery of my lecture, which lasted an hour and a half.

The lecture was then rewritten and revised, and then submitted to Constance Hunting, one of American poetry's guardian angels, who was the founder and editor of *Puckerbrush Review*, in Orono, Maine. She had founded the journal with the advance from Charles Scribner for her premier book of poetry, *After the Stravinsky Concert and Other Poems*, which was published in 1969. She began the magazine in 1971. Although I was quite grateful to Constance for publishing the lengthy essay and accommodating all of that space in one of the issues of her journal, I was discouraged by a grad student of hers who had made so many typos in retyping the essay into another format that was needed by the printer. However, I was ameliorated by Constance calling the essay, "a significant work of scholarship, previously unwritten."

In 2009, I had been selected as perhaps a half dozen New England poets to read at the 50th Anniversary of the Modern Language Association Conference held in Boston. During that conference I spoke with Herbert Richardson, Editor of The Edwin Mellen Press, primarily a publisher of Ph.D. dissertations and a distinguished academic publishing house. After speaking with him regarding my idea for the essay as a biographical literary monograph, he offered me a contract to sign, within twenty minutes. Publishing the essay without typographical errors, and with footnotes and an index was an experience I delighted in.

Although the title the book was given is *The Friendship of Two New England Poets: Robert Frost and Robert Francis,* inflecting

BIOGRAPHICAL LITERARY MONOGRAPH

Frost for obvious marketing reasons, I present the essay herein, with some further polishing, in its original title, which Constance Hunting published in *Puckerbrush Review*: "High-pressure Weather and Country Air: The Friendship of Robert Francis and Robert Frost." The essay really is about Francis's friendship with Frost and not the other way around.

With that in mind, I believe it is germane of me to offer three poems I either wrote for Robert Francis or wrote after one of his poems. "Sweet Woodruff" is a poem I wrote in 1986 or 1987, during the time I was visiting Robert. "Tone Poem for Summer Solstice" is a poem I worked on for some years after a walk in Northwest Park in Windsor, Connecticut, a veritable nature reserve near Bradley Airport, and is written in the spirit of Robert's poems consisting of mostly nouns. I finished the poem in 2011. "Skiers" is a recent poem written in 2016, after Robert's poem, "Skiers," and similarly explores the ethos of the athlete and the sport as does Francis in his own original poem.

When Robert's manuscript, *The Orb Weaver*, which Richard Wilbur praised, was accepted by Wesleyan University Press, as one of its original titles, he mentioned to Frost that he was pleased by this because the book would be issued by a university press in *his New England*. My experience in knowing Robert Francis and in living at Fort Juniper is emblematic of finding delight in *my New England*—paralleling Robert's deep love of the sense of place that emanates from the land itself and its rocky soil and pine woods.

Sweet Woodruff
for Robert Francis

Those slips of sweet woodruff
you gave as gift stand in tribute
to our visits. We brought fruit,

looked up words you had saved
so they could be as crystalline as
our friendship, and grounded in trust,

like those slips of sweet woodruff
that have taken root with an aroma
that permeates our memory.

* * * *

Tone Poem for Summer Solstice
after Robert Francis

Say oxeye daisy tansy yarrow orange hawkweed
purple clover Say skipper mourning cloak silver-

bordered fritillary monarch clouded sulfur Say
blue-eyed grass blue toadflax ragged robin *rosa*

rugosa shinleaf *pyrola* jewelweed white campion
Say bluebird swallow purple martin Say dragonfly

honey bee bald-faced hornet Say downy brome
curly dock barnyard grass hop clover Say warbler

* * * *

Skiers
after Robert Francis

They unroll strokes in a scroll of incandescent
calligraphy down the slope,

flaring white powder behind them across the blue
snow shadow of the mountain.

BIOGRAPHICAL LITERARY MONOGRAPH

>The sibilance of their skis only increases the quiet
>within them as they write their signatures
>
>in the weave of the slalom
>in their descent, leaving behind them the sound of
>
>the wind in the pines.
>They finish in a flourish, the blades of their skis
>
>cutting grooves into
>the snow crust as they brake their motion in wide
>
>arcs at the bottom,
>taking their entire run down with them as they might
>
>spangle a ribbon in
>its many arcs, in not only an act of strength but also
>
>to exhibit what is essential—
>a resplendent aesthetic; pure form in a cold world
>
>of white on white; agility then speed in a display
>of inner fire, sheer release.

HIGH-PRESSURE WEATHER AND COUNTRY AIR: THE FRIENDSHIP OF ROBERT FRANCIS AND ROBERT FROST

A Lecture Delivered at The Frost Farm, Derry, New Hampshire

I was initially introduced to Robert Francis in the summer of 1982 when, on one of his walks into downtown Amherst, he paid a spontaneous visit to the Jeffrey Amherst Bookshop where I held the position of paperback book buyer. The owner of the store, Howard Gerstein, asked me to help Francis sign cloth copies of his *Collected Poems, 1936-1976* (Amherst: University of Massachusetts Press, 1976). The assistance I was called on to deliver was to hold each book open as Robert signed it, since his hands sometimes shook uncontrollably. He was sporting a distinguished straw hat with a black band, and although I remember him being thin to the point of emaciation, he was tan and in the appearance of good health. It was only later, after assisting him with the signing of his books, that I learned he not only walked into town, but also walked back to his home on Market Hill Road in Cushman, three and one half miles away.

Over the next two years, I would occasionally observe Robert walking in Cushman, North Amherst, and Shutesbury. His presence possessed a sunny quality, but perhaps this is because I would often see him walking in the morning, and I may have associated the light of summer mornings with his coming and going. It was at this time I began not only to read his poems, but also to espouse his work to anyone who appeared puzzled as what to read when standing in front of the poetry section at the Jeffrey Amherst Bookshop, as well as other bookshops I was later to serve as manage and buyer. I was surprised, if not astonished, at the number of Amherst readers and residents who had not heard of the man or his work. It was at this time I began to refer to him publicly as someone who had composed several dozen perfect poems that could be used as examples in defining *what poetry could be*.

After quite coincidentally moving into an apartment in a refurbished barn on East Leverett Road in Cushman in July of 1984, I actually met Francis only a few months later that early autumn. Not unlike Mrs. Hopkins, whom he both describes in his autobiography as "extraordinary" and "a born entrepreneur," who had Francis chauffeur her, as a ruse, to a certain house on Sunset Avenue in Amherst where Robert Frost lived, my late wife, Donna, also devised an impromptu drive upon which, in quite a circuitous fashion, we eventually found ourselves in front of his home on Market Hill Road. What she could not plan for, however, or implement, but was in keeping with both the felicity and serendipity of my meeting Francis, was that Robert was outside in his garden in full regalia with his straw hat holding a brimful of sunlight.

Although I balked at Donna's suggestion of getting out of the car and announcing to Robert that I had recently become a neighbor of his in Cushman, it was too late. He seemed to be already aware of the presence of the orange Volkswagen parked near his mailbox just beyond his driveway in the shade of the tall white pines that bordered his land. After I decided to risk rejection, I approached him and began to speak. We may have interchanged only a few sentences at the most. It appeared as if Robert had been expecting me, and I was just fashionably late. His face opened with a radiance that assured me he was gentle, genuine, and kind-hearted. I spoke to him about my interest and support of his work, that I had Mondays off from my new job as manager of Johnson's Secondhand Bookstore in Springfield, and queried him as to the possibility of paying him an extended visit someday. I believe I also nervously inserted somewhere the information that I was attempting to become

THE FRIENDSHIP OF ROBERT FRANCIS AND ROBERT FROST

a serious writer. Francis suggested that "tomorrow afternoon about one o'clock" would be fine. It would be my first Monday afternoon visit with Robert. I felt he had already befriended me. It was a relationship that would extend to the last two and a half years of his life, whereupon he would not only become a dear friend, but a kindly mentor, and whereupon I would only miss three of those Monday visits over the course of the next two and a half years.

What I could not foresee were not only the years, but also the decades, to follow. In the years I would visit Francis I would look up words he had saved during the week for such a purpose as referencing them in his large clothbound edition of *The Merriam-Webster Dictionary*, which took up my entire lap. We would also make trips into Amherst to pick up refills of his prescriptions from the Rexall Pharmacy, at the main intersection in the center of town (where a Subway Sandwich Shop is now), and several containers of Ensure in an attempt to boost his weight. Robert also agreed to do what was to be his last poetry reading for me in *The Readers & Writers Live* series sponsored by the Globe Bookshop in Northampton where I would continue to further my career as a bookstore manager and a buyer. Although, quite naively, I would totally disregard his blindness, he could not. This was not a display of my insensitivity to him, but by my exhibiting the peculiar trait we humans possess of often being unable to be fully aware of the physical limitations of those we love, especially when those individuals are elderly or infirmed. Robert would spend the next six months, with the help of his literary trustees, committing twenty minutes of his poetry to memory. Fortunately, I exercised the prudence to record the reading, and to make a gift of a copy of the tape to Special Collections of the Jones Library in Amherst. Jones Library is significant not only because it is where Robert was given a room in which to write, but also where carefully assembled Emily Dickinson and Robert Frost memorabilia, along with Francis material, are exhibited behind glass.

I would also open and read Robert's mail to him at his direction, nearly always make the gift of fruit or some holiday treat, and on occasion open the trap door in his tiny kitchen to climb down the three steps to read the electric meter. It was not infrequent when I would read new work to him. Although these were new poems, they were very scrupulously chosen. Sometimes Robert would say absolutely nothing, make no suggestions, and the very air would become heavy with his silence, but he would smile and we would move on to something else. Other times, he would phrase his words with deliberate appreciation, and would remark, "That poem will be included in your next collection." Once or twice he even said, in response to the short nature poems and haiku I was writing at the time, "Never stop writing those poems." Then he would pause before continuing: "In those poems you write about what you love."

One week before the last reading Francis was ever to give, in October 1986, I visited him. Robert asked me to open a specific drawer in the large hutch that extended from floor to ceiling in his living room to the right of his front door. In the drawer, Robert instructed me to take out a cigar box. He told me to open the box, and in the box were dozens upon dozens of shiny white plastic spoons.

He asked me if I had planned to have coffee at his reading, and I politely responded that I was unsure, but that we might. He then suggested that whatever the case may be that I take the spoons with me, and to make good use of them. The plastic spoons contained in the cigar box had all been saved by Robert from his writing room in the Jones Library where the librarians supplied him with coffee. I not only took this as a testament of his Yankee prudence but also as his penchant for Thoreau-like simplicity. Francis wasted little, if anything. Although he was awarded with an Academy of American Poets Fellowship for *distinguished poetic achievement* in 1984, that brought him several thousand dollars, just before his death, few individuals,

THE FRIENDSHIP OF ROBERT FRANCIS AND ROBERT FROST

if any, could have survived as well as he did on an annual income of an average of only six or seven hundred dollars a year. I remain unsure, but I believe it was at this time I began to refer to Robert Francis as *a secular saint*.

The final salient anecdote I need to offer with respect to Francis is to recount our drive to Northampton on the night of what was his last reading that was held at the Northampton Center for the Arts in the Old Schoolhouse Building near the gates of Smith College. Robert whistled as I drove across the Calvin Coolidge Bridge over the Connecticut River and farther into the autumn dusk that flamed above the horizon of the city. He asked me, rather nonchalantly, what I thought of Thoreau. Robert then hinted that Thoreau could have possibly achieved more if he had been aware of the soybean and the nourishment and protein that it provides. He concluded that: "Thoreau lived at Walden Pond for only twenty-six months, but I have lived like Thoreau in my home at Fort Juniper for over forty-five years."

Robert Francis was born in Upland, Pennsylvania on August 12, 1901. For a rather tongue-in-cheek and thoroughly delightful account of his life, I highly recommend *The Trouble with Francis: An Autobiography by Robert Francis* (Amherst: University of Massachusetts Press, 1971). For my purposes here, however, I need to begin with Robert's arrival in Amherst in 1926 to teach English at the high school. Francis, fresh out of Harvard where he earned both his undergraduate degree and master's degree in education, began his years in Amherst by living with his father, Reverend Ebenezer F. Francis, who had taken over as pastor of the South Amherst Baptist Church.

Although Robert Francis had seen Robert Frost passing on the street or engaged in conversation with Charles R. Green, Head Librarian of the Jones Library, at the Amherst Post Office, it was not until January 24, 1933 that the two actually met. Francis writes in his journal for this date, briefly, but with unforgettable resonance: "Today I started a savings account with a ten-dollar deposit; and I met Robert Frost.[1]

Francis had published a poem, entitled "Robert Frost in Amherst" in the *Springfield Republican and Union*, the previous April, honoring and welcoming Frost who had just purchased a home on Sunset Avenue in Amherst. However, it was not until after the New Year did Francis and Frost meet through what I interpret as a kind of maternal concern exhibited by Mrs. Arthur John Hopkins (Margaret Briscoe Hopkins) for Francis. She arranged the meeting by asking Francis to be so kind as to drive her to an errand she needed tending to *somewhere in town*. While Francis waited outside of the Frost home on Sunset Avenue, she broke the ice by showing Frost a copy of the poem published in the *Republican*.

Francis writes in his autobiography about his previous years in Amherst without making contact with Frost:

"That I had lived over six years in the town of Amherst without meeting Frost, without being introduced to him by anybody or bumping into him by chance, is evidence of several things: my obscurity, my timidity, my caution, and my pride. I was unwilling to face him with nothing to bring, nothing to show. I could endure well enough being a nobody, but not when confronting so much of a somebody."[2]

Francis describes meeting Frost as follows:

"On the aforementioned evening she (Mrs. Hopkins) told me she had an errand somewhere in town and asked me to chauffeur her. We drove down to Sunset Avenue and stopped in front of a Victorian sort of house standing well back from the street. Leaving me behind, she went up to the door and disappeared. Within a few moments Robert Frost came out on the porch, peered down at me through the darkness, and beckoned me to come up and in. I remember how white his hair looked under the bright porch light. He was then not quite fifty-nine. When I went in with him, I found that Mrs. Hopkins had shown him my little tribute of a poem.

"If I ask myself what it was in Frost that impressed, attracted, and fascinated me most in the years before I met him as well as in the years afterwards, the answer is power. He was a poet and he had power; the combination was striking. According to popular notion at least, a poet, however good he may be in his poetry is otherwise generally ineffectual and inadequate. But here was a poet to whom the stock jokes couldn't be applied. He was a match for any man he ran into on the street, and usually more than a match. He could speak to any man in that man's language and on that man's terms, be he banker, merchant, farmer, senator, college president, or U. S. President. You had only to catch a glimpse of him anywhere to sense his solidarity, his weight, his sanity. And his power was not in spite of his being a poet but because of it. Everything had come first from the poems, poems that in themselves could speak to any man or so it seemed. They were poems no one could dismiss or laugh aside. They had a sureness, a balance, a relevance that was like a fact of nature. But though the poems were the basis of his ascendancy, the man himself kept increasing and enriching that ascendancy. Unlike some poets he always seemed more than his poems, inexhaustible. What he said was fresher and terser than what others said. Like a boxer his mind stood on tiptoe for the next parry and thrust. People listened because they were too fascinated not to. Yet no matter how playful and teasing his words, his face kept its Newfoundland gravity, its Great Dane sadness. What made Frost's power the more impressive was, of course, its effortlessness. Celebrity? A plain man, rather bulky, white-haired, going about his business."³

And about the first meeting of Frost, Francis concludes:

"... Even in my poetry I felt myself so little the poet that I didn't want to be called one. I suppose that if I hadn't felt so deficient my contact with Frost could not have been so exhilarating. It was tonic, life-enhancing, like high-pressure weather and county air.

"Frost never smiled in greeting me at the door. He simply looked me in the eye gravely, candidly, mildly, then led the way to his study. It was not so much his not smiling that struck me—after all he was not given to much smiling—as it was that cool, level glance, that utter absence of mask or role. It set the tone of our friendship. And, of course, it contrasted with other Frosts, especially the platform Frost so conscious of his audience and of himself. When he came to the door and merely looked at me, I felt I was confronting the essential man."

Francis continues, "If I had brought some of my new poems, he would slump down in his big leather chair and go through them broodingly, mumbling them to himself. I had the uncanny feeling that he was inside my poem and that anything he said about them would be from inside. What he said was brief and unforgettable.

"... Everything he touched on was so interesting that one didn't question just why he should be touching on it. He could just start anywhere and end anywhere. Like a Roman fountain he just kept on flowing."[4]

At this point, I think it is clear that in my presenting Francis's impressions of Frost that I am offering salient characteristics of Frost as well as those of Francis, and we will see how the two personalities blended, melded, and reciprocated one another. Although, to buttress my dubbing Francis a *secular saint*, I believe this is corroborated by the following passage, again from the autobiography. If anything, by quoting this passage, it should serve to flesh out the man.

THE FRIENDSHIP OF ROBERT FRANCIS AND ROBERT FROST

"I have already spoken of my need for a balance between people and no people, between literary people and plain people. Another trinity of values was even more distinct in my mind: nature, leisure, solitude. If these words sound pale and conventional, what they meant to me was vivid and precise. By "nature" I meant the whole heavens and earth except for those spots where human concentration was a blight and poison. I meant sun and sky and clouds and hills and rain and rivers and snow and country roads and farms and country people. By "leisure" I meant not the absence of work but time for the work I most wanted to do. I meant the obliteration of the line between work and play. By "solitude" I meant the freedom to choose from hour to hour whether to be with friends or alone."⁵

Francis's home—nicknamed by him as Fort Juniper, because juniper, he assessed, was indestructible—was constructed out of *hurricane pine,* or the trees felled by the devastating hurricane of 1938, that served as inexpensive building material. The Francis home still stands today, nearly eighty years later. After his death, the trustees of the Francis estate have maintained the house as a residence for artists and writers. In recounting Frost's first visit to his home, Francis writes:

"His first visit here was on May 21, 1950, when Fort Juniper was nearly ten years old. His delay in coming was partly due, no doubt, to the fact that my house was built at a time when he was not associated with Amherst College (1938-1946) and was coming to town less often and more briefly than either before or later."⁶

However, it is Francis's interpretation of Frost that is striking. It is striking because of his intimation that Frost's visits, infrequent as they were, provided him more than just calling on someone whom he considered a friend and an ally. By visiting Francis, Frost not only enjoyed the aesthetics and utility of Fort Juniper but found it a place that facilitated relaxed conversation.

Francis writes, "If he came first partly out of curiosity, he continued to come because Fort Juniper proved the best possible place for uninterrupted conversation. Perhaps he had a special reason to feel at home here since my house was comparable to his cabin in Ripton, Vermont. I think he liked to think that he and I lived in much the same way, whereas some young poets he knew might talk about doing something like this but never did.

"There were three Frosts I knew. First was the Frost of the poems, the man in or behind the poems. This Frost I met years before I met the poet himself face to face. Second was the platform Frost, the mischievous, teasing sparkling entertainer. And not on the platform only but at any evening gathering where he sat in a comfortable chair and did all the talking and sparkled from first to last. The third Frost was the man I sat across from when there were just the two of us (with at most one other in the room). Completely relaxed, no effort to shine now, the tone kindly rather than teasing still. He did most of the talking and he talked mostly about himself, yet this always seemed the most natural thing in the world for him to do (as indeed it was) and equally natural for any hearer to want to listen to.

"One thing I know is that what he said to me about my work was immensely encouraging, and I believe his criticism and appreciation of other younger poets *must have been equally sensitive and generous.*"[7]

In appraising Francis's first volume, *Stand with Me Here* (New York: Macmillan, 1936), Frost wrote in a letter to Francis:

"I am swept off my feet by the goodness of your poems this time. Ten or a dozen of them are my idea of perfection. A new poet arrives into my ken. I can't refrain from strong praise no longer. You are achieving what you live for. I shall always honor Dave for his part in your coming out. You have not only the feeling of a true lyric poet, but the variety of a man with a mind."[8]

THE FRIENDSHIP OF ROBERT FRANCIS AND ROBERT FROST

Although Francis may have appeared to lack passion by some observers, it was Frost who consistently reiterated that the younger poet had quite a mind of his own. The *Dave* referred to in Frost's letter is David Morton, a professor of English at Amherst College, who was nearly solely responsible for seeing *Stand with Me Here*, Francis's first book of poetry, into print, since he was a reader for Macmillan at this time. Morton also had a hand in the publication of Francis's second volume, *Valhalla and Other Poems*, that he also recommended for publication to Macmillan. Francis was awarded the prestigious Shelley Memorial Award after the publication of *Valhalla and Other Poems* in 1938.

Not unlike the construction of *The Trouble with Francis: An Autobiography by Robert Francis*, that does not follow a chronological timetable, but is more *Janus-faced* in its approach of looking backward and forward into time, it is at this point I would like to bring attention to yet another visit of Frost's to Fort Juniper. In doing so, I will also cite the recording of a subsequent visit to prove, in my estimation, the reconciliation of the two poets from what appears to be the only transgression in their friendship.

Francis lists Frost's visits from memory, and recounts the essential facts of this specific one:

"I think he came to Fort Juniper nine times between 1950 and 1959, twice with Armour Craig, twice with Charles Green, twice with Hyde Cox, and twice with Samuel French Morse. Once he came and went by taxi.

"This taxi visit occurred on October 30, 1956. The weather was mild enough for us to sit outdoors for a while, but as a precaution I put around Mr. Frost a big sheet of cardboard as a screen against the light breeze. He said it reminded him of a time long past when he and Ezra Pound had been in a London restaurant together. Pound had spouted poetry so loudly that a waiter came and put a screen around them."⁹

It is important to note here Francis's solicitousness with regard to Frost. Also, it is significant to mention that Francis always referred to Frost directly as "Mr. Frost," and *never* on a first name basis as *Robert*.

I have chosen to splice Francis's continuation of the description of this momentous visit of Frost's from *Frost: A Time To Talk; Conversations and Indiscretions Recorded by Robert Francis* because it is fuller, richer, and more complete:

"As soon as we came in, I built a fire in the fireplace. F. had mentioned my being in *The Faber Book of Modern American Verse*. Since he spoke of the book again but hadn't seen a copy, I got out mine and sat beside him on the couch. I had the pleasure of showing him the place of honor of his poem "The Gift Outright." He liked the other selections from his poems too, and made comments on them. Surprised that the Grafton witch rather than the witch of Coos had been chosen. I suggested that Auden might have been influenced by Randall Jarrell's praise of that poem. F. said he had not read what R. J. had written. "Two Look at Two" he had sent to Harper's long ago but it was returned by them. H. S. Canby had advised them that it was not up to F's standard. They haven't got anything of mine since. "Design," though published *rather recently*, was written early. "Never Again Would Bird's Song Be the Same" had never been singled out before. He was glad that two of his later poems were included, " The Middleness of the Road" and "Directive." The latter, he said, had been made much of, but the former had aroused little attention.

"Then he turned to my poems. He seemed familiar with the first two. When he came to the third, "Apple Peeler," something remarkable happened. I was still sitting beside him.

"Oh," he exclaimed with a mischievous smile and looking round at me as if he had caught me in the act, "this poem." At first I hadn't the faintest idea of what he was getting at. But he kept smiling at me and making hints, and at last I caught on. He thought I was taking a dig at him in the poem, possibly that the whole poem was really about him. He supposed that his sonnet "The Silken Tent" was the only sonnet in one sentence in the English language. He suspected, therefore, that he was the "virtuoso" turning out "trick" poems after his real inspiration had been exhausted. What a thought! I hardly knew what to say to disabuse him. I didn't deny that I knew about his sonnet and that it might have been in my mind when writing the poem. But I insisted that I had not been thinking of him in particular, certainly not trying to disparage him, or that I used the word "trick" in a disparaging sense even as applied to the actual apple peeler. I could see he was not entirely convinced. "Mr. Frost," I said, "your poem 'The Silken Tent' is as beautiful as anything you ever did, and there is no trick about it. As for sonnets in one sentence, David Morton does them all the time."

"He does, does he?" asked F. with a trace of mischief in his smile. "Then that makes it all right."[10]

I take this opportunity to quote each poem. Although "The Silken Tent" does not figure prominently in this particular argument, at least in regard to strict comparison with "Apple Peeler," per se, I cite it for the sake of clarity. In doing so, I attempt to corroborate Francis's saying to Frost that his achievement in the poem was as beautiful as anything he ever did.

Apple Peeler

Why the unbroken spiral, Virtuoso,
Like a trick sonnet in one long, versatile sentence?

BIOGRAPHICAL LITERARY MONOGRAPH

> Is it a pastime merely, this perfection,
> For an old man, sharp knife, long night, long winter?
>
> Or do your careful fingers move at the stir
> Of unadmitted immemorial magic?
>
> Solitaire. The ticking clock. The apple
> Turning, turning as the round earth turns.[11]

This poem, as well, is included in *New Poems by American Poets* (New York: Ballantine Books, 1953), *The Orb Weaver* (Middletown: Wesleyan University Press, 1960), *Come Out into the Sun: Poems New and Selected* (Amherst: University of Massachusetts Press, 1965), that in my opinion should have been kept in print because it presents the best selection of Francis's poems in the most accessible format, and *Robert Francis: Collected Poems, 1936-1976* (Amherst: University of Massachusetts Press, 1976). I only list the above bibliographic information to prove that Francis thought so highly of "Apple Peeler" he reprinted it several collections, and in doing so displayed that he had nothing to be ashamed of.

Now, to quote the sonnet in one sentence of Frost's.

The Silken Tent

> She is as in a field a silken tent
> At midday when a sunny summer breeze
> Has dried the dew and all its ropes relent,
> So that in guys it gently sways at ease,
> And its supporting central cedar pole,
> That is its pinnacle to heavenward
> And signifies the sureness of the soul,
> Seems to owe naught to any single cord,
> But strictly held by none, is loosely bound
> By countless silken ties of love and thought

> To everything on earth the compass round,
> And only by one's going slightly taught
> In the capriciousness of summer air
> Is of the slightest bondage made aware.¹²

As Francis has made apparent, he attempted that afternoon to plead with Frost that he had meant nothing untoward in the poem. He also reveals that:

"He had fallen into the very error that he took other people to task for: reading into a poem what was not there and failing to see what was. My poem was not about an old poet but about an old apple peeler, and the person responsible for the image was no other than old Mrs. Boynton, the Mrs. Bemis of *We Fly Away*."¹³

The trouble, perhaps, could have been prevented if Francis had used the feminine pronoun in the poem if, as he offers, Mrs. Boynton, an Amherst resident from whom Francis rented a room and for whom he performed various chores and odd jobs, inspired the character to whom the poem is attributed to. *We Fly Away* (Chicago & New York: Alan Swallow & William Morrow, 1948) is the title of Francis's only published novel. Mrs. Boynton, portrayed as Mrs. Bemis, is one of the book's gentle and wise protagonists.

On April 24, 1959, Frost paid Francis his next visit, accompanied by Samuel French Morse, professor of English at Mount Holyoke College at the time and later at Northeastern University. Although there is a lapse of two and half years without a visit from Frost, the recounting of the two hour visit by Francis is without the least intimation of any lingering animosity between Frost and himself. On the contrary, Frost is stated to have left with a bottle of Francis's homemade dandelion wine and a pair of magnifying glasses Francis had recently purchased for which Frost exhibited a fondness. Francis even recounts that he thought Frost had made off with his recipe for dandelion wine, but later found it *tucked inside a book*.

It is my belief that Frost exonerated Francis from any *mischief* he might have initially indicted him with due to his writing and publishing of "Apple Peeler." And I believe that Francis had forgiven Frost for originally making the accusation in the first place, or in the very least, let the incident go by the boards, especially in the fashion he recounted it personally to me. Even before I had come to read accounts of Frost's initial misunderstanding of "Apple Peeler" in either *The Trouble with Francis* or *Frost: A Time To Talk*, Francis referred to the event in quite a congenial manner. He brought the anecdote to my attention one Monday afternoon quite spontaneously, and in doing so spoke to me of it with his characteristic trace of humor, that was in my opinion, directed at both parties.

A difference worth noting between the two poets was how each managed *success*. And where the two poets perhaps differed most remarkably may have been in *the way* they lived. Although both Frost and Francis can be described as having embraced living in rural New England and were naturalists in love with its nature, these differences are best relayed by Francis with, I might add, an amount of alacrity.

"Of all the memorable things I heard Robert Frost say, two have stuck in my mind most persistently and have continued to tease me. Sitting in my home on the evening of December 10, 1950, he remarked casually that he had never lifted a finger to advance his career and that what had come to him had just come to him.

"I thought how magnificent it was that success, recognition, and high honor could come to a man without his seeking them, indeed, could come all the more because he had not sought them. At the same time I was asking myself how this policy might apply to me. If I lifted not a finger to advance my career, what would happen? Precisely nothing. My problem was not whether or not to lift a finger but how to lift it. I felt there were appropriate ways and inappropriate ways for me to exert myself, and I had faith that the appropriate ways had the better chance of being effective.

"After Frost's death when his letters to Louis Untermeyer were published I discovered a Frost I had never known, a fourth Robert Frost, shall we say? What I had taken him to mean by not having lifted a finger was evidently not what he meant."[14]

I believe the simple interpretation of these last passages of Francis may be unabashedly obvious. Frost moved through the real world and through the world of poetry with confidence and savvy. Francis chose to live rather steadfastly on his own terms, but it was removed from the world, and oftentimes his living his life was apart from the world of poetry as well.

Francis further addresses the question of the differences of *the way* they lived their lives as follows.

"The other thing I keep thinking about is a question he asked me (on October 23, 1952). "What do you do when you're not actually writing?

"That he could ask such a question made me feel helpless to answer it. But he scarcely waited for an answer. 'You can't just lie on your back,' he added. And then he spoke of something he had learned to do to fill up his time, something both useful and recreational: sharpening the cutter bar of the mowing machine.

"Frost may have thought that he and I lived in much the same way, but how vastly different our daily lives were! His life was all laissez-faire except for the poetry. He gave himself to that and let everything else take care of itself. There was always somebody to do the needed things he hadn't done or had only half done. He puttered about his farm. Now and then he prepared a meal.

BIOGRAPHICAL LITERARY MONOGRAPH

"But if I didn't prepare my meals, I wouldn't be eating. Marketing, cooking, dish-washing. Washing, ironing, mending, bed-making, floor-mopping. Gardening, grass-cutting, leaf-raking, snow-shoveling. Storm windows off and screens on, screens off and storm windows on. And then the letters to answer and the books to get from the libraries and return on time. The entertaining of friends, the refreshments to serve that wouldn't be served if I didn't do it, and always the dishes. If I wanted flower wine to offer my guests, I had to gather the blossoms and go through the whole procedure myself; and if I wanted wild grape jelly to sweeten the coming winter, I had to find and gather the wild grapes and do everything to the pouring of the hot wax. To say nothing of music: violin, piano, recordings. Yes, to say nothing of many things.

" . . . If he could ask what I did to keep from being bored and lazy, then what did anybody know about me?

" . . . If anyone had reason or excuse to be incessantly busy about important things, it was he. And it was I who should have found the infinite leisure to sit out under some trees like Buddha or any meditative toad."[15]

Frost thought of "Mowing" as the best poem included in his first book, *A Boy's Will* (New York: Henry Holt and Company,1913), and it stands today as one of his finest poems. The poem's rhythms capture the motion of the *mower* and his scythe as he moves through the fields of summer. The poem is silky with sinuousness and sensuality.

Mowing

There was never a sound beside the wood but one,
And that was my long scythe whispering to the ground.
What was it it whispered? I knew not well myself;

THE FRIENDSHIP OF ROBERT FRANCIS AND ROBERT FROST

> Perhaps it was something about the heat of the sun,
> Something, perhaps, about the lack of sound—
> And that was why it whispered and did not speak.
> It was no dream of the gift of idle hours,
> Or easy gold at the hand of fay or elf:
> Anything more than truth would have seemed too weak
> To the earnest love that laid the swale in rows,
> Nor without feeble-pointed spikes of flowers
> (Pale orchises), and scared a bright green snake.
> The fact is the sweetest dream that labor knows.
> My long scythe whispered and left the hay to make.[16]

Where Frost observes "lack of sound" in his idyll of mowing, Francis's "The Sound I Listened For" is nothing but the sound of mowing and the rhythms of that sound.

The Sound I Listened For

> What I remember is the ebb and flow of sound
> That summer morning as the mower came and went
> And came again, crescendo and diminuendo,
> And always when the sound was loudest how it ceased
> A moment while he backed the horses for the turn,
> The rapid clatter giving place to the slow click
> And the mower's voice. That was the sound I listed for.
> The voice did what the horses did. It shared the action
> As sympathetic magic does or incantation.
> The voice hauled and the horses hauled. The strength of one
> Was in the other and in the strength was no impatience.
> Over and over as the mower made his rounds
> I heard his voice and only once or twice he backed
> And turned and went ahead and spoke no word at all.[17]

How acute of both Frost and Francis to imbue these poems of mowing with both the sound and the *silence* of the mower's art. Although one poet speaks of the mower and his scythe and the other of a farmer's tensile direction of equestrian choreography, it is the portrayal of the actual music, if not to mention, the particular joy made specific to the labor of each task itself *and* that music. Both poems are odes, spoken songs, in praise of the work of mowing. Contemporary society may have lost something here, on many levels, by the disuse of *labor intensive tools*, to invoke E. F. Schumacher and his socio-economic classic *Small Is Beautiful* (New York: Harper & Row, 1973), but still these poems endure.

Jay Parini writes of Frost's "Mowing," for example, that it was "probably written in the spring of 1900... He called it "talk song," and it catches in uncanny ways the sound of the speaking voice, although there is nothing casual about it. Frost has made sure to lace the voice tightly to the frame of a sonnet format."[18]

Francis makes light several times of Frost's comparing *his formula for writing poetry* to *a piece of ice of a hot stove that rides on its own melting*. Whereas Frost wrote formidable poems in a demonstrative fashion, Francis made many drafts of poems until they were finished. The entry for October 22, 1952 in *Frost: A Time To Talk* provides illuminating insight.

"Two afternoons ago I spent an hour with Robert Frost in his room at the Lord Jeff (The Lord Jeffery Inn, Amherst's leading hostelry located next to Grace Episcopal Church and near Amherst College). America's greatest living poet, the most successful, recognized, honored, sat in undramatic fashion and chatted with one whom he himself called "the best neglected poet." I am the poet whom the editors reject; Frost is the poet who rejects the editors. He had declined to contribute to *Poetry's* current Fortieth Anniversary Number. He said he had told Shapiro he would give him a poem sometime.

THE FRIENDSHIP OF ROBERT FRANCIS AND ROBERT FROST

"I took with me a manuscript copy of *With the Year's Cooling* (tentative title of my then current collection of poems for publication, which became ultimately *The Orb Weaver* (Wesleyan University Press, 1960). Have you written a book? he asked. Only poems, I said. I spoke of much revision, not only of the new but of some of the old. Frost shook his head, so to speak. I hadn't thought at the moment that I had been violating one of his pet theories: that a poem not only should but must be written in a single free-flowing run. Frost likened the process to Benvenuto Cellini's casting the statue of Perseus: it had to be done all at once. I suggested that he, Frost, wrote his poems with the speed of working of a water colorist; whereas I worked and reworked mine like an oil painter. I hadn't meant to flatter myself. Question from Frost: "Why were all the greatest paintings oils?"

"He took a hard crack at Yeats as an extreme revisionist. Yeats who had chewed pencils and sweated blood till the time came (for a time) he wrote no more poetry. But Frost was equally hard on his sexiness, both personal and poetic.

"Abbot at Buffalo (Charles D. Abbot, librarian of the Lockwood Memorial Library of the University of Buffalo, and founder and director of its collection of materials in contemporary poetry), who has the collection of worksheets of poems he called a fool. Forty versions of a poem by Auden. As if a poem's value were to be measured by the trouble it cost. He himself took pains to hide the few changes he had made in his own poems. He said people always resented his changes, and yet overvalued them, sometimes when they were mere accidents of copying. Once he wrote out one of his poems for a woman, with some variations from the printed version. Later she told him she had lost the holograph when her house burned down. Frost asked her if she knew who had set the fire."[19]

In writing about *Come Out Into the Sun: Poems New and Selected* (Amherst: University of Massachusetts Press, 1965), Francis offers:

BIOGRAPHICAL LITERARY MONOGRAPH

"One new feature that few readers would be aware of was the presence of eight word-count poems. It amuses me to remember that when I hit upon this technique I was uneasy lest it be stolen from me. After a few word-count poems were in print under my name, I felt safer. But far from wanting to help themselves to my invention, my fellow poets didn't even notice what I was doing.

"What is word-count? It is a way of controlling the length of a line of poetry, not by the number of syllables it contains, and not by the number of clusters of syllables called feet, but by the number of whole words. My first word-count poem was about dolphins and I thought they would need a long line of seven words. The unregulated rhythm turned out to be quite choppy, but not inappropriately so, I felt. What disappointed me a little was the fact that readers would not be aware that there were seven words in each line unless told; and even if told, would not be able to have a sense of seven as they read.

"'Stellaria' was my next poem, and it contained five words to a line. Here the eye could take in the fiveness. And the rhythm was smoother. My third attempt was the small poem "Museum Vase" with only three words to a line. A reader could hardly help noticing what was going on. As for rhythm, there was hardly any at all—a static effect good for certain subjects."[20]

I quote for good measure the short poem, "Museum Vase," as per example of Francis's inventiveness with respect to word-count poems and his exploration of the form. Francis's experimentation of form is achieved in such a good-natured and measured manner. There is nothing rambunctious about his word-count poems or his inventive explorations of poetry. In fact, the poem resonates, most appropriately, with a classical elegance, and, in fact, to disagree with Francis, the poem displays both an inner music and rhythm.

THE FRIENDSHIP OF ROBERT FRANCIS AND ROBERT FROST

Museum Vase

It contains nothing.
We ask it
To contain nothing.

Having transcended use
It is endlessly
Content to be.

Still it broods
On old burdens—
Wheat, oil, wine.[21]

Besides becoming the originator of word-count poems, Francis also embarked upon the discovery of tone poems. Much more than being simple lists of words, these poems pulse with the rhythms of nouns. Tone poems, at their best, at least those by Francis, are carefully assembled and playful linguistic jigsaws, each offering a thematic poetic archetype. A tone poem can not only be described as a catalog of images or a wish list of *sober merriments* but more specifically it approximates, if anything, a Calder sculpture in words. What has more felicity than a mobile designed by Alexander Calder or a tone poem by Robert Francis?

Blue Cornucopia

Pick any blue   sky-blue   cerulean   azure
cornflower   periwinkle   blue-eyed grass
blue bowl   bluebell   pick lapis lazuli
blue pool   blue girl   blue Chinese vase
or pink-blue chicory alias ragged sailor
or sapphire   bluebottle fly   indigo bunting
blue dragonfly or devil's darning needle
blue-green   turquoise   peacock   blue spruce
blue verging on violet   the fringed gentian

> gray-blue   blue bonfire smoke   autumnal
> haze   blue hill   blueberry   distance
> and darker blue   storm-blue   blue goose
> ink   ocean   ultramarine   pick winter
> blue snow-shadows   ice   the blue star Vega.[22]

In comparison to Francis's unique poetic sensibilities, Frost blended an uncompromising unity of aesthetics and utility. If both the poems of Frost and Francis are enduring literature, as we are fortunate that they are, and Francis's poems can be likened, at least on occasion, to the felicitous mobiles of Alexander Calder, then Frost's poems possess the heft and grace and security of a W.P.A. bridge.

Jay Parini, in his *Robert Frost: A Life* (New York: Henry Holt and Company, 1999), best portrays this notion of Frost's predilection for not only weighty themes but for an ideological largesse that is quite poignant. The chapter is entitled "In a Yellow Wood, 1914-1915," and it serves to relate Frost's years in England. In it Parini cites portions of letters Frost wrote to John Bartlett, as well as one written to Sidney Cox, to illustrate Frost's theory of the breaking of the words of New England speech across the line of a verse.

Frost writes: "You listen for the sentence sounds. If you find some of those not bookish, caught fresh from the mouths of people, some of them striking, all of them definite and recognizable, so recognizable that with a little trouble you can place them and even name them, you know you have found a writer." He elaborates in another letter to Sidney Cox: "Just so many sentence sounds belong to a man as just so many vocal runs belong to one kind of bird. We come into the world with them and create none of them."[23]

Frost explained to Bartlett that the way to hear "the abstract sound of sense is from voices behind a door that cuts off words."

THE FRIENDSHIP OF ROBERT FRANCIS AND ROBERT FROST

A poet must learn "to get cadences by skillfully breaking the sounds of sense with all their irregularity of accent across the regular beat of the metre." He was arguing here, implicitly, against Robert Bridges, the new British poet laureate, who believed in the fixed quantity of English syllables. Frost understood that the speaking voice is, somewhat paradoxically, both idiosyncratic and dependent upon the formal structures of English sound patterns. He praised "the abstract vitality of our speech"—a vitality that connects every speaker to the language itself, a community of shared signals. But what both separates and connects the true artist to this community is an original way of "breaking the sounds."

Two factors are always at work in a line of verse: the abstract possibility of the line and the poet's individual way of "breaking" words across it. The poetry, indeed, resides in the difference between these two possibilities. Thus, a line such as "There was never a sound beside the wood but one," the first line of "Mowing," can be scanned as iambic pentameter—in the abstract; in its vocalization, however, any number of different ways of scanning the line would seem more appropriate. Certainly, in reading the poem, a poet would be unlikely (and unwise) to stick to the iambic flow. The pleasure of poetry inheres in the contrast, then, between this abstract potential (the iambic regularity) and the vernacular embodiment of the line, which is governed by the poet's own voice and coded into the language. As Frost put it, "The living part of a poem is the intonation entangled somehow in the syntax, idiom, and meaning of a sentence. It is only there for those who have heard it previously in conversation. It is not for us in any Greek or Latin poem because our ears have not been filled with the tones of Greek or Roman talk. It is the most volatile and at the same time important part of poetry. It goes and the language becomes a dead language, the poetry dead poetry ... Words exist in the mouth, not in books."[24]

BIOGRAPHICAL LITERARY MONOGRAPH

For comparison's sake, I quote Frost's "After Apple-Picking," to display his breaking speech across a line of verse, then provide Francis's "Remind Me of Apples," that serves as an example of how rhythms and music of words can be captured by the means of free verse.

After Apple-Picking

My long two-pointed ladder's sticking through a tree
Toward heaven still,
And there's a barrel that I didn't fill
Beside it, and there may be two or three
Apples I didn't pick upon some bough.
But I am done with apple-picking now.
Essence of winter sleep is on the night,
The scent of apples: I am drowsing off.
I cannot rub the strangeness from my sight
I got from looking through a pane of glass
I skimmed this morning from the drinking trough
And held against the world of hoary grass.
It melted, and I let it fall and break.
But I was well
Upon my way to sleep before it fell,
And I could tell
What form my dreaming was about to take.
Magnified apples appear and disappear,
Stem end and blossom end,
And every fleck of russet showing clear.
My instep arch not only keeps the ache,
It keeps the pressure of a ladder-round.
I feel the ladder sway as the boughs bend.
And I keep hearing from the cellar bin
The rumbling sound
Of load on load of apples coming in.
For I have had too much

Of apple-picking: I am overtired
Of the great harvest I myself desired.
There were ten thousand thousand fruit to touch,
Cherish in hand, lift down, and not let fall.
For all
That struck the earth,
No matter if not bruised or spiked with stubble,
Went surely to the cider-apple heap
And of no worth.
One can see what will trouble
This sleep of mine, whatever sleep it is.
Were he not gone,
The woodchuck could say whether it's like his
Long sleep, as I describe its coming on,
Or just some human sleep.[25]

///

Remind Me of Apples

When the cicada celebrates the heat,
Intoning that tomorrow and today
Are only yesterday with the same dust
To dust on plantain and on roadside yarrow—
Remind me, someone, of the apples coming,
Cold in the dew of deep October grass,
A prophecy of snow in their white flesh.
In the long haze of dog days, or by night
When the thunder growls and prowls but will not go
Or come, I lose the memory of apples.
Name me the names, the goldens, russets, sweets,
Pippin and blue pearmain and seek-no-further
And the lost apples on forgotten farms
And the wild pasture apples of no name.[26]

BIOGRAPHICAL LITERARY MONOGRAPH

The exhaustion of both the harvest and those who participated in the harvest is abundant in the Frost poem. It is as if nature herself were limp and drooping with fatigue. "After Apple-Picking" is another of Frost's impressive odes to work. Frost makes us feel the *ache* of *our instep arch from the pressure of a ladder-round*. Whereas Francis offers a delicious if not mysterious lyric that invokes the orchards to bear fruit. His invocation contains such mystery it conjures *yugen*, a characteristic of Japanese poetry that signifies *unknowable mystery*. In both poems, we may inhale the fragrance of apples in the air, a veritable abundance of them.

To explore further differences and similarities between the poetic styles of Frost and Francis, it is necessary to quote in some depth not only Francis's ideas about free verse but composition itself. In my opinion, the defense of free verse Francis makes, at least in part, should annotate or be included in any definition of the form.

Francis writes, "Yes, if I could chat with him today, here in my home or in perhaps some less tangible place, I should like to say, "Mr. Frost"—or maybe I would finally call him "Robert" to his face as I think he sometimes hinted I should—"Robert, there are other games than tennis that can be played on a tennis court, games in which a net would be irrelevant and even a hindrance, yet games fully as exacting as tennis. Further, on a tennis court dancers could dance and for them a net would be only in the way. A modern dance, you know, is not regulated by rules or other external demands but is guided only by the inner compulsion of his art. I am all with you that art demands a limit, a challenge, but meter and rhyme are not the only available limitations and challenges. Anglo-Saxon poetry did it with alliteration and a strong beat, regardless of the precise number of syllables. Japanese haiku does it by counting syllables themselves, not by grouping syllables into metrical feet. There are many potential ways (including my own technique of "word-count,") of providing the needed element of resistance.

And furthermore, can't the very stuff of a poem be so shaped and molded and formed that a more external and explicit formality would be superfluous? Perhaps it comes down to what one means by "free verse." Admittedly verse that is merely free is flabby; but verse that is controlled, though not by meter and rhyme, perhaps should not be called free verse.

"I think he would listen sympathetically. He might even give in to me, as he once did on another of his pet notions. As I tell in the entry for October 22, 1952, he had asked me what I had been doing and I said I had been trying to make my poems better. Disdainfully he asserted that poets don't improve, they only change. A poem must be written in one impulse, at one sitting, like a piece of ice on a hot stove that rides on its own melting. (See The Complete Poems of Robert Frost (1949), the last paragraph of the preface called, "The Figure a Poem Makes.") But a moment later he admitted that it had taken Gray eighteen years to complete his Elegy. I think Frost, if put in a corner, would concede that spontaneity sometimes has to be labored for."[27]

Also, I cannot help but give in to the temptation of quoting what Francis would have told Frost about what it is to be a realist and what it is not if he had the chance to. I do so primarily for the sake of illustrating the former's fondness for cognitive agility as well as his perspicacious sense of humor.

Francis writes, "I should also like to challenge his well-known witticism about the potato. There are two kinds of realist, he said, one that wants the potato with all its dirt clinging to it, and one that prefers the potato scrubbed clean. He himself is for the clean potato. That is what art does for life: "clean it and strip it to form. (Quoted by Dr. Calvin H. Plimpton in his "Reflections" at the Frost Memorial Service in Johnson Chapel, Amherst College, February 17, 1963.) But Robert, doesn't it all depend on what you are going to do with your potato? If you're going to plant it, you'd never think of scrubbing it first. Instead of doing the potato any good, scrubbing

BIOGRAPHICAL LITERARY MONOGRAPH

could only do it harm by breaking the sprouts. But if *you're going to* boil that potato, you or anyone else would scrub it as a matter of course. If you're going to bake it and eat the skin with the rest of the potato, you'd probably do more than merely scrub it. This is not a world in which we need and welcome both. And it's precisely the realist who understands and accepts this fact. Didn't you yourself once say: "It's knowing what to do with things that counts?"[28]

Although it is Francis's respect of Frost, of holding him in unquestionable high esteem, that is the norm. Francis provides us not with just a caricature of Frost but a full-fledged portrait in oils:

"Robert Frost in any group makes the other men seem like boys. Whatever their age, he always looks the oldest. No one not profoundly old could in repose look so profoundly sad.

"Most men have to prepare what they have to say. Having prepared, some of them speak well. Frost no more bothers to prepare than he bothers to brush his hair. His whole life has been his preparation. Since he can't be caught off guard, he doesn't bother to guard. He has trusted himself so far so long that he now differs from us in kind as well as degree. He has a dimension of his own. When he speaks, we do not criticize what he says and how he says it. He is. If he stumbles, his stumbling is more eloquent than our dancing."[29]

Two pertinent examples of Frost's *dancing*, as Francis puts it, occur in *Frost: A Time To Talk* for the entries of April 21, 1954 and November 1, 1954:

"F. complained that so many poets today are satisfied with poetry as texture. Their poems are like the pieces of cloth hung up instead of pictures in some arty houses. His advice to such poets is to make something out of their cloth. Make a pair of pants."[30]

"You write on subjects," said Wallace Stevens to Frost when they met in Key West nearly twenty years ago. "And you," retorted Frost with equal scorn, "you write bric-a-brac."

"So the two classmates (Harvard, 1901) became friends. Friends enough for Stevens to send Frost his books as they came out. "Some more bric-a-brac," was the inscription on the latest."[31]

Did Francis record every visit Frost paid him or that he paid Frost? The answer is no. Was Francis to Frost what Boswell was to Johnson? The answer is again no. Francis was scrupulous in his attention to his poetry and his *Way of Life*, and Frost was a true mentor to him with respect to his poetry for many years of his life. With respect to unrecorded visits, Francis discloses the following, and I quote these passages at length for their full import, especially since the last visit Frost paid Francis was one of the last times the two ever saw one another. Certainly, it very well may have been the last extended conversation between Frost and Francis in the ambience of such comfortable surroundings as Fort Juniper.

Francis writes, "For instance, Frost came once to the Old House by the Brook (an account of my life at the Old House by the Brook may be found in Chapter 11 of my autobiography, *The Trouble with Francis*) where I lived from 1937 to 1940, but there is no mention of his visit in my journal. I brought him out in my little second-hand Model-A Ford roadster. Together we poked about among the cobwebs of the eight tiny unused bedrooms upstairs. It was up there that he advanced the theory that this had been a rooming house for people working in the mill nearby. What else was the meaning of the big bell that could be rung from downstairs?

"I will remember also an unrecorded visit with Frost twenty years later. I had happened to see him on the street near Converse Library (Converse Library was at that time the library of

BIOGRAPHICAL LITERARY MONOGRAPH

Amherst College. The present library is the Robert Frost Library, at the laying of whose cornerstone President Kennedy spoke a few weeks before his death.), and my greeting led to his inviting me to lunch that day at the Lord Jeffrey Inn. There were just the two of us at a small table. Since the main dining room was temporarily out of use, we were in a smaller room where the tables were rather close together. All through the meal I had the problem of trying to answer Frost's rather personal questions loud enough for him to hear but not loud enough for the whole room to listen to. He chided vegetarian me for ordering—was it an omelet?—for my main dish. What I had to drink I have forgotten, but Frost had a daiquiri. He was about to go to England to receive honorary degrees from both Oxford and Cambridge, and I was soon to leave for Rome (I had been given a "Rome Prize Fellowship" by the American Academy of Arts and Letters and the closely linked National Institute of Arts and Letters, providing for me to live during 1957-8 at the American Academy in Rome, an entirely distinct institution.). He spoke of my little honor as if it were comparable to great ones.

"I am sure that there was a second visit, unrecorded, with Frost and Hyde Cox; and a second visit with Frost and Samuel French Morse. But the unrecorded visit I remember most vividly took place on June 14, 1959, which was Baccalaureate Sunday that year at Amherst College. Late in the morning a car drove into my yard and three men got out: Frost, Armour Craig (George Armour Craig, professor of English at Amherst College), and Alfred Edwards whom Frost introduced as his publisher. For a while we talked about *Vermont Folk Medicine*," which Holt had recently published. Then the three men discussed Frost's recent eighty-fifth birthday dinner in New York at which Lionel Trilling had made a significant and somewhat controversial speech.

"Frost remarked that he was now a member of the Holt firm with the privilege of choosing four books a year, two to make money and two not. (I inferred that if mine were to be one of those books, it would be one of the two not to make money.) He asked how I stood with Macmillan. I replied that Macmillan was no longer interested in me, had rejected my current manuscript. It seemed to me that the moment had come when Frost or Edwards would make a proposal. But before that moment could arrive, I said that I was no longer an unpublished poet, that less than a week ago Wesleyan University Press had accepted my poems for publication (*The Orb Weaver*).

"Oh, why did you do that?" exclaimed Frost.

"I answered that if I was to be published at all, it seemed to me appropriate and fortunate that it would be by a university press concerned more with the quality of a book than with its chances of making money, a press, moreover, that was away from any big city and here in my New England.

"The three men left soon afterwards. Though the friendly tone of our conversation had been marred, Frost was obviously disappointed. As he went out the door he said, "Too late, too late." This was the last time he was ever in my home."[32]

To describe this rite of passage between the two men is nothing less than bittersweet: Frost most likely about to offer Francis a chance to come on board with *his* publisher, Holt; and Francis striking out on his own with Wesleyan University Press. It is of significance to add that besides Francis's *The Orb* Weaver, Wesleyan also began its series with *Silence in the Snowy Fields* by Robert Bly and *The Branch Will Not Break* by James Wright, two volumes that still stand as emblematic definitions of the new American poetry, nearly six decades later.

Poetry was not only the very core of the friendship between Frost and Francis. It was the very *essence* of it, if not its entirety. There *were* topics the two did not touch on. One was sexuality. This was felicitous for both. Frost did not approve of homosexuality, and Francis's sexuality was initially latent (he did not partake in a sexual relationship until he was almost sixty). So, as Francis does address his sexuality in the shortest chapter in his autobiography,[33] "Eros," one that numbers just five pages, he makes it clear that he is homosexual. His intimation, though, is that he had only one relationship in his entire lifetime, and that being one of trans-Atlantic magnitude that spanned the course of several years: both in its intensity and in the protracted periods of time that separated the lovers.

Religion was another issue the two did not dwell on. It is my opinion that there is an amount of *spirituality* found in both the poems of Frost and Francis, but my definition of what is spiritual is quite different from both of them. As I have done thus far, I have Francis speaking for himself as well as for Frost.

Francis writes, "As for Frost's religious views, I might be a bit cautious. If I were too inquisitive about his God, might he not feel I was taking unfair advantage since he could not question me about mine, I who had none? What I could do would be to sketch the God I found in his poems and then ask if this were a true interpretation."[34]

What is important, and vastly so, are the poems the two left behind, and what is significant is the friendship they shared. They not only appraised one another shrewdly, but with felicity and a grace in that both enjoyed a kind of reciprocal gratitude that, although sometimes peripherally, they shared a part of each other's life, and were allies to one another. Francis relates an example of such in a letter Frost wrote, then expresses his own appreciation and esteem of the work of the man who was his mentor. Although Francis did develop and grow past that specific facet of their relationship, as can be seen in what may have been one of their last meetings on June 14, 1959.

THE FRIENDSHIP OF ROBERT FRANCIS AND ROBERT FROST

Francis writes, "I think Frost would respect my point of view and respect me for speaking it. Writing about me to Louis Untermeyer on February 13, 1936, he said: 'Neither I nor anybody else owns him or very much influences his thinking. His opinions are no pushovers. He never starts a subject one way and then at the first sign or look of dissent from you steers it another way (*The Letters of Robert Frost to Louis* Untermeyer, New York: Holt, Rinehart, and Winston, 1963, page 270; Frost's letter is dated February 13,1936).'[35]

"Still it is the lyrics I keep coming back to. If I could have the luxury of a volume of them for myself, I would certainly include the following . . . These are cut and shining gems. They burn with the singleness and purity of candles, but unlike candles they never burn out. Here, finally, are Frost's "momentary stays against confusion."[36]

Francis's list of these *cut and shining gems* includes twenty poems of Frost's, and among these he includes "Spring Pools" and "Oven Bird." Both are quoted below.

Spring Pools

These pools that, though in forests, still reflect
The total sky almost without defect,
And like the flowers beside them, chill and shiver,
Will like the flowers beside them soon be gone,
And yet not out by any brook or river,
But up by roots to bring dark foliage on.
The trees that have it in their pent-up buds
To darken nature and be summer woods—
Let them think twice before they use their powers
To blot out and drink up and sweep away
These flowery waters and these watery flowers
From snow that melted only yesterday.[37]

BIOGRAPHICAL LITERARY MONOGRAPH

///

The Oven Bird

There is a singer everyone has heard,
Loud, a mid-summer and a mid-wood bird,
Who makes the solid tree trunks sound again.
He says that leaves are old and that for flowers
Mid-summer is to spring as one to ten.
He says the early petal-fall is past,
When pear and cherry bloom went down in showers
On sunny days a moment overcast;
And comes that other fall we name the fall.
He says the highway dust is over all.
The bird would cease and be as other birds
But that he knows he frames in all but words
Is what to make of a diminished thing.[38]

Then what of Francis's poems, that fall, now as well as before, into the category of exemplary poetry that is often all but forgotten. How could this be with so many individuals writing poetry now? How could Francis's work be so overlooked with as many books of poetry being issued? How could so many writers of poetry who so much desire to publish a book of their own so overlook the work of Robert Francis? Should we not study such a fine example of *what poetry can be*, as "Cedar Waxwings," for instance, if we can lay any claim whatsoever to even being remotely interested in poetry at all?

Cedar Waxwings

Four Tao philosophers as cedar waxwings
chat on a February berrybush
in sun, and I am one.

Such merriment and such sobriety—
The small wild fruit on the tall stalk—
was this not always my true style?

Above an elegance of snow, beneath
A silk-blue sky a brotherhood of four
birds. Can you mistake us?

To sun, to feast, and to converse
and all together—for this I have abandoned
all my other lives.[39]

Perhaps we can refer to this poem, that certainly offers Francis's philosophy of not only choosing as his preference living *a simple life* but his actual living that *Way of Life*, as his own *momentary* stay *against confusion*. The question is: what would Frost say? Perhaps it is Francis who is not only able to provide the best answer, but who may be the only one who can offer us an answer at all. Once again, I quote from Francis's *Frost: A Time To Talk*.

Francis concludes, "But now comes a last question. Why "momentary," Robert? Why aren't they permanent stays against confusion, enduring as long as the poems endure?

"He might answer that they are effective stays only while in a reader's mind. But I would argue that even when a reader is not thinking of them consciously, they may still be in his mind, and of course he can always go back to them, again and again.

"Frost might agree with me. Who knows?"[40]

BIOGRAPHICAL LITERARY MONOGRAPH

Notes

1. *Frost: A Time To Talk, Conversations & Indiscretions Recorded by Robert Francis*, Amherst: University of Massachusetts Press, page 49, 1972.
2. *The Trouble with Francis: An Autobiography by Robert Francis*, Amherst: University of Massachusetts Press, page 201, 1971.
3. *The Trouble with Francis: An Autobiography by Robert Francis*, pages 201-202.
4. *The Trouble with Francis: An Autobiography by Robert Francis*, pages 202-203.
5. *The Trouble with Francis: An Autobiography by Robert Francis*, page 18.
6. *The Trouble with Francis: An Autobiography by Robert Francis*, page 86-87.
7. Ibid..
8. Reprinted from *The Trouble with Francis: An Autobiography by Robert Francis*, page 19.
9. *The Trouble with Francis: An Autobiography by Robert Francis*, page 87.
10. *Frost: A Time To Talk, Conversations & Indiscretions Recorded by Robert Francis*, pages 36-38.
11. *The Trouble with Francis: An Autobiography by Robert Francis*, page 88.
12. *The Poetry of Robert Frost*, New York: Henry Holt and Company, 1975, page 331.
13. *The Trouble with Francis: An Autobiography by Robert Francis*, page 88.
14. *The Trouble with Francis: An Autobiography by Robert Francis*, pages 88-89.
15. *The Trouble with Francis: An Autobiography by Robert Francis*, pages 89-90.
16. *The Poetry of Robert Frost*, page 17.
17. *Robert Francis: Collected Poems, 1936-1976*, page 125.
18. *Robert Frost: A Life*, New York: Henry Holt and Company, 1999, page 76.
19. *Frost: A Time To Talk, Conversations & Indiscretions Recorded by Robert Francis*, pages 11-12.

20. *The Trouble with Francis: An Autobiography by Robert Francis*, page 127.
21. *Come Out Into the Sun: Poems New and Selected*, page 37.
22. *Robert Francis: Collected Poems, 1936-1976*, page 241.
23. *Robert Frost: A Life*, pages 135-136.
24. *Robert Frost: A Life*, pages 135-136.
25. *The Poetry of Robert Frost*, pages 68- 69.
26. *Robert Francis: Collected Poems, 1936-1976*, page 178.
27. *Frost: A Time To Talk, Conversations & Indiscretions Recorded by Robert Francis*, pages 84-85.
28. *Frost: A Time To Talk, Conversations & Indiscretions Recorded by Robert Francis*, pages 84-85.
29. *Frost: A Time ToTalk, Conversations & Indiscretions Recorded by Robert Francis*, page 79.
30. *Frost: A Time To Talk, Conversations & Indiscretions Recorded by Robert Francis*, page 21.
31. *Frost: A Time To Talk, Conversations & Indiscretions Recorded by Robert Francis*, page 29.
32. *Frost: A Time To Talk, Conversations & Indiscretions Recorded by Robert Francis*, pages 46-47.
33. *The Trouble with Francis: An Autobiography by Robert Francis*, page 209.
34. *Frost: A Time To Talk, Conversations & Indiscretions Recorded by Robert Francis*, page 86.
35. Ibid.
36. *Frost: A Time To Talk, Conversations & Indiscretions Recorded by Robert Francis*, pages 97-98.
37. *The Poetry of Robert Frost*, page 245.
38. *The Poetry of Robert Frost*, pages 119-120.
39. *Robert Francis: Collected Poems, 1936-1976*, page 118.
40. *Frost: A Time To Talk, Conversations & Indiscretions Recorded by Robert Francis*, pages 98-99.

7. What Is Psychospirituality?

INFUSING THE BLOG WITH LITERARY PANACHE

When I was 20, and working in my first bookstore, Book World, in New Haven, I had occasion to begin to read Eastern classics, under the guidance of Ed Bednar, who was a co-founder of the New Haven Zen Center, and with whom I was invited to sit in Zen meditation both in the basement of Yale Divinity School Chapel,; and at a colleague's of Ed's whose husband was not only a Master at Branford College but also a Nobel Prize-winner in Economics, at Yale. She just happened to have constructed quite a lovely zendo in a portion of her living space. I was also guided as to what to read, early on, by the book buyer for the Eastern and Western Religion section at the store, Kenny Angus, who was especially knowledgeable not only in what constituted a core selection of titles from world religion and comparative religion but also regarding occult studies. The latter would include his stocking the store with titles from Samuel Weiser, then in New York City, located on Book Row, publishing the likes of Aleister Crowley and Madame Blavatsky. Although I never pursued reading these authors, or the occult, in any manner, the expansiveness of the tenor of the books collected in the religion and philosophy sections that Kenny gathered there could lead just about anyone toward an illumined life, if they should wish it. Through these early experiences I continued my study of comparative religion and philosophy throughout my life over the last forty years and more.

My reading the works of Joseph Campbell came surprisingly late in my life and not until my late thirties. However, when I caught on to what Campbell had to offer and who he was affiliated with as a young man—John Steinbeck, who he was

WHAT IS PSYCHOSPIRITUALITY?

acquainted with and with whom he would become mutual enemies with due to a crush Steinbeck's wife had on Campbell; and Ed Ricketts, who was portrayed as "Doc" in Steinbeck's *Tortilla Flat* trilogy, and who was Steinbeck's muse, as well as Campbell's—I couldn't quite get enough of reading much of what Campbell wrote. Over the period of five years, or so, I devoured Campbell's work, rereading books such as *Myths to Live By* (New York: Viking, 1972), thirteen lectures he was invited to give, one every spring, at Cooper Union, which nugget his thought; and *Transformations of Myth through Time* (New York: Harper Perennial, 1990), another set of thirteen lectures he gave towards the end of his life, which also exhibit his encyclopedic knowledge of comparative religion and world mythology in an expansive, yet encapsulated, fashion. What I found in these books of Campbell's, and others, was the possibility of how to live one's life—often with an interpretation of daily life, and its challenges, seen through the context of myth. Reading Campbell opened a whole new cosmos of ideas to me, and, as the opening of doors that Campbell spoke of revealed yet other new vistas of thought, so very often I hadn't even known any of those doors previously even existed before.

What followed after reading Campbell was immersing myself for some half dozen years in the work of Caroline Myss. She is not the erudite academician that Campbell was, but I did learn more of a meditative approach to my inner life, as her being a self-described *healing intuitive,* one which offered more challenges as I apparently became not only more informed but also filled with more awareness and possibly even with more of an opening to higher consciousness. By Myss proclaiming that once you forgive one person you then get *x* number of more people to forgive is the beginning of a master class, or a post-doc, in what I refer to as *psychospirituality.* There truly comes a time when you have invested yourself in a lifetime of reading through which you then need to leave the confines of your room, to paraphrase the 20th-century Armenian mystic

INFUSING THE BLOG WITH LITERARY PANACHE

George Gurdjieff, and to brave moving about in the world with the spiritual knowledge one has accrued, only to feel the pull of the reigns of the wild horses which you need to tame, as Gurdjieff intimates—a metaphor for the rigors of the practice of spiritual disciplines within, and without, oneself when one reenters into the world.

Another way of stating this is being engaged in the work of the fourth chakra, the heart chakra, and realize, whether you are Christian or not, that you are walking into the marketplace of life having electrified the sacred heart of Jesus and the ensuing consciousness of that. This is soul work at one of its highest levels, and it offers its lessons in humility and compassion. This is not for everyone. It is not just an *evangelical* assumption, or notion, of the teachings of Christ. It is a full-fledged opening and practice of Christ consciousness, in action.

My mentors, through the reading of their books, also have included Pema Chodron, especially *No Time to Lose: The Timely Way of the Bodhisattva* (Boulder, CO: Shambhala Publications, 2005), through which Chodron extrapolates upon *The Way of the Bodhisattva* (*Bodhicharyavatara*), written by the 8th-century sage Shantideva. My favorite anecdote from the book is when Shantideva, who is shunned by his fellow monks, is requested by them to deliver a Dharma talk in the meditation hall, as a tease, obviously to shame him for what little ardor or knowledge they think he might posses, truly surprises his peers by then delivering the tenets of the *Bodhicharyavatara*, after which he ascends, bodily, into a pillar of light. In minor ways, I have experienced a similar beneficence, especially when someone has offered an insult, or an unjust aspersion, inferring my inferiority, and little do they know, nor do I, often enough, that by my staying centered, similar to the Buddha in his finding the *immovable spot*, that I transcend their impertinence and readily feel myself lifted into another plane of consciousness, which is, veritably, filled with not only more light but also

WHAT IS PSYCHOSPIRITUALITY?

more spiritual resonance, a more palpably alive existence that is exponentially clearer as it is brighter—as in a bolt of light sparkling on clear water.

One morning after I had meditated, when I was managing the general bookstore at UMass, the doyenne of the MFA department came in to dress me down verbally for my PR for the reading series I was hosting being confused with theirs. She was so angry she was shaking. The fusillade of her verbal attack just rolled right off me, and I was able to wish her a nice day, with a smile. Being centered can save us from some of the more stressful and anxiety-ridden situations we can imagine. I will never forget how red this woman's face was—due to her own overblown ego. I will never forget how calm I was.

However, I have also gained immense spiritual nourishment in reading other books by Pema Chodron, such as *When Things Fall Apart: Heart Advice for Difficult Times* (Shambhala Publications, 1996) and *The Places That Scare You: A Guide To Fearlessness* (Shambhala Publications, 2001). These are books that can be readily assimilated when one is moving through one's own dark night of the soul. What I gleaned most from Pema Chodron, and a practice I still use to this day, is her *Tonglen* meditation, which is done during the course of one's daily life. It is a meditation of one's indrawn and outdrawn breaths but with the inflection of focusing energy, and blessings, on those who are in need. Whenever I am driving and see an ambulance and hear its siren, I begin practicing *Tonglen*, and sending healing energies to *the people or person who are being attended to by that ambulance,* repeatedly until at least the siren is no longer heard, and many times for quite a while afterwards. I may have heard the siren fifteen minutes earlier and I am now out of my car and doing my grocery shopping when I notice that I am still repeating the mantra of *bless the people or person who are being attended to by that ambulance.* There are worse way to live one's life. This isn't one of them.

INFUSING THE BLOG WITH LITERARY PANACHE

Regarding dark night, there is no better book than Thomas Moore's *Dark Night of the Soul: A Guide to Finding Your Way through Life's Ordeals* (New York: Avery/Penguin, 2005). I read the book in only a handful of sittings in the summer of 2005, when I was managing the general bookstore at University of Massachusetts, Amherst. I was so taken with the wisdom regarding dark night contained in the pages of this book that I invited Thomas Moore to speak at the University that autumn, which he did, to a rather avid and receptive audience. The offering of compassion and resilience that this book offers is immeasurable.

Combined with the work of Caroline Myss, in which she also discusses dark night, and which Moore accurately proposes is not only unrecognized in American society, especially, but also that the consciousness gained through this spiritual ordeal is frowned upon with the presupposition that the individual suffering through their own dark night is marked as having something considerably wrong with them. However, Moore lends great approbation to the process of dark night as part of a supreme stage of spiritual growth. Myss posits that when an illumination—of which could also be of an archetype itself—is so charged within an individual that afterwards they experience what is a natural process of enduring a dark night of the soul. The spiritual formula then would read as: *illumination equals dark night which then results in transformation as spiritual resurrection.* The soul is imbued with an illumined state followed by a state in which it moves through a process of its own resurrection. The next time you see someone going through a dark night offer them not only some compassion but congratulations since they recently may have been illumined to such a degree that they have been thrown into the belly of their own whale, so to speak, and are about to issue forth as a new spiritual being, once again.

Psychospirituality is actively living by depth psychology, the interpretation of world mythology, and daily spirituality—the

WHAT IS PSYCHOSPIRITUALITY?

kind not just found during Saturday or Sunday services and sitting in the front pew of your church but every day all week long. In fact, living this way is maintaining your spiritual practice on the path to active presence, which is attempting to be awakened each moment of the day and each day of the year. It is work. This is what is our life's work, all of us, and as imperfect as I am, too many times, the practice of presence leads me back to focus on the eternity in the evanescent, the consciousness of the ever-present moment, which is all we have, and in having it and then letting it go, we live more fully and more compassionately, so much more essentially, and in a more empathetic way.

The following six blogs were originally written between December 2016 and January 2017 for the purposes of being published online by a psychotherapy association in Boston. I am including the following poem with the idea that much of the time, if not all of the time, we are able to access not only the divinity in the world around us, especially in the natural world, but also a similar divinity within ourselves—and then not just access it but also, in the very least, be able to curate it and recognize it for what it is.

* * * *

Daylilies

When I left this morning,
    under a deep cerulean sky,
        the orange daylilies were thronging

the mailbox beside
    the road, petals still
        closed, beaded with droplets of dew;

so much green in the grass, in the trees,
    the sunlight streaking everything,
        making all sparkle, infusing every color

with shades of gold and yellow.
>   When I returned just before noon,
>   >   the daylilies had opened their supple

orange mouths,
>   tasting the air, savoring the breeze
>   >   with tongues of anther and pistil;

the chiffon of their
>   throats offered the coolness
>   >   of song and practical shade and nectar

for a pollinating bee.
>   They hold as much
>   >   gladness as we can imagine, filling us

with orange rapture,
>   the orange of daylilies,
>   >   rising on stems by the roadside farm;

the lithe cups of their mouths,
>   spilling over with urgency,
>   >   with exultation, unfolded and full,

blooming with heedless
>   abandon, with pleasures
>   >   so tantalizing they invite us to look,

to breathe the diligence
>   of their color, to be as bedazzled
>   >   as they at the pinnacle of their lives.

* * * *

So readers may be aware of just who Ed Ricketts was, I am including the next poem. His iconic book *Between Pacific Tides*, originally published by Stanford University Press, in 1939, is

WHAT IS PSYCHOSPIRITUALITY?

now in its fifth edition. The book was, and remains, an ecological and environmental classic in its exploration of intertidal ecology of the Pacific coast. It has sold more than 100,000 copies. Ricketts, who provided the inspiration for both Steinbeck (portrayed as "Doc" in his novels) and Campbell (who sailed with Ricketts and whose landmark book *Hero with a Thousand Faces* just may have been either inspired or encouraged by him) attended the University of Chicago but did not finish his studies for a degree. A book worth reading regarding the life of Ed Ricketts is *Beyond the Outer Shores: The Untold Odyssey of Ed Ricketts, the Pioneering Ecologist Who Inspired John Steinbeck and Joseph Campbell* by Eric Enno Tamm (Boston, MA: De Capo Press, 2005).

In relation to the blogs that follow the poem, "Homage to Ed Ricketts," which offer an awareness of what anxiety is, in Ricketts dying as tragically as he did, we also are able to remain open to a much greater realm of feeling, and truth, which can be accessed in being *present* for the greater inflection of what his essence was, and is, which is what resonates throughout the memory that remains of him and what he bequeathed to us for an enduring and felicitous posterity.

* * * *

Homage to Ed Ricketts

When you drove up Drake Avenue that evening,
You had just spoken with your sister Alice over the phone.

Your last words to her being, *I have never been any happier
In my entire life.* You had just married a young woman,

You were only days away from leaving on another
Expedition to the Queen Charlotte Islands with Steinbeck

INFUSING THE BLOG WITH LITERARY PANACHE

To write a book that was to be entitled *The Outer Shores*.
Was it your musing about the sea worm that distracted you?

Or was it the list of what you needed to pack
For the expedition? Did the rusted 1936 Packard stall

On the railroad tracks, as the Delmonte Express, on its way
From San Francisco, turned the blind curve from behind

One of the canneries, to bear down on you, as the engineer
Blew the whistle several times, before the train crashed

Into the car, carrying you down the tracks three hundred
Feet away, spilling you and the Packard off to the side?

The collision startled most of the saintly bums from
Their dreams at the foot of the hill along Cannery Row.

At that moment, Monterey would never be any quieter.
Nothing would ever be quite the same again.

John Steinbeck's Doc and Joseph Campbell's *Hero with
A Thousand Faces* would pass from this specific incarnation

Three days short of their fifty-first birthday. Described as
Having a face that was *part Christ, part satyr*, the wise voice

That everyone seemed to listen to was silenced because
Of either a stalled car or the distraction of your thinking

About the ecology of sardines, instead of paying attention
To an oncoming passenger train crossing an intersection

Without the safety of a wigwag. I imagine that you reside
In your own version of paradise: dawn at low tide on one

WHAT IS PSYCHOSPIRITUALITY?

Of the most remote of the Queen Charlotte's, off the coast
Of British Columbia, the tidal flats spread out before you

For your prospecting of marine specimens, stretching out
In the bracing cold and the pink brightness of the new day—

The innumerable starfish dotting their universe over
The expanse of the abated Pacific tide, and you persevering

In the perpetuity of the perigee and the apogee in gathering
Nothing but grace from the abundance of the sea.

ANXIETY, TIME, AND BEING PRESENT IN THE MOMENT

Time presses upon us in innumerable ways. Marcel Proust wrote, "When a man is asleep, he has in a circle round him the chain of the hours, the sequence of the years, the order of the heavenly bodies." Not only can time weigh heavily on our psyche but it may also appear to control us in ways which seem even beyond its measure, as William James wrote, "All my life I have been struck by the accuracy with which I will wake at the same *exact minute* night after night and morning after morning." Alan Burdick recently provides insight into the psychological aspect of time in a *New Yorker* article, offering the elucidation that "most likely it's the work of the circadian clocks, which, embedded in the DNA of my every cell, regulate my physiology over a twenty-four-hour period. At 4:27 A.M., I'm most aware of being at the service of something; there is a machine in me, or I am a ghost in it."

"Ghosts" and "machines" in congruence with each other can precipitate a kind of horror. Similarly, as in Edgar Alan Poe's short story, "The Tell-Tale Heart," time can, in the very least, produce within us an anxiety, possibly reigning chaos in our daily lives: in our relationships, in our careers, in every waking moment.

However, Burdick points out that in waking up at 4:27 a.m., in an incantatory prose which is vibrant, that "as worried as I am in these waking moments, I also find them oddly calming. It's as if in falling asleep I'd fallen into an egg and woken as the yolk, cushioned and aloft on an extended present. It won't last, I know. In the morning, the hours and minutes will reassert

WHAT IS PSYCHOSPIRITUALITY?

themselves and this seemingly limitless breadth of time will seem unreal and unreachable—the dream of boundless time, dreamed from the confines of an egg carton. But that's a thought for tomorrow. For now, it's now, and the tick of the bedside clock is the muffled beat of a heart."

Burdick has successfully taken the ire out of the illusion that time needs to be the perpetrator of any anxiety whatsoever. The Amherst poet, Robert Francis, who lived very much as did Henry David Thoreau for nearly a half-century in a cottage he had built for himself and his wife, *Patience*, wrote a poem, entitled "Glass." In it he creates a working metaphor for what a poem, or poetry, could actually be, and, in fact, what life could be, if we remove all that it isn't: "If the impossible were not/ And if the glass, only the glass,/ Could be removed, the poem would remain." Essentially, this is what Alan Burdick has accomplished for us in taking time and the illusion of time away from what it really isn't, and that being the ever-present moment that Buddhists have always propounded we live in—each changing moment being what is our eternal now.

There actually is little room for anxiety if we are present for the words of Plato, writing in the 4th-century B.C.E, "The instant, this strange nature, is something inserted between motion and rest, and it is in no time at all, but into it and from it what is moved changes to being at rest, and what is at rest to being moved."

Alan Burdick suggests experiencing how time "unfolds in a sentence. Recite a poem or a psalm by heart: your mind strains to recall what you've said and reaches forward to grab what you will say next." Expounding upon a passage from St. Augustine, in *The Confessions*, written circa 397, Burdick intimates a cogent theory of time—*and consciousness*, "Vital energy: that's the essence of Augustine, and of you, too, right now, as you absorb these words, strive to remember, and wonder what comes next. 'Time is nothing other than tension,' Augustine wrote, 'and I would be very surprised if it is not tension of consciousness itself.'"

References

Burdick, Alan, "The Secret Life of Time," *The New Yorker,* December 19-26, 2016, 68-72.

Burdick, Alan, *Why Time Flies: Mostly a Scientific Investigation,* New York, NY: Simon & Schuster, 2017.

Francis, Robert, *The Collected Poems of Robert Francis,* Amherst, MA: University of Massachusetts Press, 1976.

ANXIETY: NOT BEING NEEDED AND WHAT TO DO ABOUT IT

The recognition of our identity is essential to the health of both our human soul and our psyche.

"Compared with 50 years ago," there are "five times as many working-age men completely outside of the workforce" the Dalai Lama and Arthur C. Brooks cite in a 2016 New York Times article. This idea implies what the American poet Bert Meyers wrote regarding the haunted feeling of being unneeded in his poem entitled "One Morning" from *The Dark Birds*: "I told myself/ a single man's/ like water where/ nobody swims."

Social isolation precipitates a whole host of negative emotions and can result in ill health. Research has revealed that seniors of both sexes who experience the anxiety of loneliness are three times more likely to succumb to premature death than those who are active and making themselves useful. The keys for preservation are significant here: staying engaged and, through that practice, finding emotional resilience in preserving one's integrity. These are priceless prescriptions for health on multiple levels.

Sharing isn't often thought of as a possible panacea by many of us who suffer from loneliness and the anxiety, which can usurp our best intentions to remain positive and proactive. However, the Dalai Lama suggests a question that can actually become a guided meditation to begin our day: "What can I do today to appreciate the gifts that others offer me?" Such a question completely takes oneself out of a continuous circle of self-pitying thinking—a lugubrious dialectic of self-abnegation.

We can each be taken out of ourselves if we take on what the Dalai Lama prescribes as our need "to make sure that global brotherhood and oneness with others are not just abstract ideas that we profess, but personal commitments that we mindfully put into practice." In other words, we affect others as we do ourselves. The result of such positive psychological karma is possibly as the 13th-century Buddhist priest, Nichiren, advised: "If one lights a fire for others, it will also brighten one's own way."

Even if one finds the wherewithal and courage to set forth on such a path, what about today's truculent political climate? How do we go about lighting fires for others to see by if the one that brightens our ascent out of the shadowy realms of anxiety and loneliness isn't the flame by which others are able to see clearly enough at all to find their own way?

The Dalai Lama answers such questions with an intrinsic gleam of wisdom:

> The problems we face cut across conventional categories; so must our dialogue, and our friendships . . . Many are confused and frightened to see anger and frustration sweeping like wildfire across societies that enjoy historic safety and prosperity. But their refusal to be content with physical and material security actually reveals something beautiful: a universal human hunger to be needed.

For the Dalai Lama to reveal the answer to our questions within the experience of anxiety itself is a relevant philosophical axiom worth our time contemplating daily.

References

Gyatso, Tenzin, The 14th Dalai Lama and Brooks, Arthur C., "Dalai Lama: Behind Our Anxiety, the Fear of Being Unneeded," *The New York Times,* November 4, 2016.

Meyers, Bert, *In a Dybbuk's Raincoat: Collected Poems*, Albuquerque, NM: University of New Mexico Press, 2007.

ANXIETY AND SYNCHRONICITY: LIVING IN THE REAL WORLD

The concept of synchronicity was initially posited by the psychoanalyst C. G. Jung as being an incident in our lives that reveals itself as a significant, or consequential, coincidence which apparently has no causal relationship to one another yet seems to be, in fact, directly related. The psychic healer and medical intuitive, Caroline Myss, claims that synchronicity is prevalent in our daily lives. Some writers, for instance, experience typing the same word as it is being spoken as they may hear it when they have the radio on while working. You think of your best friend in fifth grade while shopping at the mall, and when you turn your head, arms full of wrapped gifts, there she is, smiling, having stopped right in front of you.

What if you organize your life to such a degree that all is laid out the night before— as ritual? *What if* you are having Sunday breakfast before going to the mall, the day after a snowstorm? If there was an anxiety meter, you wouldn't be registering any. You have just finished reading your daily affirmation in *Words to Live By* by Eknath Easwaran (*Ish*-war-an), a spiritual teacher who founded the Blue Mountain Center of Meditation in Berkeley, California.

Easwaran prefaces his thought for the day by using a quote from literature, or from a spiritual text, such as *The Upanishads,* from which he was an expert interpreter. *What if* the quote was from William Wordsworth, from his Ecclesiastical sonnet, "Inside King's College Chapel, Cambridge," which reads: "Give all thou canst; high Heaven rejects the lore/ Of nicely-calculated less or more?" *What if* Easwaran's last

WHAT IS PSYCHOSPIRITUALITY?

paragraph of the guidance for the day reads, "But the spiritual approach is very simple. Whatever you give—it may be a check to a worthy cause, it may be clothes to a person who is cold, it may be food to the hungry, it may be medical help to the sick—do it without thinking of getting anything in return. Do it as a service to God, not reluctantly, but with joy."

Then *what if* the plowman who is clearing a part of the iced-over driveway, where your car is parked, knocks on your door? It could be he is just the person who plows your driveway. It could even be a neighbor who you have known for many years. It could be *all or any* of those people rolled into one. He is angry because he phoned you earlier but you were in the shower, and you didn't hear the phone ring. He is angry because of many reasons: he had to wait several hours to borrow the plow truck, he has been salting the driveway since early morning, he is tired, and he is cold—all of the above.

Standing outside with him beside your car, which you are about to move, the weight of *his* anxiety snaps his otherwise taciturn nature and normal good intentions, and he says, "We need to live in *the real world*. If I am offending you, I can't help it. I am not sensitive [with the ellipsis filling the air with 'like you']," his eyes burning directly into you.

Well, here it is: your opportunity to accept this moment of synchronicity in either accepting a challenge to engage in a verbal exchange you immediately know you will rue, even by only defending yourself, or by just uttering one inconsiderate word. However, you can, indeed, offer him "not reluctantly, but with joy" by giving "all thou canst." Your intuition is ringing like a bell: there is nothing you can do to assuage him or the situation. Your inner voice is exclaiming, "Let go of his insinuation that you don't live in *the real world*. Just let go. Let go of being right. Let go of being wrong."

Driving over to the mall in the winter rain, tapping lightly on the hood of the car, you feel a sense of peace. No amount of preparation could have prepared you for just being in the moment, being present, being in harmony with a moment of synchronicity in your life in which *your* anxiety wasn't a determining or detrimental factor. As Easwaran intimates: doing something "without thinking of getting anything in return" is veritable joy enough to fully grasp "High heaven" rejecting "the lore/ Of nicely-calculated less or more."

You don't even really feel a need to share your new secret with anyone that you feel you are, at this instant, truly, living in the real world.

References

Easwaran, Eknath, *Words to Live By: A Daily Guide to Leading an Exceptional Life,* Tomales, CA: Nilgiri Press/The Blue Mountain Center of Meditation, 2005.

Wordsworth, William, *The Collected Poems of William Wordsworth,* Ware, U.K.: Wordsworth Editions, Ltd., 1998.

ATTACHMENT: HOW IT AFFECTS YOU
AND HOW YOUR PARENTS ARE CULPABLE

Kate Murphy, contributing writer to *The New York Times*, conveys in her article, "Yes It's Your Parents' Fault," that despite what our culture of independence and individualism may signify "more than anything else, our intimate relationships, or lack thereof, shape and define our lives." Although she mentions the spectrum of schools of psychological thought regarding the understanding of attachment, it is the landmark work of English psychologist John Bowlby whose "attachment theory is now having a breakout moment, applied everywhere from inner-city preschools to executive coaching programs."

Bowlby's theory of attachment, which was validated by developmental American psychologist, Mary S. Ainsworth, espouses that depending upon the quality of our earliest attachments as children our experiences directly determines our adult behaviors. Expressing the gravity of this situation quite adeptly, Murphy writes that the psychological fallout from these patterns "has special resonance in an era when people seem more attached to their smartphones than to one another."

Murphy relays that our brain, as a baby, is ingrained with our own, albeit limited, experience of the working of relationships, based on how our primary caregivers related to us. This, she writes, makes sense since our evolutionary origins predicate our "need to figure out early on how to survive in our immediate environment."

Miriam Steele, co-director of the Center for Attachment Research, is quoted as clarifying the magnitude that attachment influences

ATTACHMENT

our lives, "If you're securely attached, that's great, because you have the expectation that if you are distressed you will be able to turn to someone for help and feel you can be there for others." Steele also posits, quite demonstratively, on our behalf, that "by later forming secure attachments that help you override your flawed internal working model" you can, as the German poet Rainer Maria Rilke wrote, "change your life."

However, with a 40-50% divorce rate, forming attachments of consequence may not may be facilitated by the experience our caregivers instilled in us. We may choose abusive relationships as adults due to how are brains were imprinted. Murphy writes that we may "act in ways that elicit insensitive, unreliable or abusive behavior, whatever is most familiar." "Or," she continues, we "may flee secure attachments because they feel unfamiliar."

Dr. Amir Levine, a psychiatrist at Columbia University, who has just co-authored a book, *Attached*, relays that how we respond to the attachments we make in our lives are based on our past experiences. An expert in the ways in which attachment inflects upon brain neurochemistry, Levine succinctly renders attachment, and its ramifications, with respect to how our brains function as "searching in Google where it fills in based on what you searched before."

What is exciting is the work that the New School at the University of Delaware is performing with assisting at-risk teenage mothers. What has been proven there is that how much our destinies might otherwise appear as being carved in stone they can be augmented and redirected. Murphy reports that "attachment-based intervention strategy called the Circle of Security, which has 19,000 trained facilitators in 20 countries, has also proved effective."

With attachment categories ranging from secure, insecure anxious, insecure avoidant, and insecure disorganized it should be

WHAT IS PSYCHOSPIRITUALITY?

relatively obvious to us as to which one we identify with, as well as with those individuals of consequence in our lives. Children's responses to unreliable caregivers can fluctuate from defiant behavior to a behavior of exhibiting not much interest at all in a lack of a caregiver's attention. The adult who was influenced by a caregiver's unreliable behavior may obsess about their relationships. Also, they may annoy their love interests by being overbearing. They may find it impossible to adopt an attitude of taking things slow. The latter behavior pattern ruled by an adult's inattention may affect the child as grownup by their proclivities for abandoning relationships early or to not return phone calls from their significant others if they persevere to remain involved.

Abusive caregivers who inculcated threatening behaviors in the children they reared effect the adults those children become with what Murphy notes as an expressions of "both anxious and avoidant behaviors in an illogical and erratic manner." Determinates in assessing one's behavior in relationship to attachment can be employed in such tests as the Adult Attachment Interview, which ascertains dominant attachment patterns, and self-report questionnaires such as the Attachment Styles and Close Relationship Survey. However, results may largely be based upon the physician administering the tests. Reports have shown that someone taking both tests could result in registering in quite different categories at the same time.

Peter Fonagy, a professor of psychoanalysis at the University of London, offers the keen discernment that "you need a social context to sustain your sense of security." Murphy frames attachment quite brilliantly in the axiomatic tautology of "people in the insecure categories can become more secure when they form close relationships with secure people, secure people can become less so if paired with people who are insecure." In other words, it is quite pertinent to be aware of who you partnered with and to possibly gain understanding as to why.

Not being partnered at all also hinges on a pertinent theory of attachment, and discovering the underlying reason would be nothing less that liberating.

Murphy offers us the guidance that it is not in finding what may be the perfect partner that assures us to maintain balance of our attachments, since perfect partners do not exist, but she quotes, Dr. Fonagy, who gifts us with the key to the problem of attachment itself, by his saying, "if free flow of communication is impaired, the relationship is, too."

References

Bowlby, John, *Attachment* (New York: Basic Books, 1969).

Levine, Amir, and Rachel F. S. Heller, *Attached: The New Science of Adult Attachment and How It Can Help You Find—and Keep—Love,* New York: Tarcher/Penguin, 2010.

Murphy, Kate, "Yes, It's Your Parents' Fault," *The New York Times,* Sunday Review/News Analysis, January 7, 2017.

ORIGINS OF THE INNER VOICE: DIFFERENCE BETWEEN DIVINITY, CONSCIOUSNESS, AND MADNESS

When we hear voices apparently not our own, and Jerome Groopman summons examples from the Hebrew Bible in which "God's voice, in midrash, was heard communally, but was so overwhelming that only the first letter, aleph, was sounded." In an article published in *The New Yorker,* entitled "The Voices in our Heads: Why Do People Talk to Themselves?," he continues that "in later prophetic books the divine voice grows quieter. Elijah, on Mt. Horeb, is addressed by God (after a whirlwind, a fire, and an earthquake) in what the King James Bible called a 'still small voice,' and which, in the original Hebrew (*kol demanah dakah*), is even more suggestive—literally, 'the sound of slender silence.'"

Groopman cites Martin Luther King hearing the voice of Jesus and the instructions to continue "to fight on" after the beginning of the Montgomery, Alabama bus boycott in 1956. Groopman also mentions "other celestial powers" in 15th-century France when Joan of Arc "testified to hearing angels and saints tell her to lead the French Army in rescuing her country from English domination." He also cites the example of 15th-century English mystic Margery Kempe who "reported that Christ spoke to her from a short distance in a 'sweet and gentle' voice."

Julian Jaynes and *The Origin of Consciousness in the Bicameral Mind*

What is quite enlightening is Groopman's revivification of the landmark work by Princeton psychologist, Julian Jaynes, who published his seminal book, *The Origin of Consciousness in the Breakdown of the Bicameral Mind,* in which he, as Groopman writes, "proposed a biological basis for the hearing of divine voices." The great interest here is Jaynes' theory that about the time of the writing of the *Iliad* human brains were "bicameral," or constituted of two separate chambers. Jaynes formulates that then the brain's left hemisphere did, indeed, comprise the area where language functions.

However, the right hemisphere, as developed as it was at that time, "spoke" when under the provocation of stress. Jaynes writes, "The characters of the *Iliad* do not sit down and think out what to do. They have no conscious minds such as we say we have, and certainly no introspections." Jaynes mentions how Achilles goes into battle clothed "in a golden fire reaching up to heaven and screams through his throat across the bloodied trench at the Trojans, rousing in them ungovernable panic. In fact, the gods take the place of consciousness."

Marius Romme and the Hearing Voices Movement

Jaynes also posits that the writing of *The Odyssey* transpired more than a century later than the *Iliad*, and that during this time "the development of nerve fibres connecting the two hemispheres gradually integrated brain function."

Groopman mentions the Hearing Voices Movement, initiated by Dutch psychiatrist, Marius Romme, which was precipitated by his treatment of a patient, Patsy Hage, who was afflicted by "malign voices."

Groopman writes, "Hage insisted that her voice-hearing was a valid mode of thought. Not coincidentally, she was familiar with the work of Julian Jaynes. 'I'm not a schizophrenic,' she told Romme. 'I'm an ancient Greek.'" The Hearing Voices movement has centers 80 centers in England and has now

WHAT IS PSYCHOSPIRITUALITY?

networked into 24 countries. It has given credence to the phenomena of hearing voices, worldwide.

Kay Redfield Jamison's *Robert Lowell, Setting the River on Fire*

Groopman also cites Kay Redfield Jamison's new book, *Robert Lowell, Setting the River on Fire: A Study of Genius, Mania, and Character* (New York: Knopf, 2017), in which she relates how Boston's own poetic genius Robert Lowell found an alter ego in Achilles and his translating the first word of the *Iliad*, which is *menin* in Greek, as "mania," instead of "wrath" or "rage," as other translators had.

Groopman writes that Jamison "shows that Lowell sometimes saw his episodes of manic inspiration in a more coldly medical light. After a period of intense religious revelation, he wrote, 'The *mystical* experiences and explosions turned out to be pathological.' Splitting the difference, Jamison suggests that his mania and his imagination were welded into great art by the discipline he exerted between his manic episodes."

We can only what speculate what "mania" transpires, as it did recently at a press conference with President Donald Trump, and his hostile displays of aggression, cheered on by his own retinue, whose support of him can be heard much like the *menin of* a tragic Greek chorus.

References

Groopman, Jerome, "The Voices in Our Heads: Why Do People Talk to Themselves?," *The New Yorker,* January 9, 2017, pp. 70-73.

Jamison, Kay Redfield, *Robert Lowell, Setting the River on Fire: A Study of Genius, Mania, and Character* (New York: Knopf, 2017).

Jaynes, Julian, *The Origin of Consciousness in the Breakdown of the Bicameral Mind* (Boston: Houghton Mifflin, 1976).

POST-ELECTION COLLECTIVE TRAUMA: HOW TO MANAGE THE STRESS OF HAVING AN AUTOCRATIC PRESIDENT

Neil Gross, writing in an article, "Are Americans Experiencing Collective Trauma?," in *The New York Times*, makes note of "damage to an individual's psyche caused by an extremely distressing event," however, he also mentions "another kind of trauma: a collective disturbance that happens to a group of people when their world is suddenly upended."

With Donald Trump losing the popular vote by nearly 3 million voters and just managing to win significant states such as Michigan, Pennsylvania, and Wisconsin by only some 107,330 cumulative votes, there are many Americans who have been traumatized by the autocratic, staunch, and all too frequently offensive rhetoric and unethical tactics that the new president abides by. To envision the first 100 days of what such a presidency might yield is a source of trauma for what constitutes most Americans never mind what this aggregate of the population will need to endure for the next four years, if Trump's unwavering tenacity to bombast isn't somehow mitigated.

The Buffalo Creek Flood of 1972

Due to a coal mining company pouring over a million gallons of wastewater and sludge into Buffalo Creek, a mountain hollow in West Virginia, insufficiently protected by a dam of diminutive dimension, on February 26th the containing walls burst. What ensued was, as Neil Gross writes, "An enormous wall of thick black waste [that] came barreling down the hollow, destroying one mining hamlet after another. Homes, churches, roads—everything was swept away. One hundred and twenty-five people were killed."

A year later, the area was visited by esteemed Yale University sociologist Kai Erikson. As Erikson writes in his eminent book on the subject, *Everything in Its Path*, "The floodwaters carried away not just physical objects but also relationships and routines that had defined life there for generations. Without these social anchors, residents struggled to find meaning and purpose. They were disoriented and disconnected in ways that could outlast even the effects of their individual psychological traumas. Socially, they were in a permanent state of shock."

Emile Durkheim and the Significance of Social Order

20th-century French sociologist Emile Durkheim's main tenets were grounded in his research in collective trauma. He contended that "norms, values, and rituals" established the groundwork for social order. Without the foundation for societal norms, when any collective trauma splits the framework that ties people together then that community suffers the fracturing of such an occurrence on a deeply personal level.

A flood such as the one that washed away a town at Buffalo Creek had such an effect. Ron Everyman wrote a book regarding the effects from Hurricane Katrina, *Is This America?*, which was based on Kai Erikson's findings at Buffalo Creek. Neil Gross speculates, in his article, that "Wars, genocide, financial crises, even large-scale movements of population can radically challenge established ways of living together."

Factory Closings and Trumped-up Rhetoric

Gross, who is a professor of sociology at Colby College and the author of *Why Are Professors Liberal and Why Do Conservatives*

Care?, relates that 24% of Americans held manufacturing jobs in 1960. That figure is 8% today. The mills and factories in which mostly American men worked not only provided financial means for families but also became institutions of pride within working class communities themselves. As those factories closed, men who weren't college educated needed to take lower sector jobs for meager salaries. The result was an increase in alcohol and drug dependency. An entire way of life was lost along with the factory closings.

Trump rode the rhetoric of his promises into the White House in his assurances of bringing manufacturing jobs back to America. Whether or not this is even possible is only one of the questions regarding the larger electorate of the country since they voted for Hillary Clinton and a more progressive vision of a brighter America for everyone.

Although Democrats and Republicans have argued on the ways in which issues should be resolved, never has there been a candidate who completely eschews not only political norms but shows no regard whatsoever for what Neil Gross calls "fundamental ethical" sensibilities such as espousing that an opposing candidate should be jailed for what are uncorroborated actions, as Trump threatened Clinton, or a candidate who as Gross cites as "celebrating sexual assault," as Trump unceremoniously denied.

We can also add to this list, since collective American memory appears to be short-lived: Trump bragging that he could still be elected even if he had shot someone on Fifth Avenue.

Reclaiming Our Identity and Where to Go from Here

Lines of propriety have not only been crossed but they are now blurred and redefined by an active barbarity. Gross writes,

WHAT IS PSYCHOSPIRITUALITY?

"Rightly or wrongly, memories have been activated of historical traumas linked with anti-democratic politics, such as the emergence of fascism in interwar Europe and the rise of Senator Joseph McCarthy in the 1950s."

Visionary in title, Ron Everyman's book, *Is This America?*, regards the collective trauma that was precipitated by Hurricane Katrina. Similarly, we hear many people discussing the current predicament of America with regard to its new president, Donald Trump. Gross writes, "It's a telltale sign of collective trauma, a grasping for identity when the usual bases for community aren't there anymore. If research on other collective traumas is any indication, it may take years, and a great deal of political imagination, for us to figure out where to go from here."

Where we go on from here is all up to us—each and every individual in our American society—and it is within our power to call up within ourselves the greater angels of empathy and compassion to assist not only ourselves in coming through this next era in the history of our country but also to offer the best of who we are to those around us so that we may stand tall on high moral ground and to preserve the fundamental democratic values we esteem.

References

Erikson, Kai, *Everything in Its Path: Destruction of Community in the Buffalo Creek Flood*, New York, NY: Simon & Schuster, 1976.

Everyman, Ron, *Is This America?: Katrina as Cultural Trauma*, Austin, TX: University of Texas Press, 2015.

Gross, Neil, "Are Americans Experiencing Collective Trauma," *The New York Times*, December 16, 2016.

Gross, Neil, *Why Are Professors Liberal and Why Do Conservatives Care?*, Cambridge, MA: Harvard University Press, 2013.

A Pair of Forewords and a Meditation

TOWARDS AN ACTIVE SPIRITUALITY

In the summer of 1973, one of the most distinct memories I have is my avidly reading the Gia-Feng Fu and Jane English translation of the *Tao Te Ching* (New York, NY: Vantage/Random House, 1972). Reading *the watercourse way*, as it is called by scholars, was written by ancient Chinese writer and philosopher, Laozi, also often spelled as Lao Tzu and Lao Tze, who was born in 6th-centry BCE and who died in 531 BCE. The eighty-one verses which compose *The Daodejing*, spelled as in the new English version, is a recent interpretation by three poets and scholars, Steven Schroeder, of Chicago, Illinois; David Breeden, of Minneapolis, MN; and myself. Steve is a painter, a translator, a poet, a professor of philosophy who occasionally still teaches at the University of Chicago, and the Editor and Publisher of Virtual Artists Collective. David is a Universalist Minister, who studied writing at Iowa Writer's Workshop and acquired a Masters in Divinity from Meadville Lombard Theological School. This *translation* was published rather beautifully, including Steve's watercolors, by Jerry Craven, Editor and Publisher of Lamar University Press, in Beaumont, Texas, in January 2015.

When I first read Laozi, I was transported to a transcendent realm—and still am. In my late teens, I had weaned myself on the translations of Kenneth Rexroth, the inspiration of the San Francisco Literary Renaissance in the late 1940s and 1950s. Rexroth's *100 Poems from the Chinese* and *100 Poems from the Japanese* (both from New Directions) provided some of the basis from which I initially discovered my love for poetry. It is realistic to believe that those books and my reading of *The Daodejing* led to my persevering to work in the forms of lyric poetry, haiku, and when I was invited, by Steve, some forty years later, to compose my own interpretations of Laozi's eighty-one verses of his Taoist classic, which is sometimes referred to as poetry but it is always thought of as a philosophical and spiritual work of major proportions.

If anyone had whispered in my ear that I was to interpret—the word I use instead of *translate* since I don't read or speak Chinese—a new version of Laozi several decades later, I would have simply gotten down on my knees and offered them my absolute gratitude. As Steve referred to Laozi in emails and then in a launching of the book at the Broadside Bookshop in Northampton, Massachusetts in May 2015, for himself, David, and me, Laozi is *our old master*. The three of us had read not only the Feng and English translation but so very many others. *The Daodejing* is much translated and rendered in many different ways, with any number of inflections. I have had my favorites, which include the translations of Feng/English, of Ursula K. Le Guin, and of Steven Mitchell—whom I knew when he was a grad student at Yale.

The anecdote of the sheer serendipity of the occasion of such a creative endeavor is the result of an unusual brand of thoughtfulness and of colleagueship. Steve had finished his own translation of *The Daodejing*, and was invited to publish it by Jerry Craven, of Lamar University Press. Before going ahead with the preliminaries of publishing his version alone, he asked Jerry if he wouldn't mind him asking two friends—David and myself—to contribute to an *interactive* version of Laozi. Jerry agreed. What transpired between early January and the first week of March 2014 was a highly charged creative interchange between the three of us, which for me was, undoubtedly, the most inspired and visionary two months of my entire writing life.

During those first snowy weeks of early 2014, I locked in to Steve sending one of his versions of each of the eighty-one verses in

TOWARDS AN ACTIVE SPIRITUALITY

an email, which David and I would then *render*—which is my verb choice, instead of translate. I would then meditate on the verse, and it would eventually *speak* to me. The process was far from linear. I didn't necessarily begin with line one of each verse. Sometimes an image or a phrase from the very middle of the poem would resonate to me, and then afterwards it would be followed with a kind of fluidity, a music and a rhythm, and often a torrent of words, which lyrically sang within me. Initially, I compared translations with the Le Guin and then the Mitchell versions, both of which were different from any of ours, but quite soon discarded this practice since the *interactive* nature of what the three of us were doing was intrinsically different. What grew between us was synergetic and I actually felt the power of three poets who loved what they were doing so much that their egos were not at all in the way. I may never have felt freer and so connected with two other people at the same time. However, it was also being connected to *our old master,* Laozi.

Twice, I believe, during the interactive, but separate, composition, did David and I compare notes. We had sent emails to each other, which ostensibly exclaimed, "Can you believe that we are doing this?" Or "I have always *dreamed* of doing this." There was remarkable camaraderie and colleagueship. In early March, when we finished our interpretation of the eighty-one verses, we had a chance to revise any lines we thought might need further work, and for all intent and purpose, finished the project in about two months. The heat of the composition, which sometimes included two verses per day—one in the early morning and one in the evening—was like nothing I had ever experienced before. The fact that I was also engaged in a freelance writing project made this even a richer creative time for my writing. Living and breathing Laozi, I recall having my feet firmly planted on the planks of the yellow pine floor of my studio but with my consciousness coursing along *the watercourse way.* Quite simply, I felt that I was writing with such an active spontaneity that I was, as the phrase goes, out of my head.

A PAIR OF FOREWORDS AND A MEDITATION

Synchronicity occurs every day of our lives—all day long. Some days we notice it, others we don't. Sometimes it is not just the synchronicity of the moment but one of greater significance, as in a larger pattern, such as Steve Schroeder knowing my longstanding friend Jay C. Rochelle, who is now known as Father Gabriel. Steve and Jay had met in Chicago when they were grad students. For them to know each other, and for my first being acquainted with Steve through Virtual Artists Collective in his publishing two of my books, *Winding Paths Worn through Grass* (Chicago, IL: VAC, 2012) and *Velocity* (Chicago, IL: VAC, 2013), then after more than three decades reconnecting with Father Gabriel, all of that is all quite electric—as far as synchronicity goes.

Also being invited by Father Gabriel to provide an introduction to his *A Staff to a Pilgrim: Meditations on the Way with Nine Celtic Saints* (Emmaus, PA: Golden Alley Press, 2016) provided me with an opportunity to offer my gratitude to Father Gabriel for the years in New Haven which he invited me to be a part of his family: to dine with his children and himself, to meet with me in his study once a week every Monday, to be touched by his friendship and the confidence he placed in me, especially during the years in my early and mid-twenties when I was hardly wayward but sometimes slightly awry in navigating the coordinates of my life craft. Our luminous conversations regarding poets and philosophers, theologians and saints, novelists and calligraphers, kept me from veering too much astray from the solace occasioned by a safe harbor. Therefore the foreword I provided Father Gabriel for his new book was not only a joyous experience for me but also my coming full circle, as Joseph Campbell might say, a return home from a hero's journey. Being able to accomplish writing that foreword brought me spiritually closer to Father Gabriel and in doing so made me appreciate the best of my own beginnings sitting across from him in that booklined study in his brownstone on High Street in New Haven on those marvelous Monday mornings.

TOWARDS AN ACTIVE SPIRITUALITY

The Guided Meditation enclosed here is also a piece of writing I had wanted to achieve and fortunately found reason in doing so after being hired to write a few blogs for a psychotherapy association in Boston. I evoke my old mentor Joseph Campbell and my newer teacher Caroline Myss in my creating my own guided meditation using the seven chakras, which are explained to at least some degree in the piece itself. It is a morning meditation using the chakras in ascending order. Although the reader can use this as a frame of reference for their own chakra meditation using their own knowledge and predilections regarding the chakra system to either augment the morning meditation, or to fashion their own evening meditation by descending the chakras. I intuited that concluding this book with such a meditation could not be a better way to offer my gratitude for any reader who may have invested their time in reading it.

CO-TRANSLATOR'S PREFACE, *THE DAODEJING: A NEW INTERPRETATION*

My process in what I term *rendering* Laozi was initially reading the translation that Steve Schroeder would present in the Google Docs program, which I would then copy into my hardcover journal whose sole purpose was a workbook for *The Daodejing*. My approach was to place my *self* in the forefront of Steve's translation with an amount of veneration, then, and this was always crucial, to find, and more appropriately discover, where the lyric core of the poem arose from. When I found that, then my own *rendering* flowed. However, it may have been one or two of the middle lines, perhaps an image at the end, and most usually, especially toward the conclusion of *The Daodejing*, with the beginning lines, that I was able to locate the *source* of the flow of each particular verse.

My attempt was not only to *render* 'our old teacher,' Laozi, but to *play* off of Steve's translation—much like how John Coltrane released the sweet torrent of sound from his saxophone in harmonizing with Johnny Hartman's voice, and Johnny Hartman's debonair baritone rising to meet that effusion of Coltrane's grace notes—but also my purpose was to limn Steve's meaning; to shadow a phrase, here and there; and to offer both clarity and a mirror to the perpetuity of the sage's import and wisdom.

Steve's invitation for me to participate in this interactive *rendering* of *Dao,* is a watershed event for me—one in which I have prepared for all of my writing life. I am grateful for the opportunity to work with both Steve Schroeder and David Breeden, who both provided the appropriate *alchemy* for my own lyrical

CO-INTERPRETER'S PREFACE, *THE DAODEJING*

contributions to the project. I first came across the Gia-Fu Feng and Jane English translation of Laozi when I was twenty, over forty years ago in New Haven, when I was also reading every Eastern classic I could assimilate, as well as practicing Zazen with a small group of people in the basement of Yale Divinity School Chapel. Although I augmented my reading of Steve's translations with the Feng and English version, and often enough chose to strike a balance between the two to actually and effectively fashion a new *rendering*, I have also treasured Ursula K. LeGuin's translation, as well as Stephen Mitchell's, who, on occasion, as I recall, was one of the other participants in sitting meditation in the basement at the Divinity School Chapel, when he was grad student at Yale.

So, my being invited to *render* Laozi has been completing an enormous circle for me, as Joseph Campbell, whose voluminous works of comparative religion and mythology I have studied, might point out as being *the hero's journey*. In that time it is not only Campbell who I found both inspiration and guidance from, much after my discovery of Laozi, but also the psycho-spirituality of the modern mystic Carolyn Myss, and the high octane spirituality of *The Guide Lectures*, channeled by Eva Pierrakos, among many others, whose writing regarding higher consciousness have affected me, such as Pema Chodron, Katherine MacCoun, and Eckhart Tolle—all of whose insights, at least partially, I have integrated, and that have lent themselves to becoming some of the very philosophical underpinnings of my *renderings* of *The Daodejing*.

It is with gratitude, and an active humility, that I thank everyone here that I have mentioned by name, including, of course, 'our old teacher,' and offer a deep appreciation for the verses themselves, as well as for Yinxi, the sentry at the western gate, who, aprocryphally or not, stopped Laozi, and asked him to record his wisdom before moving on, into the frontier, beyond, which as a result was *The Daodejing*—for it is as if I have come

A PAIR OF FOREWORDS AND A MEDITATION

to meet them both, stepping out of the western frontier of the future, to greet them in the *eternal now of the present*, in which we all have come together, with our hands placed firmly palm to palm, bowing to one another, in unison, not to affect benefit for ourselves, but for the positive intent and good will of every reader.

South Amherst, Massachusetts
March 2014

CO-INTERPRETER'S PREFACE, *THE DAODEJING*

* * * *

#1

Walking the way is not the true walk
of the way.
When we speak the name of the way,
it is not the real name.

When everything began, it grew out of
the name;
and the name of the word is
the mother of the ten thousand things.

When we desire nothing, we see what is;
when we want more, we become blind.
What transpires, transpires, as a spring—
and the fountain runs, from the source.

However, there are two names for
what is but one; the one that is whole—
when these are found together,
we enter a realm of mystery.

This mystery opens
when we no longer see it as mystery—
again, on its threshold,
the door to self is no door at all.

* * * *

#81

Reliable words that exact truth sometimes lack aesthetics.
Aesthetic words that express what is genuine

may not always be reliable.
Those who are wise, and whose actions originate

from their center, do not quarrel.
And those who are contentious are not only unwise but

they can also be as dishonorable as they are disagreeable.
The sage is never one to accrue

or collect anything—either bad or good, except maybe rainwater.

The practice
of the sage, is to do as much that can be done for others—

which only increases the inner wealth of all.
The more the sage

gives to others, the more abundance there is to keep on giving.

Dao of heaven
is incisive, but the diamond of its divinity never does any

harm.
Dao of the sage, always with the propensity of being active,

if only
it is accessed, through *the practice of no practice*, is—

not to endeavor; but to move in harmony with
what is without and within—the greater force of nature.

FOREWORD TO *A STAFF TO A PILGRIM: MEDITATIONS ON THE WAY WITH NINE CELTIC SAINTS*

I first met Fr Gabriel in New Haven forty years ago, when he was a campus minister at Yale. We would meet every Monday morning in the front office of the brownstone he and his family lived in. Lined floor to ceiling with shelves of books, the room faced the sidewalk on High Street. Our conversations were as nourishing as the bread and pasta Fr Gabriel made for family dinners, which I was often enough invited to. These were conversations of magnitude and depth, as we discussed poetry and spirituality from Wendell Berry to Tomas Transtromer, from Thich Nhat Hanh to Henri Nouwen. We talked of *The Practice of the Presence of God* by Brother Lawrence and the Jesus prayer.

These Monday conversations were springboards to transcendent moments in which the air filled with the intensity of a psychic pointillism. They offered me both clarity and a renewed vision, which would provide me with grist for thought and contemplation during the rest of the week. My initial source and first taste of discovering the numinous in the commonplace, the main thing I strive for in my poetic practice, may well have come from that book-lined front room. As Fr Gabriel writes in the mediation after the life of St Melangell in this volume, "to see the holy in the ordinary, the transcendent in the momentary, vast infinity within the confines of place . . . this is sometimes called seeing 'the cosmic Christ.'"

I am drawn to the rigorous philosophical investigation of the practice of maintaining an actual spiritual life as laid out in *A*

A PAIR OF FOREWORDS AND A MEDITATION

Staff to the Pilgrim. Fr Gabriel gives an historical recounting of each of the nine saints, and each one serves as a touchstone for his meditative, and sometimes lyrical, extrapolations to help us in our spiritual practices of paying attention to one's inner voice, the practice of presence, and finding guidance in our lives. His discussion of *hiraeth* as spiritual mystery, or nostalgia, draws me in as I am drawn to Federico Garcia Lorca's literary trope of Duende, or mysterious spirit.

I found in Fr Gabriel's book parallels and complements to other works of spirituality that have nourished me over the years, both in philosophy and the quality of the craft of the writing itself. In his meditation upon the life of St Cuthbert, Fr Gabriel offers that "quiet is the threshold, not the doorway, but there can be no door without the threshold." This brings to mind the small book that offers large dimensions, Thomas Merton's *Thoughts in Solitude: Meditations on the Spiritual Life and Man's Solitude Before God.*

In portraying St Brigid in her spiritual valor, reminding us that "anyone without a soul friend is like a body without a head," Fr Gabriel also befriends each of us. He befriends us by offering us spiritual guidance on our way to real healing. There is nothing about the path that is not *de rigueur*, since it is distinguished by integrity, and it is beyond anger, beyond coldness in others.

As Fr Gabriel writes, "the allure of the divine" is "beckoning us toward fulfillment." To me, this echoes with tones resonant in the poetry of Rainer Maria Rilke. As the eminent translator Stephen Mitchell writes of Rilke in conjunction with his composition of the *Sonnets to Orpheus*, he suggests that at first he was writing about Orpheus; at the end of the sequence he, himself, became Orpheus. The same can be said about Fr Gabriel—we move with him as he discusses the saints with us, then he graciously hands us our own staff to be pilgrims on our way.

FOREWORD TO *A STAFF TO A PILGRIM*

Even in those long-ago years, Fr Gabriel's interests lay in baking, calligraphy, and bicycling. It is a pleasure to recognize these three enduring threads interwoven in the tapestry of *A Staff to the Pilgrim*. We read about Fr Gabriel's encounter with the famous French bread baker, Lionel Poilâne, for whom bread was the heart of his spiritual vision. I recall Fr Gabriel's passion for the craft of calligraphy and our sharing a reverence for the work of Frederick Franck, whose spiritual ethos informed what was then a recent book, *The Zen of Seeing* (New York, NY: Vintage, 1973).

My friend's zeal for bicycling continues to lead him to explore the spiritual presence therein. Reminiscent of Robert M. Pirsig's ontological explorations in *Zen and the Art of Motorcycle Maintenance* (New York, NY: Harper Torch, 1974), Fr Gabriel tells us, "God is waiting if only we don't hold back and try to hold on to whatever has already gone by." That may be the mantra of the universal bicyclist, breezing on through the wind, sweeping past the countryside on physical and spiritual aerodynamics as both sacred exercise and devotional practice.

A Staff to the Pilgrim is iconic, inspirational, and provident in its offering of guidance for all of us in leading an active spiritual life. It offers us the beneficent combination of erudition and wonder—as in awe—with which it springs forth. When we are provided with a new and fruitful way of leading our lives in the world that combines the material and the physical with the spiritual and the transcendent, we are given an auspicious and true gift—a gift which this book marvelously makes to readers everywhere.

South Amherst, Massachusetts
April 2016

GUIDED CHAKRA MEDITATION

The chakras, or energy centers in our ethereal body, offer an energized guided meditation either in the morning or the evening, or both. In the morning meditation, you are entering the world anew, rising through chakras one through seven. In the evening meditation, you are withdrawing from the world, and before you go to sleep, and set your soul free, you descend from chakras seven to one.

Joseph Campbell, aided by his encyclopedic knowledge of comparative religion and mythology, provides some of the best insight into the chakras in his book, *Transformations of Myth through Time* (Harper Perennial, 1990). In it, Campbell discusses in depth both the practice of Kundalini, which makes use of the chakras, and *The Tibetan Book of the Dead*. There may not be more clarity found anywhere which elicits what the chakras are and what powers they possess.

Additionally, there is a rather in depth practicum of use of the chakras in Caroline Myss's 2-CD set, *Spiritual Power, Spiritual Practice: Energy Evaluation Meditations for Morning and Evening* (Louisville, KY: Sounds True, 2000). In it, Myss guides the listener through the chakras and readies them for the day they are about to live and aids them in reflecting in a daily review before they enter sleep, and release their soul.

Practical Guided Meditation with Chakras

What is proposed here, as a guided meditation using the chakras is a gloss on what Myss offers with some backstory of Campbell's interpretation, obviously, along with a more poetic elucidation of the various meanings which each chakra resonates. After using this specific guided meditation, it might be useful to read what Campbell writes about the chakras, and to listen to the Myss morning/evening meditation employing the chakras. However, what the practitioner may eventually find is that they may develop their own interpretations of the chakras in relation to both what they are, as power centers, and what they might signify for the individual themselves.

* * * *

Morning Meditation—Chakras, to Get Ready for the Day

First Chakra

Think of the color, red, as in the dawn sky. This is the color of the first chakra. It is often referred to as alimentary. This is also where the base of the spine rests. You can choose to hold tight to your own existence, or you can make the decision to release your grip. You are free to do so. Identify your fears. As you release your hold, you open within yourself. As you identify your fears, feel the strength in your replacing them with something other than fear. You can smell the rich fragrance of damp earth. You feel the delight of the morning wind, lightly over your body. You revel in the blueness of the sky.

Second Chakra

Think of the color orange, as in the sun after it has ascended the mountain ridge. This is the color of the second chakra. It contains the energy of sexuality. It is found in the hips, the genital area. This is the power of union, but it is also infused with creativity. This chakra radiates with energy. Who are you going to meet today? How are you going to respond? How are you going to honor others today? Be in touch with your creative energy today. Feel the warmth within you, and over your body enjoy the heat of the sun.

A PAIR OF FOREWORDS AND A MEDITATION

Third Chakra

Think of the color yellow. Think of the sun rising in the sky. Think of that power. This is the chakra of conquest. This chakra is located at the level of the naval or the solar plexus. Breathe in. Breathe out. There is power in this. Although the power of this chakra has been associated with violence, you can use this energy in turning it around to yourself. Reflect on your own sense of dignity. Imagine how you want to live your life today. Think of your integrity. Think of your strength in action in being courageous. Are you in need of someone's approbation today? Or are you able to find that within yourself, while being kind to others. Imagine the sawgrass blowing in the wind in a cove beside the ocean. Imagine the powerful waves rolling in from the sea.

Fourth Chakra

The color of the fourth chakra is green. It is as verdant as a meadow. Its Sanskrit name is *Anahata*, which means "no hit." It is located at the heart. It is also the touchstone of spirituality. It refers to the sound made when two objects are struck together. This is the sound of the manifestation of the universe. This is the center of love. Think of who you love today. Imagine those who you need to forgive. If you are unable to forgive them today, release a prayer to find a way to do so. Remind yourself how much forgiveness is difficult. Remind yourself how much you might want to forgive yourself today. Feel the love that is shining forth from your heart. Walk into this day with that love. Walk into the day in gratitude, whether or not certain things you want to happen occur today. Radiate the warmth in your heart today. See how the forest is backlit by the sun. Listen to the branches crackle in the light breeze. Inhale the resin of the pines.

Fifth Chakra

The color of the fifth chakra is blue. It is the chakra of purification. It is located at the larynx. This is the chakra of spiritual purification; of holding back all of the animal energies of the lower chakras. Allow *divine will* to flow through you. This is the chakra of placing others above yourself. Think how you can assist others today. Relinquish your own will to that of a power other than yours. When you speak, speak confidently. This power, located at your throat, will assist you in talking clearly and communicating honestly. Think of a flowing brook, the clarity of the water, the surge of it rushing over the stones, its spray bristling across your face. Feel the freshness of that. Open to that, as you open to the love flowing within you.

Sixth Chakra

The color of this chakra is indigo or purple. The Sanskrit name for this chakra is *Anja,* which is "lotus of Command," and located between the eyebrows. It is also known as "the chakra of heaven" or the "highest level of incarnate forms." The 13th- and 14th-century German mystic, Meister Eckhart wrote, "The ultimate leave-taking is the leaving of God for God." This is the chakra of the transcendent. Imagine the realm behind your eyes. Seek to learn what your divine plan is and not the one you might desire yourself. Feel clear today. Feel that you will not perpetuate any grievances or illusions about yourself or others. They no longer serve you. Enter your day in full knowing that what has happened in your life has occurred for a reason. Be grateful for your own truths. Be open to the truths of others. Know this is the only way, that you are on the path, the sunlight shining through the leaves of the trees, and the shadows darkening into purple.

Seventh Chakra

The color of this chakra is either violet or white. The Sanskrit for this chakra is *Sahasrara,* meaning thousand-petaled. This is the lotus at the top of the head. What exits here is undifferentiated consciousness. There is no "I." There is only silence—upon which life originates from and to which it returns. This

A PAIR OF FOREWORDS AND A MEDITATION

is also the chakra of the eternity found in the present moment. Reflect on being present for this moment and for each moment during the course of your day. Know that this is all you have and all that will ever be. Allow yourself to let go of what happened yesterday and everything that has occurred to you in the past. Reflect on mindfully living your life today—without any anticipations of tomorrow.

POETICS AND PRACTICE

Wally Swist in Conversation with Lynne DeSilva-Johnson

Greetings comrade! Thank you for talking to us about your process today! Can you introduce yourself, in a way that you would choose?

My name is Wally Swist. I practice in a variety of genres: poetry, haiku, poetry translation/interpretation, nonfiction, children's literature, and memoir.

Why are you a poet/writer/artist?

Becoming a poet and a writer is a calling. I was drawn to literature and writing in my mid-teens. The gestation, or the journey, of becoming a writer or a poet is a one of an entire lifetime. It is life-altering and life-augmenting.

When did you decide you were a poet/writer/artist (and/or: do you feel comfortable calling yourself a poet/writer/artist, what other titles or affiliations do you prefer/feel are more accurate)?

I never introduce myself as a poet, but do offer that I am a writer and an editor. My favorite anecdote regarding this is what the Israeli poet, Yehuda Amichai, said to me, once many years ago, upon meeting him. He said, with his characteristic humility: "I am only a poet when I am writing."

What's a "poet" (or "writer" or "artist") anyway? What do you see as your cultural and social role (in the literary / artistic / creative community and beyond)?

WALLY SWIST IN CONVERSATION

True writers and poets write because they need to. Poems and stories are edicts. The best literature had to have been written—and the work reflects that urgency and need. Cultural and social forces shape any writer's or poet's work. You may live in the mountains and write mountain poems. However, since Trump has been elected president you will more than likely begin writing poems about Trump trying to take away the mountains.

Talk about the process or instinct to move these poems (or your work in general) as independent entities into a body of work. How and why did this happen? Have you had this intention for a while? What encouraged and/or confounded this (or a book, in general) coming together? Was it a struggle?

Life is struggle. Politics are, too. To understand this we must be cognizant that struggle is not anything that is mitigated by progressive social gains. Struggle continues at all times. It is ongoing. Our struggle against our oppressors is what lights the darkness.

Books, early on, that made a difference were *The Stranger* by Albert Camus, the plays of Henrik Ibsen, Ginsberg's *Howl* and Corso's *Gasoline*, Robert Creeley's *For Love*. Also, reading *Sailor on Horseback*, Irving Stone's memorable fictional biography of Jack London offered me hope that I could one day become a writer. Reading Joseph Campbell some three decades later also opened doors and made me rich.

Did you envision this collection as a collection or understand your process as writing or making specifically around a theme while the poems themselves were being written / the work was being made? How or how not?

I am at an age when one thinks of what one has possibly accomplished. *Singing for Nothing from Street to Street: Selected Nonfiction as Literary Memoir* brings together 40 years of scrupulously selected nonfiction interspersed with memoir. The editor of The Operating System, Lynne DeSilva-Johnson offered direction on the project in my writing memoir that might push the genre of just an ordinary nonfiction collection. It was her brilliance that sparked me into writing the memoir, and I am grateful to her for her guidance. She is an exemplary editor and a visionary publisher.

What formal structures or other constrictive practices (if any) do you use in the creation of your work? Have certain teachers or instructive environments, or readings/writings/work of other creative people informed the way you work/write?

For decades, I found a friend in perseverance. The last decade I have found my angel in what I call *listening to guidance*. *Listening to guidance* may be for some another way of learning to be vigilant to hearing one's inner voice. Also, even though one more than likely, whether writer or poet, has had mentors or teachers, the real work needs to have been developed by you and spoken through your voice. Finding one's own voice is part of the journey. There are no secrets, except for executing the work itself. Through the work one discovers the power of one's voice. Through the work one comes to terms regarding how one lives and then through that process the work just might possess some life of its own, beyond the writer.

Speaking of monikers, what does your title represent? How was it generated? Talk about the way you titled the book, and how your process of naming (individual pieces, sections, etc) influences you and/or colors your work specifically.

My book's title was generated by lines of a poem by the late Californian poet, Bert Meyers, wrote:

> Be like the rain
> that wears a ragged coat

    and finds the lamp
    in the smallest stone
    and sings for nothing
    from street to street

from *In a Dybbuk's Raincoat: Collected Poems* (Mary Burritt Christiansen Poetry Series/University of New Mexico Press, 2007).

However, many poets and writers influence my work. Nonfiction writers include Joan Didion, Peter Matthiessen, John McPhee, and John Hanson Mitchell. Poets include Walt Whitman, Lorine Niedecker, Bert Meyers, Robert Francis, Federico Garcia Lorca, Juan Ramon Jimenez, Richard Wilbur, Mary Oliver, and too many others to mention.

What does this particular work represent to you
... as indicative of your method/creative practice?
... as indicative of your history?
... as indicative of your mission/intentions/hopes/plans?

When one assembles and crafts any *Selected* volume it is an enormous endeavor. It is a privilege to have lived and to possibly have written well enough to find reasons enough to gather work for such a tribute. The tribute being to the work itself and not so much the author. A *Selected* volume is really meant for readers now and in the future. Hopefully, such a book will contain enough guideposts it will be worth for readers and writers to glean from in the present and for many years to come.

What does this book DO (as much as what it says or contains)?

This book, if anything, is a testament. It is a testament of 40 years of belief, of perseverance, of diligence, and of courage. The book at its best should mirror the times: from the late 1970s to the mid-21st century teens. The book really is more than just a memoir and certainly more than just a *Selected Nonfiction*. It is a book about writing and the shaping of a writer. The book is also about espousing literature and the love of reading writing that is well written.

What would be the best possible outcome for this book? What might it do in the world, and how will its presence as an object facilitate your creative role in your community and beyond? What are your hopes for this book, and for your practice?

My practice continues. However, as is previously offered, any *Selected* volume is its own watershed. My best hopes for the book are that writers of any age might find camaraderie and possibly inspiration in reading the work.

Let's talk a little bit about the role of poetics and creative community in social activism, in particular in what I call "Civil Rights 2.0," which has remained immediately present all around us in the time leading up to this series' publication. I'd be curious to hear some thoughts on the challenges we face in speaking and publishing across lines of race, age, privilege, social/cultural background, and sexuality within the community, vs. the dangers of remaining and producing in isolated "silos."

Publishing writing is a public act. If we, as writers, are fortunate to publish, and actually, initially, to have written well at all, then what we publish is definitely an example of social activism, especially if there is any consciousness whatsoever that is exhibited in the work whatsoever. It is more important, as well as significant, to write about racism or ageism, for instance, which is close to my own struggle, and/or privilege, which is what I would call *entitlement,* as it is to write a poem about clouds.

However, it is how you might write a poem about clouds. If you are Vladimir Mayakovsky, then you may be brilliant enough to write about "a cloud in your trousers" or how "the material is words from the vocabulary of soldiers" and "the tools of production—a pencil stub," as can be found in his marvelous book, *How Verses Are Made* (Jonathan Cape, 1971).

We are never thoroughly isolated as writers. Emily Dickinson wrote in seclusion but her poems were her "letters to the world." Miklos Radnoti, the Hungarian poet, whose body was found in a mass grave after World War II by his wife, discovered that there was a manuscript of poems in his coat pockets, which was published as his inimitable collection (of hope), entitled *The Clouded Sky*.

Writing is a very social act.

Is there anything else we should have asked, or that you want to share?

Yes, there is. I am so very honored and grateful that my book is on the same list as those by the great Jerome Rothenberg and the perennially inspiring Margret Randall. Frankly, I couldn't be any happier.

ACKNOWLEDGMENTS

These essays, haiku, poems, and reviews, etc. have appeared in the following periodicals and books, nearly all in an earlier form, and appear here in quite often refreshed, revised, and/or updated versions.

All of the brief quotes from various works cited in this volume originally appeared in the essays and reviews as they were originally published in the publications listed below and were used for the sole purposes of extolling the works themselves.

Adelaide Literary Magazine (New York & Lisbon): "Anxiety and Synchronicity: Living in the Real World," "Anxiety, Time, and Being Present in the Moment"
all roads will lead you home: Poetic Alchemy: Wislawa Szymborska's *Map: Collected and Last Poems*
Anchor Magazine: Where Spirituality and Social Justice Meet: "Anxiety: Not Being Needed and What to Do about It"
Appalachia: "Daylilies"
Connecticut River Review: The Kingfisher's Reign by Jonas Zdanys
Empirical Magazine: "Homage to Ed Ricketts"
Frogpond: The Journal of the Haiku Society of America, review of *Not Asking what if--Selected and New*, Adele Kenny (Libertyville, IL: Issue 39:3, 2017), Christopher Pachtel, Editor
The Galway Review (Ireland): "Sooey"
Grolier's Masterplots: Being Here by Robert Penn Warren, *The Dream of the Golden Mountains* by Malcolm Cowley; *Field Work* by Seamus Heaney; *Basin and Range* by John McPhee; *Native Realm* by Czeslaw Milosz; *Mirabell: Books of Number* by James Merrill
Many Hands: A Journal of Holistic Health: ""Skiers," Tone Poem for Summer Solstice," "Windhorse"

ACKNOWLEDGMENTS

Ocolind iazul/Round the Pond, Antologie de/An Anthology (Editura Muntenia, Romania, 1994): "The Conclusion of the Grail Legend, Trout Fishing, and the Art of Writing Haiku Poetry"
Old Crow: "Before Dawn"
Painted Bride Quarterly: "Sweet Woodruff"
Poetry East (Special *Praises* Issue, 2, 1992): "Tuning Fork on the Sidewalk of Dreams: Bert Meyers's *The Wild Olive Tree and the Blue* Café"
Puckerbrush Review: "The Friendship of Robert Frost and Robert Francis: High-pressure Weather and Country Air" (Orono, ME: Puckerbrush Press, xxi, ii, Winter/Spring 2003), Constance Hunting, Editor
Raw Nervz (Canada): "The Watershed of "Just as It Is: *Mountain* by John Wills"
ROSA: Women in Power & Politics: "Post-election Trauma: How to Manage the Stress of an Autocratic President"
The Silence Between Us (Decatur, IL; Brooks Books, 2005): "The Poetics of Walking"
Tuck: A Magazine for Discerning Readers (Canada): "Future History Books"

Portions of "The Art and Necessity of *Festschrift: Fair Warning: Leo Connellan and His Poetry* and a Review of Leo Connellan's *Death in Lobsterland*" were initially published in *The New Haven Advocate* and in *Fair Warning: Leo Connellan and His Poetry* (Tokyo, Japan: Printed Matter, 2011). The entire essay was republished online in *The Operating System*, April 2016.

"Before Dawn" was collected in *Winding Paths Worn through Grass* (Chicago, IL: Virtual Artists Collective, 2012).

The co-translator's preface to *The Daodejing: A New Interpretation* appeared in the book of the same title (Beaumont, TX: Lamar University Press, 2015). The first and last verse of *The Daodejing*, which is reinterpreted by the author, as they appears here, also appeared in the book along with the other subsequent seventy-nine verses, originally composed by Laozi.

ACKNOWLEDGMENTS

"Daylilies," "Homage to Ed Ricketts," "Sooey," and "Tone Poem for Summer Solstice" were collected in *Invocation* (Beaumont, TX: Lamar University Literary Press, 2015).

High Pressure Weather and Country Air was published as a scholarly biographical literary monograph, *The Friendship of Two New England Poets, Robert Frost and Robert Francis: A Lecture Presented at the Robert Frost Farm in Derry, New Hampshire* (Lewiston, NY: The Edwin Mellen Press, Hardcover/Library Buckram, 2009).

"Origins of the Inner Voice: Difference between Divinity, Consciousness, and Madness" was designated as a Shortlist Winner Nominee in the Adelaide Voices Literary Award for 2018 in the essay category. The essay was included in *Adelaide Voices Literary Award Anthology* (New York & Lisbon: Adelaide Books, 2018).

The Foreword to *A Staff to the Pilgrim: Meditations on the Way with Nine Celtic Saints* by Father Gabriel Cooper Rochelle appeared in the book of the same name (Emmaus, PA: Golden Alley Press, 2016).

"*The Windbreak Pine:* An Introduction," as well as the haiku "spring snow" and "snowflakes in the wind" were collected in *The Windbreak Pine: New and Uncollected Haiku, 1985-2015* (Ormskirk, U.K.: Snapshot Press, 2016).

The author wishes to offer his gratitude to the following philanthropic literary agencies for granting financial assistance while parts of this book were written: The Authors League Fund, The Carnegie Fund for Authors, and PEN Writers Fund, of New York City; and The Haven Foundation, of Brewer, Maine.

photo: Betty Wilda

ABOUT THE AUTHOR

WALLY SWIST's books include *Huang Po and the Dimensions of Love* (Southern Illinois University Press, 2012), selected by Yusef Komunyakaa as the co-winner of the Crab Orchard Series Open Poetry Competition for 2011; *The Daodejing: A New Interpretation*, with David Breeden and Steven Schroeder (Lamar University Literary Press, 2015); *Invocation* (Lamar University Press, 2015), *The View of the River* (Kelsay Books, 2017), *Candling the Eggs* (Shanti Arts, LLC, 2017), and *The Map of Eternity* (Shanti Arts, LLC, 2018).

His poetry and prose have appeared in many publications, including *Adelaide Literary Magazine, The American Book Review, Anchor: Where Spirituality and Social Justice Meet, Appalachia Journal, Arts: The Arts in Religion and Theology, Commonweal, Garrison Keillor's Writers Almanac, North American Review, Rattle, Sunken Garden Poetry, 1992-2011* (Wesleyan University Press, 2012), *The Woven Tale Press: Cybersphere's Premier Literary and Fine Arts Magazine,* and *upstreet*. Swist makes his home in South Amherst, Massachusetts.

WHY PRINT / DOCUMENT?

The Operating System uses the language "print document" to differentiate from the book-object as part of our mission to distinguish the act of documentation-in-book-FORM from the act of publishing as a backwards-facing replication of the book's agentive *role* as it may have appeared the last several centuries of its history. Ultimately, I approach the book as TECHNOLOGY: one of a variety of printed documents (in this case, bound) that humans have invented and in turn used to archive and disseminate ideas, beliefs, stories, and other evidence of production.

Ownership and use of printing presses and access to (or restriction of printed materials) has long been a site of struggle, related in many ways to revolutionary activity and the fight for civil rights and free speech all over the world. While (in many countries) the contemporary quotidian landscape has indeed drastically shifted in its access to platforms for sharing information and in the widespread ability to "publish" digitally, even with extremely limited resources, the importance of publication on physical media has not diminished. In fact, this may be the most critical time in recent history for activist groups, artists, and others to insist upon learning, establishing, and encouraging personal and community documentation practices. Hear me out.

With The OS's print endeavors I wanted to open up a conversation about this: the ultimately radical, transgressive act of creating PRINT /DOCUMENTATION in the digital age. It's a question of the archive, and of history: who gets to tell the story, and what evidence of our life, our behaviors, our experiences are we leaving behind? We can know little to nothing about the future into which we're leaving an unprecedentedly digital document trail — but we can be assured that publications, government agencies, museums, schools, and other institutional powers that be will continue to leave BOTH a digital and print version of their production for the official record. Will we?

As a (rogue) anthropologist and long time academic, I can easily pull up many accounts about how lives, behaviors, experiences — how THE STORY of a time or place — was pieced together using the deep study of correspondence, notebooks, and other physical documents which are no longer the norm in many lives and practices. As we move our creative behaviors towards digital note taking, and even audio and video, what can we predict about future technology that is in any way assuring that our stories will be accurately told – or told at all? How will we leave these things for the record?

In these documents we say:
WE WERE HERE, WE EXISTED, WE HAVE A DIFFERENT STORY

- Lynne DeSilva-Johnson, Founder/Creative Director
THE OPERATING SYSTEM, Brooklyn NY 2018

RECENT & FORTHCOMING
OS PRINT / DOCUMENTS 2018-19

Ark Hive-Marthe Reed [2019]
A Bony Framework for the Tangible Universe-D. Allen [kin(d)*, 2019]
Śnienie / Dreaming - Marta Zelwan/Krystyna Sakowicz,
(Polish-English/dual-language) trans. Victoria Miluch [glossarium, 2019]
Opera on TV-James Brunton [kin(d)*, 2019]
Alparegho: Pareil-À-Rien / Alparegho, Like Nothing Else - Hélène Sanguinetti
(French-English/dual-language), trans. Ann Cefola [glossarium, 2019]
Hall of Waters-Berry Grass [kin(d)*, 2019]
High Tide Of The Eyes - Bijan Elahi (Farsi-English/dual-language)
trans. Rebecca Ruth Gould and Kayvan Tahmasebian [glossarium, 2019]
I Made for You a New Machine and All it Does is Hope - Richard
Lucyshyn [2019]
Illusory Borders-Heidi Reszies [2019]
Transitional Object-Adrian Silbernagel [kin(d)*, 2019]
A Year of Misreading the Wildcats [2019]

An Absence So Great and Spontaneous It Is Evidence of Light - Anne Gorrick [2018]
The Book of Everyday Instruction - Chloe Bass [2018]
Executive Orders Vol. II - a collaboration with the Organism
for Poetic Research [2018]
One More Revolution - Andrea Mazzariello [2018]
The Suitcase Tree - Filip Marinovich [2018]
Chlorosis - Michael Flatt and Derrick Mund [2018]
Sussuros a Mi Padre - Erick Sáenz [2018]
Sharing Plastic - Blake Nemec [2018]
The Book of Sounds - Mehdi Navid (Farsi dual language, trans. Tina Rahimi) [2018]
In Corpore Sano : Creative Practice and the Challenged Body [Anthology, 2018]
Abandoners - Lesley Ann Wheeler [2018]
Jazzercise is a Language - Gabriel Ojeda-Sague [2018]
Return Trip / Viaje Al Regreso - Israel Dominguez;
(Spanish-English dual language) trans. Margaret Randall [2018]
Born Again - Ivy Johnson [2018]
Attendance - Rocío Carlos and Rachel McLeod Kaminer [2018]
Singing for Nothing - Wally Swist [2018]
The Ways of the Monster - Jay Besemer [2018]
Walking Away From Explosions in Slow Motion - Gregory Crosby [2018]
The Unspoken - Bob Holman [Bowery Books imprint - 2018]
Field Guide to Autobiography - Melissa Eleftherion [2018]
Kawsay: The Flame of the Jungle - María Vázquez Valdez
(Spanish-English dual language) trans. Margaret Randall [2018]

DOC U MENT
/däkyəmənt/

First meant "instruction" or "evidence," whether written or not.

noun - a piece of written, printed, or electronic matter that provides information or evidence or that serves as an official record
verb - record (something) in written, photographic, or other form
synonyms - paper - deed - record - writing - act - instrument

[*Middle English*, precept, from Old French, from Latin *documentum*, example, proof, from *docre*, to teach; see *dek-* in Indo-European roots.]

Who is responsible for the manufacture of value?

Based on what supercilious ontology have we landed in a space where we vie against other creative people in vain pursuit
of the fleeting credibilities of the scarcity economy, rather than freely collaborating and sharing openly with each other
in ecstatic celebration of MAKING?

While we understand and acknowledge the economic pressures and fear-mongering that threatens to dominate and crush the creative impulse, we also believe that *now more than ever we have the tools to relinquish agency via cooperative means,* fueled by the fires of the Open Source Movement.

Looking out across the invisible vistas of that rhizomatic parallel country we can begin to see our community beyond constraints,
in the place where intention meets
resilient, proactive, collaborative organization.

Here is a document born of that belief, sown purely of imagination and will. When we document we assert. We print to make real, to reify our being there. When we do so with mindful intention to address our process, to open our work to others, to create beauty in words in space, to respect and acknowledge the strength of the page we now hold physical, a thing in our hand... we remind ourselves that, like Dorothy: *we had the power all along, my dears.*

THE PRINT! DOCUMENT SERIES
is a project of
the trouble with bartleby
in collaboration with
the operating system